T0225866

Project Reliability Engineering

Pro Skills for Next Level Maker Projects

Eyal Shahar

Apress®

Project Reliability Engineering: Pro Skills for Next Level Maker Projects

Eyal Shahar
San Francisco, CA, USA

ISBN-13 (pbk): 978-1-4842-5018-1   ISBN-13 (electronic): 978-1-4842-5019-8
https://doi.org/10.1007/978-1-4842-5019-8

Copyright © 2019 by Eyal Shahar

This work is subject to copyright. All rights are reserved by the Publisher, whether the whole or part of the material is concerned, specifically the rights of translation, reprinting, reuse of illustrations, recitation, broadcasting, reproduction on microfilms or in any other physical way, and transmission or information storage and retrieval, electronic adaptation, computer software, or by similar or dissimilar methodology now known or hereafter developed.

Trademarked names, logos, and images may appear in this book. Rather than use a trademark symbol with every occurrence of a trademarked name, logo, or image we use the names, logos, and images only in an editorial fashion and to the benefit of the trademark owner, with no intention of infringement of the trademark.

The use in this publication of trade names, trademarks, service marks, and similar terms, even if they are not identified as such, is not to be taken as an expression of opinion as to whether or not they are subject to proprietary rights.

While the advice and information in this book are believed to be true and accurate at the date of publication, neither the authors nor the editors nor the publisher can accept any legal responsibility for any errors or omissions that may be made. The publisher makes no warranty, express or implied, with respect to the material contained herein.

Managing Director, Apress Media LLC: Welmoed Spahr
Acquisitions Editor: Natalie Pao
Development Editor: James Markham
Coordinating Editor: Jessica Vakili

Cover designed by eStudioCalamar

Cover image designed by Freepik (www.freepik.com)

Distributed to the book trade worldwide by Springer Science+Business Media New York, 233 Spring Street, 6th Floor, New York, NY 10013. Phone 1-800-SPRINGER, fax (201) 348-4505, e-mail orders-ny@springer-sbm.com, or visit www.springeronline.com. Apress Media, LLC is a California LLC and the sole member (owner) is Springer Science + Business Media Finance Inc (SSBM Finance Inc). SSBM Finance Inc is a **Delaware** corporation.

For information on translations, please e-mail rights@apress.com, or visit http://www.apress.com/rights-permissions.

Apress titles may be purchased in bulk for academic, corporate, or promotional use. eBook versions and licenses are also available for most titles. For more information, reference our Print and eBook Bulk Sales web page at http://www.apress.com/bulk-sales.

Any source code or other supplementary material referenced by the author in this book is available to readers on GitHub via the book's product page, located at www.apress.com/978-1-4842-5018-1. For more detailed information, please visit http://www.apress.com/source-code.

Printed on acid-free paper

To Ada,

It's not much of a children's book,
but that's what I have.

Table of Contents

About the Author xiii

About the Technical Reviewer xv

Acknowledgments..xvii

Introduction xix

Chapter 1: The Case for Object-Oriented Programming 1

Object-Oriented Programming Basics...1

Polymorphism and Duck Typing 5

Inheritance..9

OOP in JavaScript 13

OOP in JavaScript ES6 17

Summary..19

Chapter 2: Our First Web Dashboard 21

Everything Is a Server...21

HTTP Requests..22

HTML in a Nutshell 25

Selectors and CSS...28

Template Rendering...30

Python and Flask...31

    Coding Our First Dashboard...32

    The Flask Web Server..37

Adding Browser Interactivity 38

Node.js and Express.js 45

A Little Help 47

    jQuery 47

    Bootstrap 49

Summary 49

Chapter 3: The Live Dashboard 51

HTTP Requests 51

The Case for HTML Classes 54

WebSockets 56

    Introduction to WebSockets 56

    WebSockets in Node.js 56

    WebSockets in Python 59

    WebSockets in the Browser 65

    Honorary Mention: SocketIO 67

JSON 69

    JSON Communication Design 69

    JSON Message Structuring 72

    JSON Message Parsing 76

Summary 79

Chapter 4: Dashboard Design 81

Strategizing 81

Beefing Up the Project 82

Serving Static Files 83

Creating a Template 84

Data Updates 86

    Scrutinizing the Code 88

Basic CSS 90

    Tables 90

    Text 91

    Layout 93

Data-Driven CSS 98

Responsive Design 100

    Media Queries 100

    Element Sizing 103

    Device Orientation 103

HTML Graphic Indicators 104

    LEDs 104

    Meters 105

    Gradients 106

Google Charts 109

    Line Graphs 110

    Gauges 112

Real-World Examples 116

    Tidal Memory 117

    Wired Pier 119

    Internet Speed Monitoring 120

Summary 121

Chapter 5: Project Configuration 123

Motivation 123

File Formats 125

    XML 125

    JSON 127

    YAML 129

    Code 131

Interpreting the Configuration 133

    The Constructor's Argument 133

    Dynamic Instantiation 134

Command-Line Arguments 136

    Introduction 136

    Parsing 138

    Getting Help 142

Configuring an Arduino Project 144

    The Arduino's EEPROM 144

    Storing on an SD Card 152

Handling Configuration Errors 154

Configuring with Hardware 155

    Jumpers 155

    DIP Switches 157

Summary 158

Chapter 6: Machine Setup 159

User Setup 159

Where Should the Code Live? 161

Network Configuration 162

    The Settings 162

    Applying Network Configuration 165

    Accessing Remotely 167

Launching on Startup 170

    Running as a cron Job 170

Crash Recovery 175

    Python 175

    forever.js 176

    pm2 176

Running As a System Service 177

Setup Documentation 180

Summary...182

Chapter 7: Logging 183

The Good Old Print 183

    stdout and stderr 184

Where Do Logs Go? 186

Understanding Log Levels...188

    DEBUG and INFO Messages...190

    WARNING, ERROR, and CRITICAL Messages 190

Logging Libraries 191

    Python's logging 191

    Logging in JavaScript...201

    Roll Your Own 204

Log Rotation...204

    Linux's logrotate 205

    File Watching 206

    In-Program Log Rotation 207

Logging Configuration...208

What to Log..210

    Exceptions 210

    Callback with Error Arguments...211

    Initialization Sequences..212

Entering and Leaving Functions 212

Parameters 213

Data 213

Reading Log Files 213

Summary 214

Chapter 8: Advanced Logging, Monitoring, and Alerting 217

How Big Tech Companies Do It 218

Email Alerts by Log Handlers 219

Logging As a Microservice 222

The Service 223

The Client Library 225

Monitoring 226

A Simple Monitoring System 227

Alerts Throttling 231

Monitoring the Machine 232

The Playbook 235

Playbook Content 235

Playbook Hosting 236

SMS Alerts 237

Online SMS Services 237

SMS Alerts with Hardware 239

IFTTT 243

Summary 248

Chapter 9: Best Practices **249**

Fake Classes 249

Exceptions and Errors 255

    The Basics 255

    Operational vs. Programmer Error.......................................256

    Python 257

    JavaScript..259

Software Recovery 264

Version Control and Rolling Back 265

    Getting Started 267

    The Development Cycle 269

    Rolling Back...270

    Git Best Practices 271

Hardware Reliability..271

    Strain Relief...271

    Custom Shields..273

Real-Life Recovery Planning 274

More Microservices 275

    Microservices Revisited 275

    A Case Study 276

    Microservices Best Practices 278

It's Best to Practice 279

Summary...280

Index...**283**

About the Author

Eyal Shahar currently lives in San Francisco with his wife, daughter, and two cats. He works as an exhibit developer in the New Media Department at the Exploratorium, a museum of art, science, and human perception.

Dreaming of building synthesizers, Eyal got a B.Sc. in electrical engineering from the Tel Aviv University while working as a professional musician, playing with some of Israel's most prominent artists. In later years, he filled various engineering positions in music and art related startups in Tel Aviv, Paris, and San Francisco. Eyal also holds a Master's degree in Media, Arts and Sciences from the MIT Media Lab.

One day, he'll get around to building that synthesizer.

About the Technical Reviewer

Chaim Krause is a lover of computers, electronics, animals, and electronic music. He's tinkled pink when he can combine two or more in some project. The vast majority of his knowledge is through self learning. He jokes with everyone that the only difference between what he does at home and what he does at work is the logon he uses. As a lifelong learner he is often frustrated with technical errors in documentation that waste valuable time and cause unnecessary frustration. One of the reasons he works as the Technical Editor on books is to help others avoid those same pitfalls.

Acknowledgments

One last thing before we get going: writing this book has been one of the hardest and most time-consuming challenges I took on in my life. I can't testify myself to the quality of this work – you will be the judge of that – but I can say that it does not rely solely on my own efforts. First, I owe a great deal to many people – too many to name – who gave me a chance when it wasn't obvious that I deserved one. These people enabled the windy and weird path that led me to where I am today, writing a book about software for makers.

I'd like to extend my thanks to Natalie Pao and Jessika Vakili from Apress for holding my hand in this long process, to the technical reviewer Chaim Krause for his wise comments and warm words of encouragement, to Kristina Yu and Joyce Ma from the Exploratorium for their trust and mentorship and for letting me do some of the most interesting and rewarding work I have ever done, and to Troy Trimble for his professional advice and insight.

Last, I'd like to give special thanks to Julia Ma, whose presence is in every page of this book. I am extremely lucky to have had her pretty much come up with the idea for this book, proofread it and correct my awkward phrasing, fix the code segments, and comment on her experience as an on-call engineer – all that while providing all the emotional and logistical support I could have asked for.

And being married to me.

And giving birth to our daughter, Ada, right as I started writing.

This has been one crazy ride.

Introduction

On Being a Professional Maker

In 2014, I took a job at the Exploratorium, the museum for science, art, and human perception in San Francisco, California – a job that I am still holding at the time of writing these lines. In my role as a New Media Exhibit Developer, I am assigned to upcoming exhibitions[1] and charged with coming up with ideas for exhibits for them that use new media elements. This means that these exhibits feature touchscreens, physical computing components, projectors, and so forth. Some of the ideas I come up with get tossed away immediately – they might be too hard to make, too silly, out of the scope of the exhibition, or maybe they would just not make good exhibits – but other ideas show potential. I take those ideas and make prototypes. A prototype starts with something as simple as a diagram or a paper simulation, and at some point (and usually pretty quickly) it evolves into a computer program on an Arduino, Raspberry Pi, a desktop computer, or a virtual machine. I am a sub-average fabricator, but if any physical structure is needed at this point, I'll hack something together using my favorite tools – a table saw, a drill press, and a laser cutter.

A prototype is then evaluated by the project leadership and by our Visitor Research and Evaluation Department, who take the prototype to the museum floor and watch how visitors interact with it. Based on the feedback, I modify the prototype, often getting support from other

---

[1]While different museums use different terminologies, in Exploratorium lingo an *exhibit* is a single item dealing with a specific phenomenon, an *exhibition* is a set of exhibits that deal with various phenomena in a particular topic or field, and the *collection* is the entire body of exhibits that the museum owns.

departments such as the Graphics Department in designing the visual elements and the Editorial Department in refining the text content of the labels and the screens. After a few iterations of evaluation and adjustment, the exhibit is ready for production. I stabilize or sometimes completely rewrite the code, order and assemble all the parts, and ensure that the electronic circuitry complies with our standards. At that point I might get more support from our engineers and technicians in building cabinetry and manufacturing circuitry. To conclude the process, I make sure everything is documented and that the code is backed up on our servers and in the cloud.

In summary, my job is to own and shepherd the exhibit from ideation to deployment, which is what every maker does. Since this is my actual job, I guess that makes me a professional maker. Over the years, I've learned that professional makers work in many industries. They make prototypes in design companies and corporate companies' innovation teams; they create rides for theme parks and practical effects for movies and theater; they produce public art installations; and they build exhibits for science museums.

In order to make the leap from being hobbyists to professional makers, makers must add a few tools to their toolbox. Among these are the ability to create robust and reliable products and to be able to effectively monitor and control them. The exhibits that I make at the Exploratorium are used by hundreds, sometimes thousands, of people every day, and I need make sure that they **work**, that they overcome power outages, and that they know how to deal with edge cases without crashing. Also, the Exploratorium's footprint is pretty big – just the exhibit space is about 75,000 square feet and over 800 feet from end to end. This means that I need to have a way to monitor the exhibits from my desk rather than walk repeatedly to the various galleries and back to my desk all day.

Professional makers from various industries have similar needs, and I hope this book will help them formalize their process when it comes to reliability. For makers who aspire to become professionals, the primary audience for this book, I hope this book will serve as a stepping stone as they build their new career. Finally, I believe that even hobbyists who are happy to keep creating projects just for fun will find this book valuable and eye-opening.

Origins: A Short History of Reliability Engineering

Traditional Software Development

Here is an over-simplified history of reliability engineering: in the beginning, there were companies that made software. Development was done in stages: first, the company would **analyze** the market and product domain and decide on the software requirements; then the company would enter a **design** stage, where the *Software Development* team would decide upon structure and components of the software. Next, the developers set to **code** the actual components of the software, building and refining the product, adding features, and fixing bugs; the *Quality Assurance* team (QA) would then **test** the product, and when all was said and done, the *Operations* team would step in: the Operations team was mostly in charge of hardware – both the company's and its clients, network hardware and configuration, data backups, and so on. It was their job to **deploy** the product and **maintain** it.

This model, in which software development goes sequentially between the phases of analysis, design, coding, testing, deployment, and maintenance, is known as the *Waterfall Model*.

Agile Software Development

As time went by, the software development world changed. Programs became bigger, physical products became more software heavy, the number of companies making software products grew, and the lifespan of products became longer, thus requiring more software updates, and most importantly the market was changing faster. Releases and updates had to happen more rapidly than before. In the Waterfall Model, it is difficult to move backward in the process: by the time a company is in the implementation phase, the market needs may change, making it necessary to go back to analysis and design; if tests prove that the program is faulty, the coders have to start over. Another major issue with the Waterfall Model is that nobody gets to put their hands on any working product until the entire process is done. The first time the company gets to see if their product is something that people even may want to use is after all the work is finished.

In response to the Waterfall Model's shortcomings, other methodologies started to appear, with the hype around them culminating in the mid-2000s. These approaches revered speed and simplicity; they embraced change and used iterative processes, repeatedly going through phases of design, development, and testing; and they valued having a working version of the software at any given moment and as early as possible. Today, these techniques are known collectively as *Agile Software Development.*

Agile Software Development brought changes not only to the process but also to organizations' culture and structure. Companies favored face-to-face conversations and short stand-up meetings instead of long email threads, and they re-examined and restructured the way teams are built. In many cases, teams were no longer composed of people from the same discipline, but rather people who are responsible for a certain feature or component, who work on it from different perspectives. In other cases, teams that were traditionally separate were brought closer together or even completely merged.

The Birth of DevOps

That was the case when some companies specifically examined how Development and Operations work together. The idea was to put an end to some of the tensions that were manifesting between the two disciplines. Developers wanted to deploy new features, while the Operations team cared mostly about the integrity of the service the company was giving. Because of that, Operations kept pushing back on requests put by developers, an act that developers saw as slowing down the product's growth. To put an end to these frictions, companies formulated new relationships between the two teams. Various principles were put into place, such as giving each team more insight into what the other team was doing by sharing the same codebase. Tools were built to give Operations control over the configuration of the code, while developers were given agency to configure hardware and access to dashboards that visualized the systems integrity.[2] Some companies created new teams whose entire job was to bridge the gap between Development and Operations. A new philosophy was born, and it was named *DevOps*.

Site Reliability Engineering

One of the best known examples of this type of thinking happened at Google, a few good years before the term "DevOps" was coined. Due to the size of its server farms, Google was looking into automating processes such as configuring and deploying virtual machines and recovering from hardware failure. They came up with a paradigm called *Site Reliability*

---

[2]A seminal talk called "10+ Deploys Per Day Dev and Ops Cooperation at Flickr," by John Allspaw, head of the Operations group, and Paul Hammond, head of the Engineering group at Flickr, set the basis for DevOps and is available to watch on YouTube: www.youtube.com/watch?v=LdOe18KhtT4

Engineering (SRE)[3] and described it as "what happens when a software engineer is tasked with what used to be called operations."[4] By that philosophy, Site Reliability Engineers (SREs) spend about half of their time doing regular operations work, and in the remaining half, they build tools to automate and scale their work. Although SRE predates DevOps, it is considered today a flavor of DevOps, or a specific way to implement it. Others see DevOps and SRE as having slightly different functions, with DevOps addressing needs for development and SRE ensuring the integrity of the deployed product.

Philosophy of Project Reliability Engineering

Many maker projects are engineered just enough to get them to the point that they are working, a moment often commemorated by the calling "It's working! Don't touch anything!" *Project Reliability Engineering* aims to make maker-scale projects resilient to heavy usage and unexpected circumstances. To establish that, Project Reliability Engineering promotes

- **Built-in mechanisms** for logging, alerting, and recovering from hardware, software, and infrastructure malfunctions like power outages, network outages, and defected hardware

---

[3]Google literally wrote the book on SRE, called, naturally, "Site Reliability Engineering: Betsy Beyer, Chris Jones, Jennifer Petoff, and Niall Richard Murphy. 2016. *Site Reliability Engineering: How Google Runs Production Systems*. O'Reilly Media, Inc. It is also available to read online for free here: https://landing. google.com/sre/book.html

[4]As said by Ben Treynor, founder of the SRE team at Google.

- **Modular software** designed and programmed in a way that enables configurability for both development and debugging purposes

- **Ecosystem-aware design** that takes into account the maker, the user, and third parties such as clients who own and care for the finalized project and machines that interact with it

The big question is, why? Is it really worth the trouble? It depends what the end goal is. If a project is built for the sole purpose of having fun, and maybe being featured in a video posted online – a well worthy goal on its own – then building it with reliability in mind is definitely an overkill, but professional makers must consider the stability and reliability of their projects. In this book, we look at SRE for inspiration and adapt some of its underlying principles to the scale of maker projects. Although our goal is similar – keeping our projects up and running – the environment in which a maker works is very different than the one in which a corporate SRE works, and therefore our interpretation will be based only loosely on the classic SRE paradigm. Table 1 shows some DevOps principles, how they are interpreted in SRE, and how they are reflected in Project Reliability Engineering. This will give you an idea of what we are about to explore in this book.

Table 1. *From DevOps, to SRE, to Project Reliability Engineering*

DevOps	SRE	Project Reliability Engineering
Bridging between Development and Operations	Sharing tools and responsibilities across the organization	• Understanding the host platform on both software and OS levels • Building in recovery mechanisms
Accepting failure	Embracing risk and setting metrics for acceptable failure	• Building in mechanisms for logging • Implementing alerting mechanisms
Implementing gradual changes	Reducing cost of failure by gradual releases	• Having a working version constantly and from early on • Using interchangeable components for production and simulation • Making (almost) everything configurable
Using tools and automation	Automating work that is manual, repetitive, and/or unscalable	• Using open source workflow automation tools • Building custom tools and libraries • Using version control for code reuse
Measuring everything	Define metrics and treating Operations as a software problem	• Building in APIs and a dashboard for monitoring and troubleshooting

About This Book

This book is mostly about thinking on systems and code rather than being a set of tutorials. To foster that approach, I hope that as you read this book, you will not feel as if you are being **taught**. Rather, I would like you to feel as if you and I are having a conversation. For this reason, I transition between code and text fairly rapidly. I often present code that is halfway there, discuss it, and then go back and present amended code. Consider that as you are reading – I advise you not to immediately copy code to your machine and run it. If you do, know that it may not work or may not be optimal. In fact, it might be a good idea not to use any of the code in this book as is. The best way to use the code in this book would be to take whatever is relevant to your own project and make the proper modifications.

I am a great believer in understanding how things work under the hood; therefore, I usually try to start a discussion with vanilla code – code that does not rely on libraries, but rather the built-in capabilities of the language or framework in question, even if that results in code that is somewhat awkward. At times, however, I point out some useful libraries that are relevant to the topic.

What Do You Know?

This is an intermediate level book; this presents a challenge: intermediate level books assume that the reader approaches the book already having a significant amount of prior knowledge and experience. Each reader, however, knows different things, and the challenge the author faces is to determine what to assume the reader already knows, what needs some refreshing and fine-tuning, and what should be explained as if encountered for the very first time. Makers are a particularly tricky bunch, as they often come from very different disciplines, prefer breadth over depth, and pick up skills as they go. I have to resort to doing something that is a big no-no these days: make assumptions about you.

I'll assume that you have worked with a Raspberry Pi, a BeagleBone, or some other *single-board computer* (SBC) before. I will not cover how to set up your SBC, find your way around the board and the file system, edit and run code, or run basic bash commands.

You must have done some programming in Python and a little bit of JavaScript in Node.js.[5] Given that Python is more dominant in the maker community, the level of the sections that discuss JavaScript is sometimes more basic. If we use a library, I don't explicitly state whether it should be installed with `pip`, `npm`, or by directly downloading it. I often just point out the library's homepage in a footnote and expect you to figure it out.

As mentioned, we often add to or modify the code that we discuss in previous paragraphs. Instead of presenting the entire code again, I often present only the modified or added portions. This means that I am counting on you to understand where the new code goes or which lines are the ones that need to be modified. Of course, I provide help with directions in the text and sometimes in the code itself by adding a comment containing an ellipsis (`#  ...` for Python, `//  ...` for JavaScript, and `<!--  ...  -->` for HTML) signifying the previously discussed code. Here's an example in Python:

```python
#  ...
do_after_previously_discussed_code()
```

And here's one in JavaScript:

```javascript
runBeforePreviouslyDiscussedCode();
//  ...
```

All the final code that we produce in this book is on the book's GitHub page,[6] so refer to it if you feel disoriented. If you are unfamiliar with Git and GitHub, you will find a short introduction to it in Chapter 9.

---

[5] https://nodejs.org
[6] https://github.com/Apress/project-reliability-engineering

Languages

The languages of choice in this book are Python and JavaScript. These are the two languages that are most used by makers working with SBCs, they have well-maintained libraries that support the hardware capabilities of the popular SBCs, and most importantly they are not going anywhere in the near future.

At the time of writing this book, both languages had gone through fairly recent major shifts: in 2014, it was announced that support for Python 2.7, the last version of Python 2, will discontinue in 2020 and that programmers were encouraged to port their programs to Python 3. Now, Python 3 has been around since 2008, but many programmers were reluctant, or just lazy, to port their software due to lack of backward compatibility: even a simple `print` command, which in Python 2 did not require parenthesis for the argument, would not work in Python 3. Unfortunately, this applies to some useful libraries as well, and some of them are still not ready yet for Python 3. Regardless, it makes very little sense to write code examples for a language version that has an expiration date on it, so for us Python 3 it is. The code presented in the book should work with versions 3.5.3 and up, as this is the version that is included in Raspbian at the time of writing this book.

It's a completely different story when it comes to JavaScript. In 2015, JavaScript was updated to ECMAScript 2015[7] (also known was ES6). The update introduced many new features, both syntactical and functional. The new features were quickly embraced by the JavaScript community, and although ES6 and subsequent versions are backward compatible, the prevailing coding style has changed dramatically, taking advantage of JavaScript's newfangled features. In this book, we also make use of

---

[7]*ECMAScript* is the specification of JavaScript, as determined by *Ecma International*, a standards organization with members from the computer, electronics, and telecommunication industries.

the new features, but I do my best not to turn JavaScript sections into ES6 tutorials, as tempting as it is – after all, the features introduced in ES6 are still new and exciting. Having said that, I occasionally take some time to discuss new features in JavaScript, mostly when this serves to emphasize differences between JavaScript and Python or to discuss more advanced topics.

Note There is often confusion about the relationship between Node.js and JavaScript. Node.js is a JavaScript runtime library. That means that one never writes code **in** Node.js, but rather runs JavaScript code in the Node.js framework. This is important to remember when we present JavaScript code and specify that it should be run "server-side" or "on the machine," that is, in Node.js, rather than on a web browser.

Code Style

I state with great confidence, although I have no way to prove it, that every software organization, no matter how big or small, adopts a set of *code conventions* (sometimes referred to as *coding conventions* or *style guide*). A commercial program is read, used, and very often written by multiple people who need to understand exactly what the code does. Of course, adding comments to the code is one way to do that, but it is more important that the code itself is easy to read. Therefore, having agreed-upon ways to use indentation, capitalization, spacing, and variable and function naming helps programmers clearly communicate their ideas to each other, reducing development time and code complexity.

It is extremely valuable for an independent developer, even a hobbyist, to develop or adopt code conventions for their own use. Corporate software engineers are not the only ones whose code is being looked at and changed by other people – you are too, and the person tinkering with your code is your future self, who most likely will not remember what a variable called "i", a file called "project_old", or a comment reading "OMG" meant to your past self. A good way to start is to observe what other people do. Many big software companies have their conventions available to the public on the Web, and trust me, they went through endless meetings until every item was decided upon.[8] Python, by the way, has its own style guide written by some of the developers of the language itself, so that is definitely a good place to look for inspiration.[9]

The situation in this book is a little different. First, the code, as I mentioned, is not brought as a single complete file. Second, a book's page, unlike a line in a file, has limited width, so some compromises must be made in order to accommodate it. Third, I have my own preferences which sometimes deviate from the common practices, and this is, after all, **my** book. Last, at the end of the day we are using a small set of features of every language, so obviously a full-blown style guide will not be necessary, but I would like to specify a few conventions that are used. I focus on things that are significantly different than the norm, things that are specific to this book due to the printed format, and things that I think are good practice but are not always included in other style guides.

Formatting

I am using **two-space indentation** for both Python and JavaScript, mostly, in order to keep things tight on the printed page. In the great battlefield of JavaScript style, we're just picking a side, since plenty of style guides are out there with either two-space or four-space indentation. For Python, however, we're going against the mainstream, since the vast majority of developers use the four-space indentation, so do keep that in mind.

---

[8]Google's Python style guide is an interesting example, as it lists the pros and cons of every single convention (https://github.com/google/styleguide/blob/gh-pages/pyguide.md).

[9]www.python.org/dev/peps/pep-0008

ECMA 2015 lifted the requirement to end JavaScript statements with a semicolon. This started a controversy in the developer community whether or not semicolons should be used. In this book, **statements end with a semicolon**. The main argument for this decision is that I often break statements into multiple lines, so a semicolon helps to clearly see where the statement actually ends. Also, some of my favorite online style guides are on the pro-semicolon camp.

Naming

Choosing names for functions and variables is one of the key aspects of generating readable code. We are going to follow these rules:

- Variables names are nouns, for example, `motor`.

- The preferred way to name a list is not with a plural verb, but rather by adding the postfix "list" to a noun, for example, `motor_list`. When text compactness becomes an issue, plural nouns such as `motors` are used.

- Function names are verbs, for example, `set_motor_speed()`.

- The preferred way to name a loop index is by adding the postfix "index" to a noun, for example, `motor_index`. When the code is simple and easy to understand, shorter names like `i` or `idx` are used.

- In Python, both function and variable names are in snake_case (underscores separating between words), for example, `left_motor`. Class names (see Chapter 1) are an exception, using Camel case with a capitalized first letter, for example, `ServoMotor`.

- In JavaScript, both function and variable names are in
  CamelCase (words are connected, and every first letter
  of every word is uppercase), with the first letter of the
  name in lowercase, for example, `leftMotor`. Again,
  class names are an exception, using Camel case with a
  capitalized first letter, for example, `ServoMotor`.

Comments

Just as with any other aspect of programming, there are numerous
approaches when it comes to including comments in the code. The school
of thought I was brought up in asserts that if variables and functions are
named clearly, the code should be mostly self-explanatory, and therefore
comments should be used only when absolutely necessary. You may find
that in the code that is in this book I use comments even more scarcely
than that, not because it's a good practice – it's not – but rather because the
text that follows discusses the code in detail, and I try to avoid redundancy.
I stress again that code must be as easy to read as possible, and if that
means going through the tedious effort of including comments your code,
by all means do that.

Browser Compatibility

In quite a few chapters in this book, we will build web pages. The code
has been tested mostly with Chrome, but not with every browser that
is out there. If you use a different browser, you may experience some
compatibility issues. Functionally, everything is supposed to work but may
look a little different. Should compatibility issues arise, please refer to the
book's GitHub page for assistance.

CHAPTER 1

The Case for Object-Oriented Programming

We will start by reviewing some of the foundations of object-oriented programming (OOP), specifically from the point of view of a hardware-centered, SBC-powered project. Whether you are familiar with OOP or not, we will discuss some examples that demonstrate the usefulness of inheritance when dealing with peripherals such as sensors. In later chapters we will see how polymorphism helps create more elegant and scalable tools for troubleshooting, logging, and monitoring.

Object-Oriented Programming Basics

In object-oriented programming, as the name suggests, the programmer constructs objects – entities that have properties and are able to do perform certain tasks. This is very similar to how we, as humans, grasp the world around us in real life, which is why OOP is so appealing.

A *class* defines the properties that objects of that class have and the operations which they can carry out. The properties, usually referred to as *fields* or *data members*, are variables that exist in the object's scope and

© Eyal Shahar 2019

E. Shahar, *Project Reliability Engineering*, https://doi.org/10.1007/978-1-4842-5019-8_1

are valid as long the object exists. The operations, often called *methods* or *member functions*, are functions that have access to the fields and can manipulate them.

If we were to design a sensor class, for example, it might have a method that performs a measurement and a field in which the most recent measurement is stored. Let's make a class that represents a temperature sensor, namely, Silicon Labs Si7021. Looking at the sensor's data sheet,[1] we see that it communicates via I2C and its address is fixed to 0x40. The command 0xF3 tells the sensor to measure the temperature. About a quarter of a second after the command is issued, two bytes can be read from the sensor, and these express the last measured temperature, following this equation

$$Temperature\left[\,^{\circ}C\right] = \frac{175.72 \cdot \left(256 \cdot byte0 + byte1\right)}{65536} - 46.85$$

with *byte0* and *byte1* being the first and the second bytes read, respectively. Listing 1-1 shows how that can be implemented in Python code.

Listing 1-1. Si7021Temp sensor class

```python
import smbus
import time

class Si7021Temp:
    def __init__(self, name, bus_id):
        self.name = name
        self.units = 'Celsius'
        self.bus = smbus.SMBus(bus_id)
```

---

[1]`www.silabs.com/documents/public/data-sheets/Si7021-A20.pdf`. Several breakout boards exist for easier integration.

```
def measure(self):
  self.bus.write_byte(0x40, 0xF3)
  time.sleep(0.1)
  byte0 = self.bus.read_byte(0x40)
  byte1 = self.bus.read_byte(0x40)
  self.measurement =
    ((byte0 * 256 + byte1) *
      175.72 / 65536.0) - 46.85
  time.sleep(0.1)
```

This definition of a class, however, does not yet represent an actual object, but rather it describes what an object of that type looks like. The methods cannot yet be called and the fields cannot be accessed – we'll need an actual object of this class type for that. An actual object, one that can carry out its methods and store data in its fields, is called an *instance*, and the process of making one is called *instantiation*. Notice how methods, like measure, are defined. The first argument in the definition must be self, which is used to refer to the instance itself. Also note the special method __init__ that is called when the instance is created. In Python, a field, rather than a local variable, is any variable that is created in the self scope, like in the line

```
self.units = 'Celsius'
```

We can instantiate a temperature sensor like so:

```
temp_sensor1 = Si7021Temp('Temperature 1', 1)
```

This instantiates a sensor that is connected to the I2C1 bus. This immediately exposes an advantage of OOP: the Si7021 has a fixed I2C address, so we can only have one sensor connected to any I2C bus, but the BeagleBone Black, for instance, has two I2C buses that are accessible on the header pins. Now, if we wanted to connect another Si7021 sensor to the I2C2 bus, all we'd have to do is instantiate that one as well:

```
temp_sensor2 = Si7021Temp('Temperature 2', 2)
```

Or better yet, instantiate them both directly in a list:

```
sensor_list = []
sensor_list.append(Si7021Temp('Temperature 1', 1))
sensor_list.append(Si7021Temp('Temperature 2', 2))
```

Now we can do cool things, like perform actions on both sensors in a loop (see Listing 1-2).

Listing 1-2. Iterating through a list of sensor objects

```
def measuring_loop():
  while True:
    for sensor in sensor_list:
      sensor.measure()
      print('{} measured {:.2f} {}'.format(
        sensor.name,
        sensor.measurement,
        sensor.units))
    time.sleep(5)
measuring_loop()
```

Note that even though we defined the method measure() with self as an argument, we called it now with no arguments specified. The self argument is always implicit when calling an object's method. This is also true if we want a method to take arguments when it's called (see Listing 1-3).

Listing 1-3. When invoking a method, self is implicit

```
class MyClass:
  def method(self, arg1, arg2):
    # do stuff
    return

my_instance = MyClass()
my_instance(val1, val2)
```

Polymorphism and Duck Typing

Let's look at that loop again: what other kinds of objects can we push into the sensor_list without breaking our program? It seems like we can add any object that has measure() as a method and name, measurement, and units as fields. It doesn't have to be an object of the class Si7021Temp or a temperature sensor at all. We can define another class to utilize the Si7021's capability of measuring humidity, as shown in Listing 1-4.

Listing 1-4. Si7021Humidity sensor class

```
class Si7021Humidity:
  def __init__(self, name, bus_id):
    self.name = name
    self.units = '%'
    self.bus = smbus.SMBus(bus_id)

  def measure(self):
    self.bus.write_byte(0x40, 0xF5)

    time.sleep(0.1)
    byte0 = self.bus.read_byte(0x40)
    byte1 = self.bus.read_byte(0x40)
    self.measurement = (
      (byte0 * 256 + byte1) *
        125 / 65536.0) - 6
    time.sleep(0.1))
```

Note that a different command (0xF5) is written to the I2C bus to
prompt the humidity reading rather than temperature. This demonstrates
that although we call the methods and access the fields in the same way,
the implementation can be very different. As a matter of fact, we can define
a third class which utilizes a different type of sensor altogether – one
that communicates with the SBC in a whole different way. The code in
Listing 1-5 defines a class for the MPL3115A2 air pressure sensor.

Listing 1-5. MPL3115A2Pressure sensor class

```
class MPL3115A2Pressure:
  def __init__(self, name, bus_id):
    self.name = name
    self.units = 'kPa'
    self.bus = smbus.SMBus(bus_id)

  def measure(self):
    self.bus.write_byte_data(0x60, 0x26, 0x39)
    time.sleep(0.1)
    data = self.bus.read_i2c_block_data(
      0x60, 0x00, 4)
    self.measurement = (
      (data[1] * 65536) + (data[2] * 256) +
        (data[3] & 0xF0)) / 64000
```

If we want to use the new humidity and pressure sensors along with
the two temperature sensors that we've instantiated before, we just have to
push an instance of each of them into our sensor_list. For this example,
we'll only measure humidity using the first Si7021, and we'll assume the
MPL3115A2 is also connected to I2C1:

```
sensor_list.append(Si7021Humidity('humidity', 1))
sensor_list.append(MPL3115A2Pressure('pressure', 1))
```

In OOP terminology, we say that classes that have a set of identical methods and fields implement the same *interface*; this allows a program to treat objects of different classes in the same way, a concept that is called *polymorphism*. In some languages, such as C++ and Java, there are mechanisms that a developer needs to use in order to define an interface. Then, when a class is defined, the definition specifies which interface the class needs to implement. Listing 1-6 shows an example in Java.

Listing 1-6. Interfaces in Java

```java
public interface Sensor {
  public void measure();
  public void getReadAsString();
}

public class Si7021Temp implements Sensor {
  public void measure() {
    // implementation goes here
  }

  public void getReadAsString() {
    // implementation goes here
  }
}
```

Python and JavaScript, being the loosely typed languages that they are, support what is known as *duck typing*: the interface of the duck does not need to be explicitly defined, but if we define a class and give it all the methods and fields we expect a duck to have, then as far as we're concerned, it describes a duck. All three classes that we have defined so far in this chapter have a measure() method and a measurement field, which is all that we expect from a class describing a sensor. This is what allows us to execute the same operations on objects of all these classes, without knowing at the time the operation which specific class an object belongs to.

At this point, it should be clear why we didn't look for a library that already implements communication with the sensor – libraries for different sensors have different interfaces, so we would not be able to do all these cool things we just did – and will do later on. However, implementing everything from scratch is not always easy and requires some research. To get the best of both worlds, we could implement our sensor class as a *wrapper* class. Wrapper classes encapsulate other classes to simplify their interface, make them more readable, and often make them compatible with existing code, like in our case. After installing the Python library Si7021, we can rewrite the class Si7021Temp, this time as a wrapper class (see Listing 1-7).

Listing 1-7. Wrapper class for the Si7021 library

```python
from si7021 import Si7021

class Si7021Temp:
  def __init__(self, name, bus_id):
    self.name = name
    self.units = 'Celsius'
    self.sensor = Si7021(smbus.SMBus(bus_id))

  def measure(self):
    result = sensor.read()
    # we got an tuple: (humidity, temperature)
    self.measurement = result[1]
```

Note   Using a library can be much easier; but in this particular case, this approach comes with a price – when this library reads data from the sensor, it reads both temperature and humidity, which takes a little bit longer, while in our previous implementation, we treated the measurement of temperature and humidity as two separate sensor classes, which gave us more control.

From a reliability engineering standpoint, this satisfies our desire for modularity and scalability. As we will see in later chapters, using these techniques allows us to keep necessary code changes due to hardware changes to a minimum, it simplifies the process of generating web-based dashboards, and it allows for powerful troubleshooting techniques, like creating fake objects.

Inheritance

In the previous sections, we defined several different types of sensors and used duck typing which allows us to treat them all as just general "sensors." We mentioned that in other languages, such as Java and C++, we would first have to explicitly define an interface, a concept that is not supported by Python or JavaScript. There is another mechanism though, and that is *inheritance*. In inheritance, we first define a *superclass* (or *base class*), which represents a general case of the entities in question, and then we define *subclasses* (or *derived classes*), which are more specific cases of those entities and define their unique functionalities. While this sounds a lot like an interface, there are a few fundamental differences:

- Unlike a superclass, an interface cannot define data members, only methods.

- It is considered bad practice (and in some languages, impossible) for a class to inherit from more than one superclass when it's perfectly fine to implement more than one interface.

- An interface cannot include an implementation of any of its methods, while a superclass can.

Note   These are gross generalizations and are brought here to introduce the terminology, for which every language has its own nuances. As we mentioned, some terms are not even relevant in certain languages.

How can inheritance benefit our slowly growing weather station? We noted earlier that a superclass can include implementation of methods. When that happens, all subclasses inherit the methods of the superclass and can invoke them. This is useful when all subclasses need to execute something in the same way. For example, we might want all sensors to be able to provide the last measurement as a string consisting of the value of measurement along with the units string. Let us define the superclass (Listing 1-8).

Listing 1-8. Defining the Sensor superclass

```
class Sensor:
  def get_read_as_string(self):
    return('{} {}'.format(
      self.measurement, self.units))
```

We will need to change the definition of our sensors, as we now want them to be subclasses of Sensor (see Listing 1-9).

Listing 1-9. Rewriting our sensor classes as subclasses of the Sensor superclass

```
class Si7021Temp(Sensor):
#...

Si7021Humidity(Sensor):
#...

MPL3115A2Pressure(Sensor):
#...
```

10

CONCRETE THOUGHTS ABOUT ABSTRACT CLASSES

In other languages, such as C++ and Java, if some of the superclass's methods are not implemented, it is called an *abstract* class. If none of its methods are implemented, it is called a *pure abstract class*, and in that case, it is pretty much the same as an interface. Regardless, an abstract class can never be instantiated, which is the point of its existence: to make sure only subclasses of it are implemented. There are nuances between languages, one of them being that JavaScript and Python don't actually have abstract classes built into the language, and if such behavior is needed, it is up to the developer to avoid instantiating objects of the superclass in question.

Another good use of the superclass is when we want to set a default value to a member of all subclasses. Note that in all the subclasses of Sensor that we implemented, the value measurement is not set until the first time a measurement is performed. This can cause problems if the value of measurement is invoked before measure() is called. By giving measurement a default value upon instantiation, we can make sure that measurement already exists when invoked regardless of whether a measurement was taken or not. Since all sensors will benefit from this, instead of initializing the field in every subclass, we can do this just once in the superclass. We will, however, have to make sure to call the superclass's constructor from every subclass's constructor if there is one. If not, the superclass's constructor is used as default (Listing 1-10).

Listing 1-10. Initializing a superclass's data member

```python
class Sensor:
  def __init__(self):
    self.measurement = -999
  #...
```

```
class Si7021Temp(Sensor):
  def __init__(self, name, bus_id):
    super().__init__()
    #...
```

Note   The value -999 is often used to represent an invalid sensor
reading in systems where the value must be a number. If you don't
care about that too much, you can choose a string value such as
"N/A" or "NaN" or just set the value to None.

Similarly, we can also use the methods implemented in the superclass
as default behaviors, and then subclasses can, but don't have to, override
them. While in some languages it is necessary to explicitly specify that a
method of a superclass needs to be overridden, in Python all that is needed
is to define the method again within the subclass. For example, let's define
another sensor - one that just spits out the time. At first, this might be a
strange thing to do, but in fact, it's pretty elegant: let's say we wanted to
produce a file from our measurements. A simple choice for a format would
be a comma-separated values (CSV) file. As the name suggests, every line
in a CSV file consists of values separated by commas. In our case, each line
can contain the last readouts from all of our sensors, with the first value
being the time. If we implement the time readout as a sensor, producing
such a line would be just a matter of doing this:

```
','.join([str(s.measurement) for s in sensor_list])
```

We used list comprehension to generate a list that contains the values
of the measurement field of every sensor in sensor_list and then used the
join() function to generate a string that has all these values separated by
commas.

Tip   List comprehension is a very powerful feature available in Python, which creates one list from another list. We will not dive deeper than this in this book, but if you are not familiar with it, I urge you to check it out.

OOP in JavaScript

JavaScript doesn't really have classes. Instead, it uses *prototypes*, which, unlike classes, are actual objects. ES6, however, introduced new syntax that allows programmers to dodge the awkward syntax and peculiar nuances of prototypical inheritance and pretend like they are working with classes. Let's start with what really happens under the hood, and once we understand how things work, toss it all out the window and use the fancy, simpler syntax. The new class-like syntax will make our lives significantly easier.

A new object is created in JavaScript using a constructor function, as shown in Listing 1-11. Now that we understand inheritance, let's have our base class's constructor take the sensor's name as an argument.

Listing 1-11. Constructor function for the Sensor superclass

```
function Sensor(name) {
  this.name = name;
  this.measurement = -999;
}

let genericSensor = new Sensor('some_sensor');
```

What the new operator does is create a new object and run the constructor function within its scope. JavaScript's this is the same as in most other languages, and like Python's self, it is a pointer to the object in which the execution is happening, so in our example, the constructor

13

declares and initializes a new *property*, measurement. In JavaScript, functions are objects too, so the distinction between methods and fields is conceptual; hence, they are all called *properties.*

We created the object genericSensor, but we said all objects inherit from a prototype – what is the prototype of genericSensor? When we defined the constructor function Sensor, the function created a property for itself, which is the prototype, and all objects created by the constructor point to it. When the property of an object is invoked, the JavaScript interpreter looks for that property in the object itself. If it can't find it, it looks for it in the object's prototype, and so forth.

A common mistake is to define methods of superclasses in the constructor, as shown in Listing 1-12.

Listing 1-12. A wasteful way to defining a method

```
function Sensor(name) {
  // ...
  this.getReadAsString = function() {
  // ...
  }
}
```

But because this points to the instance created, every instance of Sensor will have its own copy of the function, which is wasteful. This is why we normally define methods as properties of the prototype and not in the constructor of the object itself. Listing 1-13 demonstrates how this is done.

Listing 1-13. Defining a method for the Sensor superclass

```
Sensor.prototype.getReadAsString = function() {
  if ('units' in this) {
    return('${this.measurement} ${this.units}');
  } else {
```

```
    return(String(this.measurement));
  }
}
```

For data members, of course, we still want each instance to be able to have a different value, so the constructor function is the right place to create them.

So far, we have defined the base class Sensor. It's time to define a constructor function for a specific sensor that is derived from Sensor and see prototype inheritance in action. Examine Listing 1-14.

Listing 1-14. Constructor for the Si7021Temp subclass

```
const i2c = require('i2c-bus');

function Si7021Temp(name, busId) {
  Sensor.call(this, name);
  this.units = 'Celsius';
  this.busId = busId;
  this.i2cBus = i2c.openSync(busId);
}

Si7021Temp.prototype =
  Object.create(Sensor.prototype);
```

We start by defining the constructor function of the derived class. Notice that just as in Python, we call the superclass's constructor as well. After the constructor is defined, we make Si7021Temp inherit from Sensor. For that, the derived class needs to have the same properties that its base class has. We use Object.create() that takes a prototype as an argument and returns a new object of that prototype. It's similar to what the new operator does, but without running the constructor function. In the end, what we have done here is to overwrite Si7021Temp's prototype with the prototype of its base class.

Now we can add to Si7021Temp's prototype the nuances of the subclass. In our case, that will be reading the sensor value (see Listing 1-15).

Listing 1-15. Adding a method to Si7021Temp

```
Si7021Temp.prototype.measure = function() {
  this.i2cBus.writeByte(0x40, 0xF3, 0, (err) => {
    if(err) {
      this.measurement = -999;
      return;
    }
    setTimeout(() => {
      this.i2cBus.i2cRead(
        0x40,
        3,
        new Buffer(3),
        (err, bytesRead, data) => {
        if(err) {
          this.measurement = -999;
          return;
        }
        this.measurement = (
          (((data[0] << 8) |
            data[1]) * 175.72) / 65536) - 46.85);
      });
    }, 100);
  });
}
```

Before we move on, let's discuss this code. Notice the differences that arise when writing asynchronous code: writeByte(), which we first use to send the command to the sensor to read the temperature, has a callback function that is executed once writing the byte to the I2C bus is completed.

The callback function takes an error object as an argument, or in other words, when `writeByte()` finishes execution, it calls the callback function with an argument representing an error, if such an error happened. In the callback, we can check if `err` has a value and, if so, deal with the error – in our case, we set `measurement` to a value representing missing data. If there is no error, we can move on.[2]

If we look at the Python code we wrote earlier, we can see that we put a 0.1 second (or 100 milliseconds) delay between sending the command to read the temperature and reading the bytes from the sensor. Here, we use `setTimeout()` to create this delay and perform the reading in the callback, which also starts by checking for an error.

OOP in JavaScript ES6

To programmers like me, who started in class-based languages and only later learned JavaScript, prototype inheritance can be very confusing. The new `class` syntax does a good job shielding programmers from dealing with prototypes and allows us to continue thinking in terms of classes. Let's rewrite everything, starting with `Sensor` (see Listing 1-16).

Listing 1-16. Rewriting the Sensor superclass using the ES6 `class` syntax

```
class Sensor {
  constructor(name) {
    this.name = name;
    this.measurement = -999;
  }

  getReadAsString() {
```

---

[2]We will dive deeper into error handling, with this specific example in mind, in Chapter 9.

```
    if ('units' in this) {
      return('${this.measurement} ${this.units}');
    } else {
      return(String(this.measurement));
    }
  }
}
```

So far, this is pretty clean and self-explanatory. Let's move on to Si7021Temp (see Listing 1-17).

Listing 1-17. Subclassing Si7021Temp using the class syntax

```
class Si7021Temp extends Sensor {
  constructor(name, busId) {
    super(name);
    //...
    // Copy Si7021Temp construction function code

  measure() {
    //...
    // You get the drift. Copy the code from the
    // measure() function we wrote before.
    // ...
  }
}
```

Note that we called super(), which is the constructor of the base class. When using the class syntax, we must call the base class constructor before we can refer to this. In fact, as we've seen earlier, this is usually very useful even when using the prototype syntax or when working with Python. Remember that in our example, the superclass constructor initializes measurement. This will happen in all of its subclasses, which is great.

It's important to remind ourselves, once again, that this is just syntactical magic. Under the hood, the class syntax still produces prototype. It's important to remind ourselves, once again, that this is just syntactical magic. Under the hood, the class syntax still produces prototype inheritance.

Summary

We started by introducing OOP in Python, and we implemented several classes using duck typing, which means brute-forcing different classes into sharing the same interface. Then we moved to the more traditional, structured way of doing things: proper class inheritance, as practiced in other languages like C++ and Java, and we showed how that works in Python. When we finished going through the basics, we moved to JavaScript and its version of OOP – prototypes and prototype inheritance. Finally, we reviewed the `class` syntax in JavaScript, which simplifies inheritance and creates simpler code that looks more similar to classes in other languages.

As we discussed OOP, we only hinted at the benefits we can get from designing an object-oriented system. As we progress, we will show pragmatic examples that demonstrate how object-oriented design helps build monitoring, logging, and debugging systems that scale – when we expand or modify the project itself, those systems require very little and, sometimes, no adaptations to the changes we make. In the next chapter, as we build our first dashboard, we will already see how interface compatibility saves the day.

CHAPTER 2

Our First Web Dashboard

In this chapter we will cover the basics of creating a web dashboard for a project. A web dashboard is basically a web page that can be accessed from any device with a web browser. From that page we are able to see what our project is doing, or at least what the project thinks it's doing, change its configuration, and give it instructions.

As much as this seems like an obvious thing to do, it is a rather new concept. To this day, many computer-based systems can only be controlled with a mouse, a keyboard, and a monitor connected to the computer itself. Even with the ubiquity of Wi-Fi and mobile devices, many applications and IoT devices still heavily rely on mobile apps rather than web technologies. As makers, we can appreciate web interfaces: unlike physical knobs and buttons, connected monitors or mobile apps, web pages are fast to develop and can be accessed from any computer or mobile device.

Everything Is a Server

A *server* is a computer or a program that performs some sort of task at the request of other computers or programs, to whom it refers to as *clients*. If this sounds pretty general, it's because it is, and when we think of servers, we often imagine rows of racks in fluorescent-lit basements, stacked with blade servers that mundanely process search queries from online

© Eyal Shahar 2019
E. Shahar, *Project Reliability Engineering*, https://doi.org/10.1007/978-1-4842-5019-8_2

shoppers, while in reality servers come in all shape and sizes and can have all kinds of exotic jobs – from running a multi-player online game to coordinate the efforts of astronomy fans in search for extraterrestrial life. In today's climate, where practically every piece of technology is connected, almost everything qualifies as a server. The argument that I am trying to push here is that if something can be a server, then it should be one, including maker projects.

Giving a project the capabilities of a web server offers several clear advantages. It allows us to control a project remotely, whether it is in real time or by adjusting its settings; it allows us to monitor its activity; and it allows it to communicate autonomously with other machines.

We will start by serving a single web page, functioning as a dashboard. Graphical user interfaces (GUI) for projects gain even more benefits from being implemented as web pages: while creating a GUI in many languages can often be a painful process, the web stack, consisting mostly of HTML, CSS, and JavaScript, is extremely popular and easy to use and enjoys the support of a huge community. It's not going anywhere any time soon, so even if the code of our project ever needs to be upgraded or even ported to another language, the dashboard itself will not be affected.

To allow our project to do that, we will need to incorporate a *web framework* in it. A web framework takes care of functionalities related to web connectivity, such as listening to incoming requests and responding with the desired data or web page. We will discuss Flask for Python and Express.js for Node.js. But first, let's discuss what HTTP requests are and what happens when we pull up a web page in our browser.

HTTP Requests

The *Hypertext Transfer Protocol* (HTTP) was developed primarily to enable the transmission of web pages from a server to web browsers. HTTP implements a request-response model, and what that means is that the server sits there and waits for clients, web browsers, for example, to send requests for resources, like pages, media, or data. Requests can also be made to the server to perform an action, but no matter what the nature of the request is, the server must always respond, whether it's with the resource the client asked for or just with an acknowledgment or an error message.

Because HTTP requests work this way, it means that all communication is initiated by the client. For our purposes, it means a dashboard that updates continuously must either periodically make requests from the server for the most up-to-date data or use a different form of communication, such as WebSockets, which we will explore in the next chapter.

An HTTP request can be one of several *methods*. The ones most often used are GET and POST. GET is used to retrieve data or resources, while POST is used to transfer data for the server to store. The request specifies its method type and the resource it asks for in the form of a *Uniform Resource Identifier* (URI), which, for every practical purpose, is the same as a *Uniform Resource Locator* (URL). The request also has some *header fields*, which tell the server things about the request itself, such as the type of browser it came from and the language in which users are expecting to see results. Finally, the request has a *body,* which can be used to transmit data to the server.

The names of the methods may imply that they were meant to be used with databases. This is reinforced by the names of some of the other methods, like PUT and DELETE, but different methods can be used as the programmer pleases. What matters are that the methods chosen make sense to the programmer and to other users and that the differences between methods are understood so that the method chosen has the right features for the task at hand.

A GET request either asks for a specific file, like a web page or a JavaScript file, or performs a query. In a query, the desired resource, or query, is expressed in the URI. The URI takes the form of

```
/path/to/resource?param1=value1&param2=value2...
```

There are two parts to the query, separated by a question mark, that express to the server what the client wants – the path and the query parameters. In the software world, that most often deals with databases, the path is usually used to fetch a specific item, while the query parameters are used when the client wants to filter the data in the database. Later in this chapter we will use GET requests for controlling the hardware, and we will need to consider how we want requests to be formatted.

We will not use POST requests in the book, but we should mention that the main difference between them and GET requests is that the parameters are specified in the body, which is usually left empty in GET requests – this makes POST requests a little more secure. As mentioned, POST requests are used to send data to the server, for example, when a user submits a form or uploads a picture to a web site, and this is not really something we are going to be dealing with.

After the server gets the request and processes it, it must send a response. Like the request, the response has a body which this time contains the data that the client requested and headers which contain meta-data about transaction. It also contains a status line which specifies the protocol used, for example, HTTP/1.1, a status code, and a reason phrase, which is a super short description of the status code. Table 2-1 provides a short list of some of the most common status codes and their respective reason phrases.

Table 2-1. *HTTP response status codes*

Status Code	Reason Phrase	Explanation
200	OK	Request processed successfully
400	Bad request	The server believes the client made a mistake, i.e, sent an ill-formatted query
404	Not found	The client requested a specific resource that the server could not find
500	Internal server error	The server code failed

The codes are divided into groups, which makes it easier to remember what they mean: the 100s are informational and the 300s deal with redirection, and these two groups are rarely encountered when dealing with systems in our scale. The 200s convey success, the 400s inform of a problem on the client side, and the 500s are responses dealing with failure on the server-side.

HTML in a Nutshell

Now that we have a basic idea of how a server and a client, or a project computer and a web browser, can communicate, we are ready to craft the first thing our server is going to serve – a web page. For that, we will have to dig into HTML.

HTML (Hypertext Markup Language) is the language in which web pages are written. Learning HTML thoroughly is well beyond the scope of this book, but instead of asking the reader to pause reading and take a complete HTML course, we will quickly introduce HTML at this point and address more aspects of the language as we need them while moving forward.

HTML describes the content of the page and the hierarchy of the different elements, and although the design of the page can be embedded in the code, it is usually considered good practice to leave that for accompanying CSS files. Examine the code in Listing 2-1 and the resulting web page in Figure 2-1. You can refer to these as we explain HTML in more detail.

Listing 2-1. Basic HTML code example

```
<!DOCTYPE html>
<html>
  <head>
  </head>
```

```
<body>
   <h1>Some basic HTML tags</h1>
   <p>This is a paragraph. It will be followed
      by an unordered list, that will have:</p>
   <ul>
      <li>This item</li>
      <li>and this one</li>
      <li>and also this one</li>
   </ul>
  <div id="div-example">
    <p>div elements help keep thing organized by
       defining sections, and help with styling,
       while <span style="font-family:
       monospace;">the span tag</span> just helps
       with inline styling.</p>
  </div>
  </body>
</html>
```

Some basic HTML tags

This is a paragraph. It will be followed by an unordered list, that will have:

- This item
- and this one
- and also this one

div elements help keep thing organized by defining sections, and help with
styling, while the span tag just helps with inline styling.

Figure 2-1. *Output of the HTML code in Listing 2-1*

An HTML file consists of elements, such as text paragraphs, tables, and images. An element starts with a tag that states what kind of element it is, that is, "p" for a paragraph or "img" for image. Refer to Table 2-2 for a list of some common tags. A tag is surrounded by angled brackets, like so: <input>. Some tags are empty, meaning that they directly represent the content that goes into the page; however, most elements do have either text or nested elements in them. Elements that are capable of having nested elements have an opening tag and a closing tag, with the closing tag preceded by a slash, like so:

```
<p>This is a paragraph.</p>
```

Table 2-2. *Common HTML tags*

Element Type	Tag	Empty Tag
Level 1 header	h1	No
Paragraph	p	No
Image	img	Yes
Section	div	No
Span	span	No
Unordered list	ul	No
List item	li	No

A tag, or an opening tag in the case of an opening-closing pair, can have various attributes. These describe responses to user interactions, allow JavaScript functions and CSS styling sheets to refer to the element, and define other tag-specific properties. Attributes are followed by the equal sign, followed by the attribute's value surrounded in double quotes, like so:

```
<p id="paragraph">This is a paragraph.</p>
```

We will work extensively with two attributes: the id attribute which gives the tag a unique identifier and the class attribute which groups multiple elements.

Note   A tag can have only one id, and it must be the only tag with that id. A tag, however, can have multiple classes, and multiple tags can have the same class.

An HTML file should start with a Document Type Definition (DTD), telling the browser what kind of document it's handling. These days, as the standard is HTML5, this should be <!DOCTYPE html>. What follows is the <html> tag, containing two sections: the head and the body. The head contains meta-data about the page itself, such as the page's title, keywords that are used to help search engine bots classify the page, definitions of graphic styles used in the page in the form of CSS, JavaScript code, as well as links to CSS and JavaScript files. The body contains what is actually displayed on the page, in the form of nested HTML elements.

Sometimes, people talk about the elements in the HTML in terms of the *DOM* (*Document Object Model*). These are not exactly the same thing. HTML is a language that describes the layout and content of the page. The DOM is how the browser represents the elements, grasps their relations to one another, and provides the programmatic interface to manipulate them.

Selectors and CSS

The point of having classes and id attributes has the ability to find them effectively in order to perform actions on them, such as apply styles to them, manipulate them within the page, and assign callbacks for user interactions with them. This is done with selectors, often called "*CSS selectors*" as this is their primary use. These are strings that use a specific format to express which elements need to be found. Table 2-3 shows some of the more common selector syntax rules.

Table 2-3. *Examples for CSS selectors*

Syntax	Returned Elements
`#element-id`	The element whose id is `element-id`
`.class-name`	All elements that belong to the class `class-name`
`button.class-name`	All buttons that belong to the class `class-name`
`classname button`	All buttons that are nested inside elements of the class `classname`
`.class1, .class2`	All elements of the class `class1` and all elements of the class `class2`

We can instruct the browser how to style elements using CSS, which stands for "Cascading Style Sheets." It is a programming language that has very simple syntax. Listing 2-2 provides an example.

Listing 2-2. CSS syntax example

```
selector-string1 {
  property1: value1;
  property2: value2;
}

selector-string2 {
  property3: value3;
  property4: value4;
}
```

Styling with CSS can appear in three places:

1. In an external file, and then it is included in the
    HTML file in a link tag, like so:

    ```
    <link rel="stylesheet" type="text/css"
    href="path/to/stylesheet.css">
    ```

2. In the HTML file, within a <style> element:

    ```
    <style>
    .my-class {
    background-color: black;
    }
    </style>
    ```

3. In the HTML file, within a style attribute of an
    element's tag:

    ```
    <div style="background-color: black; font-
    size: 1.5em;>Content goes here</div>
    ```

Template Rendering

Many web application frameworks, like the ones we will discuss soon, offer a feature called *template rendering*. It allows a web page to be manipulated prior to being served to the client, for example, presenting the most up-to-date data. Obviously, this is useful to us when we set to serve a status page.

Different template engines exist, and each has its own flavor, but the general gist is the same: the web page is written with placeholders for the template engine to replace with actual content. These placeholders, usually surrounded by special characters combination known as *delimiters*, are written in something that looks very much like a programming language, specific to the template engine used. This special syntax can have various levels of complexity, from merely displaying a variable's value to evaluation of `if-then` conditional blocks and loop iteration. Consider the HTML snippet in Listing 2-3.

Listing 2-3. Mustache template example

```
<div id="sensors-measurements">
  <p>Temperature: {{temperature}}</p>
  <p>Wind speed: {{wind_speed}}</p>
</div>
```

"Mustache", a popular templating engine for JavaScript, uses two pairs of curly brackets as the delimiters. When rendering the template, it expects to receive a dictionary containing keys by the same name, and it will fill the placeholders with these keys' values.

Some engines use slightly different syntax, while others, like Pug (formally known as Jade), use a significantly different paradigm altogether.

Python and Flask

Flask[1] is a microframework for Python. It is classified as a microframework due to its minimalistic set of features. It does, however, know how to route and handle HTTP requests, render templates, and serve web pages, which is all that we need at this point.

As much as I would love to dive right into the code, we do have to pause for a couple of paragraphs and talk about synchronous vs. asynchronous code. Synchronous code is code that halts after each command until it is fully executed. Reading from a file, for instance, can take time, but in a synchronous program the following instruction will

---

[1]http://flask.pocoo.org/

only be executed after the file has been read. In asynchronous code, on the other hand, after a function is called, the next instruction is called immediately, even if the first function did not completely execute. However, after the instruction has been executed, a *callback function* is called, allowing the program to handle the completed task.

Although Python does have (since fairly recently) some mechanisms that implement asynchronous programming, it is generally a synchronous language, and due to that, once we instruct Flask to start listening to incoming requests, we will block the rest of the program. It seems inevitable to move something to a different thread.

Coding Our First Dashboard

Let's move the measuring loop to its own thread. We'll delete the line that calls `measuring_loop` and instead add the code in Listing 2-4.

Listing 2-4. Moving the measuring loop to a separate thread

```
import threading

#...
t = threading.Thread(target=measuring_loop)
t.start()
```

DON'T LOSE THE THREAD

If you are not familiar with threads, it is sufficient at this point to know that a program can run multiple independent threads in (what appears like) the same time, so that time-dependent operations don't block each other, and that this is how you spawn them in Python. Although JavaScript does offer workers which run on independent threads, they are not as needed as threads in Python, due to the JavaScript's asynchronous nature.

Now we can add the code from Listing 2-5 to our weather station from the previous chapter.

Listing 2-5. Adding a Flask server to the weather station

```
from flask import Flask, render_template
app = Flask(__name__)

@app.route('/dashboard/')
def show_dashboard():
    return render_template(
      'dashboard.html',
      temperature=sensor_list[0].measurement)

if __name__ == '__main__':
    app.run(host = '0.0.0.0')
```

What this code does, after importing Flask, is define the app object that will be used to register all that Flask will need to know, like what functions to run for each HTTP request that is made. Then, it registers the show_ dashboard() function to the /dashboard/ route. This means that if we open a browser on the same computer and navigate to 127.0.0.1:5000/ dashboard (since 5000 is the default port for Flask), the show_dashboard() function will execute and will be responsible for sending a response to the client. The body of this function is simply one line that returns a template file, dashboard.html, which is rendered with the variables that follow.

DECORATORS AND HOW FLASK USES THEM

That at sign (@) in Python is called a *decorator*. It's a mechanism that allows functions to be wrapped by other functions, hence modifying or extending their functionality. The decorating function, whose name is prefixed by the at sign, decorates the subsequent function by intercepting its input and its output. The syntax allows us to decorate many functions with the same decorator, which makes this such a power feature: imagine we wanted to write to a file the output of some of our functions. All we would have to do is define the file-writing feature as a decorator and then decorate all those other functions with it.

Flask, however, uses this syntax in a sneaky way: when you first decorate a function, that function is passed to the decorator for wrapping. Flask takes this opportunity to register that function with the request's route, so that whenever a client makes a request to this route, the correct function is called.

Listing 2-6 shows what the template we render might look like.

Listing 2-6. A basic template for the dashboard

```
<!DOCTYPE html>
<html>
  <head>
  </head>
  <body>
    <p>Temperature: {{ temperature }}</p>
  </body>
</html>
```

Note Flask looks for templates in a `templates` folder that is in the project folder.

We passed the argument `temperature` to the template engine, and marked in the template file, using the Flask's templating syntax, where its value should be placed. Note how Flask uses double brackets (`{{ ... }}`) as delimiters for expressions.

We had more than one sensor in the project from the previous chapter, and although we could have had a single line in the HTML file for every sensor, let us remember that we made sure all those sensors implement the same interface and that they are all in one list. Flask's template engine allows us to iterate through lists, so all we need to pass to the template engine is just that list and then let the template engine iterate on it. We'll start by rewriting the definition of the function `dashboard()` as shown in Listing 2-7.

Listing 2-7. Serving the sensor list

```
@app.route('/dashboard/')
def show_dashboard():
  return render_template(
    'dashboard.html', sensor_list=sensor_list)
```

And then we'll change the template body accordingly as shown in Listing 2-8.

Listing 2-8. Using the template engine's iteration feature to render the sensor list

```
<body>
  <ul>
  {% for s in sensor_list %}
    <li>{{s.name}}:
        {{s.measurement}} {{s.units}}</li>
  {% endfor %}
  </ul>
</body>
```

The delimiters Flask used to indicate statements such as for-loops or conditionals are {% ... %}. You might notice that within the template, we treat the sensor_list object exactly the same way we do in Python – as a list of instances of the Sensor class whose fields we wish to display, but the notation here is JSON.[2] When the template engine acts on the template, the content of the for-loop is evaluated for each item in sensor_list, which results in a <li> element in the final HTML file. In every loop iteration, s is a temporary variable representing the current item, so that its data members can be accessed, evaluated, and rendered.

WHAT'S MY IP ADDRESS?

The address we mentioned, 127.0.0.1, is always the IP address that machines use to refer to themselves. If we want to view the dashboard from another device, like a laptop or a phone, we'll need to know the IP address of the project's machine. As a first step, there are two simple techniques to find out what it is:

1. Use a browser to open your router's administration page. Usually it's on 192.168.1.1. Then find a page that is called something like "Connected Devices." This will display the IP addresses of all the devices in your network. To help identify the project's machine, plug or unplug it from its power supply and refresh the page.

2. Connect a keyboard and a monitor to your machine, and in the terminal window enter the command ifconfig. This will print a list of all the network interfaces that your machine has. Look for something that looks like eth0 for a LAN connection or wlan0 for wireless connection. It should be followed by the device's address.

---

[2]If you're new to JSON, flip to Chapter 5 for an introduction.

This is the address that your router gave the machine. Once you have this address, you can use it to find the dashboard from any machine on your local network, and the router is very unlikely to change it. However, we will soon see how we can set it manually so that it never changes and even view it from outside the local network.

The Flask Web Server

Flask is not designed to be run from the command line. When we do run the program, by entering in the terminal

```
sudo python3 weatherstation.py
```

we will find the Flask is very opinionated about that and will show this message before running the program:

```
WARNING: Do not use the development server in a production
environment.
Use a production WSGI server instead.
```

Let's unpack that: a *web server* is a program that runs on a machine, listens to requests that come from the Internet, and decides what to do with them. These requests are probably intended to be handled by a program on that machine, so the web server needs a way to communicate with that program. This is where *WSGI*, the Web Server Gateway Interface, comes in. It is a protocol through which the web server can launch Python programs as a response to an incoming request. This means that every incoming request spawns a new instance of the program. Usually, the program will process the request, do whatever it's meant to do, send a response, and exit. This allows the web server to serve many requests concurrently.

While this is good for many types of programs, it's not what we want. We want only one instance of the program, and we definitely want the weather station to work when nobody is looking at the dashboard. Our solution is to run the program from the command line, which causes Flask to launch its own web server, but complain while it's at it. Why is it complaining? Because Flask's web server is not suitable for production environments, since it doesn't know how to deal with multiple, simultaneous requests. Rather, it handles them one by one. We, however, use Flask, at this point, for the sole purpose of serving the dashboard, so that should be good enough for now.

There are other alternatives for including a web framework in a Python project. One example is *Tornado*.[3] Tornado can work as a web server, so if it's included in a project, it is the project itself that handles the requests – no need to spawn programs anymore. Tornado is a heavier framework than Flask, though, and has a steeper learning curve. For applications where the web component is marginal, using Flask the way we are, with its own web server, is perfectly acceptable.

Adding Browser Interactivity

It can be useful to send commands from the dashboard back to the server. We could do things like adjust preferences, enable and disable functionalities, run tests, and request data. Let's create a button that enables and disables the measurement-taking loop of our weather station program. First, we'll make a small modification to the code in Listing 1-2 and add a parameter that determines whether measuring is to take place or not. We can also stop printing the results to the screen. This will result in the code in Listing 2-9.

---

[3]www.tornadoweb.org

Listing 2-9. Rewriting the measuring loop to enable and disable sensor reading

```
is_measuring = true
def measuring_loop():
  while True:
    if is_measuring:
      for sensor in sensor_list:
        sensor.measure()
    time.sleep(5)
```

We'll add a button to our HTML file. That button will send an HTTP request to the server, which in turn the value of is_measuring to either True or False. We'll start by considering what that request will be.

A GET request seems appropriate – POST requests are a little more cumbersome and usually imply that something is stored in a database. Now, you may recall that everything we want GET request to do is expressed in the URI, so to be specific when telling the server what we want, we have to decide what that URI is going to look like – this is called an *endpoint* of a server. We could use unique paths for the two functions, like /loop_on and /loop_off, but if we stop to think what that code is going to look like, we can imagine some repetition that can be avoided. We could use the dashboard's path and make use of the query string, for instance, /dashboard?loop=false, but then the server would have to test for the existence of parameters in the URI to determine whether it should serve the page, respond to a control command from the dashboard, or execute some other functionality. These don't feel like they belong together in the same function. The healthy way to do this is probably some combination of the two: for controlling the project, we can have a path that is separate from the dashboard's path, and the exact command we want to execute can be expressed by parameters in the query string. Let's choose /control?loop=true to activate the loop and /control?loop=false to turn it off and add the code in Listing 2-10 to the server.

Listing 2-10. Adding a control endpoint to the server

```
from flask import jsonify, request

@app.route('/control')
def control():
  global is_measuring
  is_measuring = request.args.get('loop')
  res = {'is_measuring': is_measuring}
  return jsonify(res)
```

Notice the flow of data that leads to the change of the button's text: the button is pressed, the command is sent to the server, and the server changes the state of the loop and returns the new state back to the client, which in turn changes the text of the button based on the response it got from the server. Why not change the text of the button at the same time that the button is clicked and the request is sent to the server, instead of having this long course for the data to go through? Well, the code works this way to enforce an extremely important principal: data representation must always be driven by the data itself and not by what we think the data should be. If the text is changed in the click event handler, how do we know that the instruction was received by the server correctly? More generally, let's say something does go wrong, and we turn to the dashboard to debug it: we click the button, and an indicator tells us that the operation has been performed. We are puzzled – we look at our hardware, and we don't see the change – but how can that be? The dashboard says it's fine! Well, if the indicator is driven by the button, it will tell us that the change has happened whether it actually did or not. This is why indicators should be driven by data, not by our actions.

Note   We gave the form of the endpoint controlling the measuring loop some thought, but that was only a glimpse into a much larger topic – designing an efficient software interface for a program. You may have heard the term *API (Application Program Interface)*. Well, this is exactly it: an API is what allows people, but also other machines and programs, to interact with a program, and designing one that is consistent, simple for the clients to access, and easy for the programmer to maintain is not an easy task and is rarely as straightforward as the process we have just went through. There is an abundance of literature[4] and online resources if you're interested in digging deeper.

Let's add that button to our dashboard. We can put the code shown in Listing 2-11 right after the list of measurements.

Listing 2-11. Adding controls to the dashboard

```
<!-- ... -->
<ul>
  <!-- ... -->
</ul>
<div>Measuring:
  <button data-initial="{{ is_measuring }}"
          id="toggle-loop">
  </button>
</div>
```

---

[4]For example: Jin, Brenda, Saurabh Sahni, and Amir Shevat. *Designing Web APIs: Building APIs That Developers Love.* Sebastopol, CA: OReilly Media, 2018.

And since this is the last DOM element, we'll follow this with the
JavaScript code in Listing 2-12 to add the functionality. Adding the
JavaScript code at the very end of the DOM promises that by the time it
runs, any elements the code refers to have already been added to DOM.

Listing 2-12. Giving functionality to the dashboard controls

```
    <script>
let loopButton =
  document.getElementById('toggle-loop');
let isMeasuring =
  loopButton.getAttribute('data-initial') == 'True';

function setLoopButtonText(state) {
  loopButton.innerHTML = state ? "stop" : "start";
}

setLoopButtonText(isMeasuring);

loopButton.addEventListener("click", () => {
  let url = new URL(
    'control', window.location.origin);
  let params = {loop: !isMeasuring };
  url.search = new URLSearchParams(params);
  fetch(url, {
    method: 'get'
  }).then(function(response) {
    return response.json();
  }).then(function(data) {
    isMeasuring = data.is_measuring;
    setLoopButtonText(isMeasuring);
    });
  });
    </script>
```

There's a lot going on here. Let's move through the code slowly. The first interesting thing you may notice is the attribute `data-initial` that we gave the button. This is not a standard attribute, and therefore the browser ignores it, but we put it there so that we'd have a way render in the initial value of `is_measuring`, and in the dashboard's JavaScript code, we read this value into the `isMeasuring` variable. We'll need to add `is_measuring` to the arguments used to render the dashboard, so the endpoint handler in Listing 2-7 should now be modified to look like this (Listing 2-13).

Listing 2-13. The modified dashboard endpoint handler also renders the measuring loop's state

```
@app.route('/dashboard/')
def show_dashboard():
  return render_template(
    'dashboard.html',
    sensor_list=sensor_list,
    is_measuring=is_measuring)
```

Are there other ways to do this? Sure there are. We could, for example, render the value right into the JavaScript, when we first declare and initialize `isMeasuring`

```
let isMeasuring = {{ is_measuring }};
```

This is an interesting solution, but not necessarily a healthy thing to do. First of all, if the page is just a little more complicated, we'd probably want to break the file into two: an HTML file and a JavaScript file, and then we'd have to render those too, going through the server's routing instead of serving static files. Also, if for some reason there's a problem with the value we are trying to render, we will break code rather than content, and that will almost always have more critical outcomes. We then need to remember that the dashboard is not the project itself, but only a means to debug and control it, and when the dashboard fails to load

43

it doesn't necessarily mean that the project broke. If there is a problem with `is_measuring` in the Python code, we want to be **informed** by the dashboard and not have that break the dashboard, having us wasting time debugging the dashboard. Having said that, I do want to show that using the templating engine to render code is an option that exists, and although we've just shown that it is probably a bad idea, I still find something magical about code that is written partially by the machine itself.

Another way is to have the page, once it loads, query the server for the value of the button. More generally, we can query the server for the entire state of the project. Then we'd have to ask ourselves – what is the point of rendering a template? We might as well write the web page without templating, serve it as it is, then have it query for the project's state, and change the page's content based on the data received. That is a perfectly valid approach, and I recommend choosing one or the other, but avoid using both querying and template rendering for the same thing. When the same functionality is performed by very different pieces of code, it creates confusion and makes it harder to maintain the code.

Let's move on. We assigned the button's DOM element to the variable `loopButton` in order to avoid looking for it every time we need it. We found it using `document.getElementById()`. There are two newer, more powerful, but also somewhat slower ways to find element in the DOM: `document.querySelector()`, which returns the first element it finds, and `document.querySelectorAll()`, which returns a list of all the elements it finds. What makes these more powerful is that they take a CSS selector as an argument, making it easier to find elements based on their place in the DOM hierarchy, which in turn can result in a much cleaner HTML file.

The button's text changes based on the value `isMeasuring` - `"Stop"` if the loop is running and `"Start"` if the loop is idle. That is taken care of by the function `setLoopButtonText()`, and to make sure there is text inside the button when the page loads, we execute it immediately. Then we attach an event handler to the button – a function that will be executed when the button is clicked. The event handler executes a `fetch()`[5] – an HTTP request. `Fetch()` returns a promise,[6] which means that when the server responds, the promise is resolved, and the function passed to `then()` is executed, and in our case, the promise returns a `Response` object. Calling `response.json()` returns another promise, which resolves with the body of the response decoded as JSON. With that data we can update `isMeasuring` by calling `setLoopButtonText()` once again.

Node.js and Express.js

The most widespread web application framework for Node.js is Express.js.[7] To set up Express.js in our program, we'll start by adding these lines:

```
const express = require('express');
const app = express();
```

and start the server by adding this line:

```
app.listen(3000);
```

Unlike Flask that comes with Jinja as its own templating engine, Express.js can work with a selection of quite a few templating engines that are available on the Web. While many of them, like Handlebars and EJS, work similarly to Jinja, Pug,[8] one of the most popular ones, works in a completely different way, by compiling and rendering Pug code into

---

[5]The `Fetch` API replaces the somewhat awkward `XMLHttpRequest` object. If you need help, start here: `https://developer.mozilla.org/en-US/docs/Web/API/Fetch_API`

[6]Promises are pretty cool and do more than just act as callbacks. However, starting a comprehensive discussion here will distract us from the topic. You can get learn more about them here: `https://developer.mozilla.org/en-US/docs/Web/JavaScript/Reference/Global_Objects/Promise`

[7]`https://expressjs.com/`

[8]`https://pugjs.org/`

HTML and JavaScript. Since we've already seen what Jinja looks like, we'll continue with Pug, as this will give us a wider perspective.

If we rewrite the template from the previous sections in Pug, we get the code in Listing 2-14.

Listing 2-14. The weather station dashboard rewritten in Pug

```
doctype html
html
  body
    ul
      each sensor in sensors
        li= sensor.name
          = ': '
          = sensor.measurement
          = sensor.units
```

Note   Pug looks for templates in a `views` folder that is in the project folder.

First, you might notice that in Pug, very much like Python, indentation matters, as it expresses code hierarchy. Personally, I am not a huge fan of indentation-based syntax, but nobody is asking me. Having said that, this does eliminate the need for closing tags, a fact that results in much shorter and cleaner code.

Next, you might notice the each loop. This operates just like a for-loop in Jinja, where each iteration of the loop is evaluated and is being rendered into the final HTML document.

The equal sign (=) tells the Pug compiler that the remainder of the line is a JavaScript expression, whose result should be rendered to the HTML page. The minus sign (-) is also available for running JavaScript code within the Pug template, but this time the result is not rendered to the page. I used multiple lines preceded with the equal sign simply for running out on page space, but it is important to remember that using the equal sign on consecutive lines does not mean that the JavaScript code can extend beyond a single line. Rather, every line executes and renders a self-contained expression.

We can tell our server to use Pug as its template engine and enable our first endpoint by adding the code in Listing 2-15 to our Node.js code.

Listing 2-15. Plugging in Pug

```
// ...
app.set('view engine', 'pug');
app.get('/dashboard', (request, response) => {
  response.render(
    'dashboard', { sensors: sensorList});
});
```

Notice the two arguments, `request` and `response`, that the handler for a request is called with. As their names suggest, `request` contains information about the source, nature, and content of the request, while `response` is a means for the program to fill in the content sent out as a response.

A Little Help

To speed up the development of our dashboard, we can use some libraries that can save us some work, simplify our code and make it more readable, and help us focus on the things that really matter to us – the project itself.

jQuery

jQuery has been around forever. The library takes care of some of the more annoying tasks a programmer has to deal with: DOM manipulation, that is, locating, adding, and removing elements in the HTML document; event handling, which basically means attaching callbacks to events such as mouse movements and window interactions; AJAX, which can be simply put as making HTTP requests; and animation of element properties.

When jQuery is loaded, its main identifier, jQuery, or its alias, the dollar sign ($), makes all the library's functionality available. To operate on an array of DOM elements, the identifier takes as an argument a CSS selector, just like document.querySelector(). The returned value, however, is an array of jQuery object, and jQuery's functions operate on such arrays. So, let's say we wanted to find all elements of the arbitrary class name and change the text to Alice. Instead of doing this

```
for (let elem of document.querySelector('.name')) {
  elem.innerHTML = 'Alice';
});
```

we could just do this:

```
$('.name').html('Alice');
```

jQuery is a little hungry for computation force, and with the release of CSS3 animation and the introduction of more modern, powerful, front-end libraries, jQuery has lost some of its popularity. However, jQuery is far from being dead. It saves a lot of typing and helps in crafting clean, concise code, and when CSS3 animation gets too aggravating, jQuery can help alleviate some of that frustration.

For making HTTP requests, jQuery also offers some straightforward syntax. For example, to toggle the loop, as we did earlier, using jQuery will result in the code in Listing 2-16.

Listing 2-16. Simplified code using jQuery

```
$.get('control', {'loop': !isMeasuring })
  .done(function(data) {
    isMeasuring = JSON.parse(data).loop_state;
  });
```

Bootstrap

Bootstrap[9] is a front-end framework which helps create pretty web pages with emphasis on mobile devices, by offering ready-to-use designs for HTML components. By applying classes to the components, fonts, colors, and animations are applied to them, creating a unified, mobile-friendly look to the page. Premium and free themes, as well as online theme builders, are available for a more personalized look and feel. Unlike the other frameworks discussed here, Bootstrap doesn't do much more, but since it is built on top of jQuery, once Bootstrap is used in a page, jQuery is also available for DOM manipulation.

Summary

In this chapter we have learned how to make a status page – not quite a fancy, updating-in-real-time, dashboard for a project, but still – a simple way to create a web page that gives us an idea of what our project is doing. For that purpose, we reviewed the basics of HTTP and HTML and introduced two popular frameworks: Flask for Python and Express.js for Node.js. We learned how to use template rendering to dynamically generate a web page that displays data from the project and how to create endpoints that let us control and query our project. We saw how an object-oriented approach toward software design in the project itself promotes simpler, cleaner, and more scalable code in our status page. In the next chapter, we'll expand our dashboard, mostly for the purpose of having it communicate with the project in real time.

---

[9]https://getbootstrap.com/

CHAPTER 3

The Live Dashboard

The dashboard that we created in the previous chapter, as simple as it is, is already a great tool and could be very useful just the way it is. We simply used template rendering and HTTP requests to convey the current state of the project and send instruction to it from a web browser; this already gives us insight about what the project is doing and allows us to control it. In this chapter we will build on top of the skills we learned and add real-time capabilities to our dashboard using both HTTP requests and WebSockets.

HTTP Requests

First, let us recall how we used a button to send a control message from the dashboard to the server. In the response, we sent back to the dashboard a JSON object describing the new state of the project. We can use a similar mechanism to display near real-time status, by continuously sending GET requests to the server, querying for the project's current state. We can do this by including a `setInterval()` in the dashboard code, as shown in Listing 3-1.

© Eyal Shahar 2019

E. Shahar, *Project Reliability Engineering*, https://doi.org/10.1007/978-1-4842-5019-8_3

Listing 3-1. The dashboard periodically queries the server for the project's status

```javascript
function queryStatus() {
  fetch('/status', {
    method: 'get'
  }).then((response) => {
    return response.json();
  }).then((data) => {
    updateDashboard(data);
  });
}

setInterval(queryStatus, 1000);
```

This makes a query to the /status endpoint every second and calls a function, updateDashboard() (which we will implement soon), with the response. The next step will be to define the /status endpoint. The code in Listing 3-2 demonstrates what that might look like in our server-side JavaScript implementation.

Listing 3-2. The status endpoint, implemented in JavaScript

```javascript
app.get('/status', (request, response) => {
  response.json({
    sensors: sensorList,
    measuring: isMeasuring
  });
});
```

Since we are sending back to the dashboard everything we have, we should re-consider our use of template rendering. Perhaps we should no longer use it for filling the page with data as we did before, since that will result in two mechanisms that are basically doing the same thing.

We might as well either wait for the first update that happens when queryStatus executes for the first time or add code to execute it right after the page loads, for example:

```
window.onload = queryStatus;
```

And since we are not rendering a template, we need to use front-end code to dynamically fill in the page's content. Let's start with a simple implementation. Our HTML can simply look like Listing 3-3.

Listing 3-3. Basic HTML to be filled by JavaScript

```
<body>
  <ul id="sensors-data"></ul>
</body>
```

And we'll let our JavaScript code replace the content of the <ul> element whenever data comes in. In Listing 3-1 we called the function updateDashboard() when the server responded with data. Let's implement this function now (see Listing 3-4).

Listing 3-4. Updating the dashboard with JavaScript

```
function updateDashboard(data) {
  let sensorListElement =
    document.getElementById("sensors-data");
  sensorListElement.innerHTML = ;
  for (let sensor of data.sensors) {
    let newItem = document.createElement('li');
    newItem.innerHTML = `${sensor.name}: \
      ${sensor.measurement} ${sensor.units}`;
    sensorListElement.appendChild(newItem);
  }
}
```

The Case for HTML Classes

In Listing 3-4, the very first action we take is to clear the element
containing the sensor data, then we move to re-populate it. This strategy
works only when we can afford to do so – in the next chapter, we will use
graphical elements to visualize the data, a scenario in which completely
rewriting parts of the DOM would not be acceptable, since some of these
elements take time to load. We could, instead, change existing elements in
the dashboard, and if an HTML element for a sensor does not exist, we can
create one. The code in Listing 3-5 demonstrates this approach.

Listing 3-5. Dynamically populating the dashboard

```
function updateDashboard(data) {
  let sensorListElement =
    document.getElementById('sensors-data');
  for (let sensor of data.sensors) {
    sensorElement =
      document.getElementById(sensor.name)
    if (!sensorElement) {
      sensorElement =
        updateDashboard.createElement('li');
      sensorElement
        .setAttribute('id', 'sensor.name');
      sensorElement.innerHTML
        = `${sensor.name}: \
        <span class=" measurement"></span> \
        ${sensor.units}`;
      sensorListElement.appendChild(sensorElement);

  }
```

```
  sensorElement
    .getElementsByClassName(measurement')[0]
    .innerHTML = sensor.measurement;
  }
}
```

We use a `<span>` element that we can locate in the DOM and change it programmatically, but notice how we locate that element: first, the desired `<li>` element that contains that `<span>` element is found by its **id** – we generate that id programmatically based on the sensor's name. Once we've found the `<li>` element, we proceed to find the `<span>` element within it by its **class** (the method `getElementsByClassName()` returns an array, since an element may have several children of the same class. We know we only have one, hence the [0]). An alternate way to this would be to give the `<span>` element an id, rather than a class, and use that id to locate the element. However, consider a slightly more complicated case – if we had to update not only the value of the measurement but also, let's say, the time in which it was taken. Now we would have to deal with two DOM elements with different ids for every sensor. We'd have to come up with some naming convention for that and recall what it is every time the code needs to reference these elements. I find that limiting the use of ids creates leaner and more readable code, both on the JavaScript and HTML sides. Following that approach, we first find the parent DOM element that handles a certain sensor by its id and then use classes to find a child element within it that contains a particular type of data from this sensor.

At this point we've moved away from using template rendering all together, but this is not to say that template rendering should be abandoned for HTTP requests. First, not every project requires real-time updates, and in that case, as we have shown in the previous chapter, template rendering offers a perfectly valid solution. Second, template rendering can still be used for other parts of the page, ones that we do not include in the real-time updating mechanism. We'll address that soon.

WebSockets

Introduction to WebSockets

The problem with getting information back and forth between the project computer and the web dashboard using HTTP requests is that any exchange has to be initiated by the client, that is, the dashboard. This is why we had to make the dashboard constantly query the server for all the information the server has. There is an alternative, however: *WebSockets*. The WebSockets protocol allows for a continuous, bidirectional connection to be formed between a client and a server. Once the connection is established, both client and server can send information to each other. This way, instead of having the dashboard constantly query for the server's state, the server can notify the dashboard only when something worth notifying has happened. It's a little bit like the difference between driving with somebody in the back seat who is constantly asking "are we there yet?" and having them wait quietly until you tell them "hey, we're there." In the following sections, we will examine how we can embed WebSockets into both our JavaScript and Python implementations of the weather station.

WebSockets in Node.js

There are quite a few libraries that implement WebSockets for Node.js. We'll use ws.[1] It has good support and a wide user base, and it keeps things simple.

Let's start by adding a WebSockets server to our Node.js project. Examine the code in Listing 3-6.

---

[1]https://github.com/websockets/ws

Listing 3-6. Adding a WebSockets server to the Node.js project

```
const http = require('http');
const httpServer = http.createServer(app);
const WebSocket = require('ws');
const wsServer = new WebSocket.Server({httpServer});

wsServer.broadcast = function(data) {
  for (client of wsServer.clients) {
    client.send(data);
  }
};

wsServer.on('connection', function (socket) {
  socket.on('message', function (data) {
    // handle incoming data here
  });
});

// change this line:
// app.listen(3000);
// to:
httpServer.listen(3000, function () {
  console.log('ready!')
});
```

In the previous chapter we launched the server with app.listen(), and that meant that we were using an HTTP server provided by Express.js. Now, however, we need a server that can also handle the WebSockets communication. To solve this, we create an HTTP server ourselves using the http module and then tell that server to use the Express.js app to handle incoming requests. Later, we tell the WebSockets server object to reuse that HTTP server.

Next, we piggyback on the WebSockets server object that we created and add our own new method to it, broadcast(), that will send data to all of the clients. Even though the purpose of this entire endeavor is to have a dashboard, of which we need only one instance in one browser tab, we do want to make sure that multiple browser tabs that show the dashboard can get the data: perhaps we accidentally left an open tab on a desktop computer but still want to access the dashboard from our phone. This is one reason why we always think in terms of "all of the clients." Another reason is that with WebSockets, in most cases, the person using a client is not the programmer, but rather one of many users, and we might as well learn how to deal with multiple connections while we're at it. Furthermore, sometimes the entity using the client is not a person, but another program, like a main server or another project. This is another reason for wanting to make sure many connections can be handled at the same time.

Notice that the code has a placeholder to show how the ws library handles incoming messages from the client: once a connection with a client is established, a callback for the connection event is executed with the client's WebSockets object as an argument. To this object we can now attach a callback for the message event that is executed whenever data comes in, but as you can see, we don't actually need to process any data coming from the dashboard to the server yet.

The next step will be to use broadcast() in the measuring loop, as shown in Listing 3-7.

Listing 3-7. Broadcasting results from the measuring loop

```
setInterval(() => {
  if (isMeasuring) {
    for (sensor of sensorList) {
      sensor.measure();
      wsServer.broadcast(
```

```
        JSON.stringify(s)
    );
  }
 }
}, 5000);
```

The data being sent and received by WebSockets cannot be something as complex as a JavaScript object. Generally speaking, it can transfer arrays of binary data, like strings. What we can do, given that, is to `stringify()` a JSON object in the transmitting side and `parse()` the string in the receiving side. We will discuss soon how to structure the JSON response that the server sends to the dashboard. For the time being, we'll just send a simplified version of the sensor object: `JSON.stringify()` will make a JSON string from any object, ignoring any functions. That's good enough for now.

WebSockets in Python

Building a similar program in Python is significantly more difficult. Python, in its nature, is synchronous, meaning that a program can't just stop whatever it's doing to run a callback when data shows up at the WebSockets server's door. Any solution that we find must take that into consideration. We will use the websockets[2] library, which will give us an opportunity to look at some asynchronous Python code, and `asyncio`,[3] which is the built-in module for asynchronous programming.

asyncio Primer

The key component to an asynchronous program is the *event loop*, which is responsible for running callbacks, *tasks*, and *coroutines*. Coroutines are functions that run within the event loop. At any point they can pause and

---

[2]https://websockets.readthedocs.io/en/stable/
[3]https://docs.python.org/3/library/asyncio.html

wait for something to happen, giving control back to the event loop, thus allowing different operations to appear to work concurrently. Examine the example in Listing 3-8. This program will print "1 second" after 1 second and "2 seconds" one second afterward.

Listing 3-8. asyncio example

```
import asyncio

async def print_later(time, text):
  await asyncio.sleep(time)
  print(text)

async def main():
  task1 = asyncio.ensure_future(
    print_later(2, '2 seconds'))
  task2 = asyncio.ensure_future(
    print_later(1, '1 seconds'))
  await task1
  await task2

loop = asyncio.get_event_loop()
loop.run_until_complete(main())
```

The first thing to notice is that coroutines are defined using the keywords async def. Then we see that coroutines can be called using the await keyword. In fact, simply doing this

```
print_later(2, '2 seconds')
```

doesn't cause a coroutine execute. Rather, this creates an *awaitable* object that can be run, as mentioned, by using the await keyword, or passed to the event loop in some other form. In this program we see two examples of how this can be done: the first is the creation of two *tasks* that can concurrently run the print_later() coroutine using the asyncio.ensure_future()

function. The second example is the direct instruction to run the `main()` coroutine using the `run_until_complete()` function.

Let's go back to what actually ends up happening in this example: the two tasks are created in the `main` function, and the event loop is asked to execute them. The code will pause right after that, and the main function will not proceed until both `task1` and `task2` are executed. In `print_later()`, the function that both tasks execute, `asyncio.sleep()`, gives control back to the event loop for the specified amount of time. This allows for both tasks to start right about the same time, go to sleep, and be woken up by the event loop at the right time, and all this regardless of which one was called first.

Using the websockets Library

But we're not here to talk about `asyncio`. Our goal is to embed WebSockets in our weather station. However, the websockets library relies on `asyncio`, and since our code is synchronous, we have to be prepared. Now that we've established the basic terms, there are a few constraints we need to pay attention to:

- Sending data to a WebSockets client is an asynchronous operation in the websockets library.

- The `await` keyword can only be used within a coroutine.

- There can only be one event loop in a given thread.

We want to be able to send messages to clients whenever new measurements are taken, an operation that happens in our measuring loop, which is synchronous. We can't just call asynchronous functions from a synchronous function. How do we solve that? We could refactor all of our code to be asynchronous and have everything run on the same thread under the same event loop, and in the case of a simple weather station, that would probably be a good idea. However, this solution is not ideal for programs that need higher time precision, so for the sake of the example, we will choose to leave the measuring loop as it is, running as synchronous code. Therefore, we will have to spawn a new thread and within that thread spawn an event loop. This will allow the thread to deal with our WebSockets server. Let's put that into code (Listing 3-9).

Listing 3-9. Adding WebSockets to the Python server code

```python
import websockets
import asyncio

client_set = set()

def websocket_thread():
  global ws_event_loop
  ws_event_loop = asyncio.new_event_loop()
  asyncio.set_event_loop(ws_event_loop)
  ws_server = websockets.serve(
    client_handler, host='0.0.0.0', port=3001)
  ws_event_loop.run_until_complete(ws_server)
  ws_event_loop.run_forever()

async def client_handler(client, data_handler):
  client_set.add(client)
  try:
    while True:
      message = await client.recv()
      if data_handler:
        data_handler(json.loads(message))
  finally:
    client_set.remove(client)
```

```
async def send_to_all(msg):
  if client_set:
    await asyncio.wait(
      [client.send(msg) for client in client_set])
```

Let's look at the code more closely. The global set `client_set` contains all the active connections that the server has. We will have to manage this set ourselves so that we can broadcast messages to all connections. We also define `ws_event_loop` globally in `websocket_thread()`, since the measuring loop will need to execute stuff within the event loop as measurements come in, as we will see soon.

Note   The `global` keyword in Python can be confusing – why did we have to use it for `ws_event_loop` but not for `client_set`? The answer lies in the assignment. As long as you don't assign anything to a variable name that exists in the global scope, the program knows you're referring to the global variable. However, if an assignment happens within a class's method, that will create a new variable within the scope of the class.

Next, we spawn an event loop in the new thread and create a WebSockets server awaitable that is then passed to the event loop to run. Note that we had to run the WebSockets server on a different port. Unfortunatly, the websockets library does not support the running the server alongside an HTTP server on the same port, but that's not that terrible. Also note how `websockets.serve()` takes a handler as an argument that is called whenever a new client makes a connection. We define that handler, `client_handler()`, next.

There's not a lot going on in `client_handler()`. The new connection is added to the clients' set when the connection is made and an infinite loop listens to data coming in, passing it to a `data_handler`, if one was specified. The loop exits (then it's not really infinite then, is it?) when an exception is raised due to the client disconnecting, and the client is removed from the clients' set.

send_to_all() is a little more interesting to talk about. This function will be used by the measuring loop to send data to all the clients. asyncio. wait() takes a list of awaitables and executes them concurrently. It is itself a coroutine and therefore needs the await keyword to execute. Notice how we generated that list with list of awaitables using list comprehension.[4] asyncio.wait() does not know how to deal with an empty list – this is why we have to check the list before we execute this function.

We are now ready to modify the measuring loop and add the spawning of the new thread to the main code (Listing 3-10).

Listing 3-10. Spawning the WebSockets server thread

```
if __name__ == '__main__':
...
  ws_thread = threading.Thread(
    target=websocket_thread)
  ws_thread.start()
...
```

And finally, we can send data to clients when measurements are performed in the measuring loop, which we might as well completely rewrite (see Listing 3-11).

Listing 3-11. The measuring loop rewritten with WebSockets support

```
def measuring_loop():
  global ws_event_loop
  while True:
```

---

[4]List comprehension is a tool for creating lists, with many powerful subtleties that are often overlooked. Learn more here: https://docs.python.org/3/tutorial/ datastructures.html#list-comprehensions

```
for sensor in sensor_list:
  sensor.measure()
  msg = json.dumps({
    'name': sensor.name,
    'measurement': sensor. measurement,
    'units': sensor.units
  })
  asyncio.run_coroutine_threadsafe(
    send_to_all(msg), loop=ws_event_loop)
time.sleep(5)
```

Here's that global ws_event_loop again. Now we can use it as an argument for asyncio.run_coroutine_threadsafe(), which does exactly what we needed – it executes an asynchronous function, send_to_all(), on an event loop, but does all that from a different, synchronous thread in a thread-safe manner. Another thing to notice here is how we construct the message to send. Unlike JavaScript, Python's json.dumps() knows only how to deal with primitives, and our Si7021Temp class, for instance, has the I2C bus it's using as one of its fields. This means that we can't just give the sensor object as it is to json.dumps() to encode, and our current solution is to be very verbose as we construct the JSON object. We'll soon examine what other options we have for constructing the JSON message that are a little more elegant.

WebSockets in the Browser

Since we are updating the dashboard now with WebSockets rather than HTTP requests, we should rewrite our HTML file, and we might as well do that from scratch. Examine the code in Listing 3-12.

Listing 3-12. WebSockets version of the HTML dashboard file

```
<!DOCTYPE html>
<html>
<head>
</head>
<body>
  <ul id="sensor-list">
  </ul>
  <script>
var ws = new WebSocket(
  `ws://${location.hostname}:{location.port}` // hard-code port
  number if needed
);
ws.onmessage = function (event) {
  let data = JSON.parse(event.data);
  if (!document.getElementById(data.name)) {
    let newLine = document.createElement('li');
    newLine.setAttribute('id', data.name);
    document.getElementById(
      'sensor-list').appendChild(newLine);
  }
  document.getElementById(data.name).innerHTML =
    `${data.name}: \
    ${data.measurement} ${data.units}`;
});
  </script>
</body>
</html>
```

All modern browsers (that I know of) offer built-in support for WebSockets, so no libraries are needed here. Notice how we instantiate a WebSockets object: the constructor function takes the host name of the server as an argument – this can be the URL or the IP address. Instead of putting the actual IP address of the machine, we are using `location.hostname`, which will have the correct host name no matter how we access the machine. Whether we change its IP address or go through the trouble of making it accessible through a domain name, an option we'll explore later on, doing it this way would always work. `{location.port}` acts the same way, but if we use different ports for HTTP and WebSockets, as we did with the `websockets` Python library, then we should hard-code the WebSockets port instead.

Next, we define the callback function that will be invoked whenever data is received by the WebSocket. For simplicity, we assume at this point that we know what the message is: a JSON object containing one sensor's name, last reading, and the units. We use the sensor's name as an id for the DOM element, so that we can update it as new data comes in or add a new line for it if one does not exist yet.

Honorary Mention: SocketIO

Now that we wrapped our heads around WebSockets while keeping support from libraries to a minimum, it is important to remember that there are other libraries out there that can make our lives easier. One of the better known ones and a personal favorite of mine is SocketIO.[5]

SocketIO boasts some cool features like auto-reconnect upon disconnection and logging. If one of the connecting parties is unable to use the WebSockets protocol, SocketIO will use a fallback protocol, like HTTP requests, to establish the same functionality. SocketIO is first and foremost a JavaScript library, so it's a good option to consider for projects written in Node.js.

---

[5]`https://socket.io/`

For projects written in Python and use Flask, there's Flask-SocketIO,[6] a package that will not only bring SocketIO's capabilities to the project but will also determine on its own, based on the system's configuration, what is the best mechanism to use for asynchronous functionality. As another bonus, it will figure out how to use the same port as the HTTP server on its own. Flask-SocketIO can be set up as demonstrated in Listing 3-13.

Listing 3-13. Setting up Flask-SocketIO

```
from flask import Flask
from flask_socketio import SocketIO

app = Flask(__name__)
socketio = SocketIO(app)
```

From this point, the most important thing to remember is that instead of using `time.sleep()` for any time delay, `socketio.sleep()` should be used. That is the key for letting SocketIO deal with the asynchronous stuff.

It's important to remember that SocketIO is actually quite different than WebSockets: first, as mentioned, it can use a different protocol if necessary; second, unlike WebSockets, its API does support communication via actual JSON objects and not just their text representation; third, events can be named, allowing different callback functions to respond to different event names. See Listing 3-14 for an example.

Listing 3-14. Event names with SocketIO in a Node.js server

```
var app = require('express')();
var http = require('http').Server(app);
var io = require('socket.io')(http);

io.on('connection', function(socket){
```

_____

[6]https://flask-socketio.readthedocs.io/en/latest/

```
// send an event named "greet"
socket.emit('greet', {text: "hey there"});

// handler for events named "user_command"
socket.on('user_command', function(data){
  // do something with the data
  handle(data);
});
});
```

Personally, I find that event names can be handy if used mindfully and more specifically if the event names themselves are chosen very carefully. On the other hand, event names can also be confusing and can bring unnecessary awkwardness to the code – remember that anything that can be done with event names can also be achieved by systemic structuring of the JSON objects that are communicated, as we will explore in the following section.

JSON
JSON Communication Design

So far, the JSON objects that we sent back and forth were very lightweight, and the programs we wrote assumed a very simple and frail communication protocol. Designing an efficient protocol can make the code handling it more compact, readable, and robust.

The key to successful communication is to make sure that the receiving party, whether it's the client or the server, knows what the content of message describes. Until now, we had the server send the dashboard a dictionary containing a name, the last readout, and the units, assuming that the dashboard knows that every incoming JSON object describes a sensor. In a more complex project, the dashboard would want to know the **type** of thing that is being described. Is this a sensor, a motor, or a user? We can solve that by treating all the sensor data as a value in a key-value pair where the key is sensor, for example (see Listing 3-15).

Listing 3-15. An example JSON object wrapped in a key-value pair

```
{"sensor":
  {
    "name": "sensor1",
    "last_read": 24,
    "units": "Celsius"
  }
}
```

Better yet, we can use a key such as sensors, with data of multiple sensors, if we choose, just like we did when we were using HTTP requests (see Listing 3-16).

Listing 3-16. An example JSON object that describes multiple sensors

```
{"sensors": [
  {
    "name": "sensor1",
    ...
  },
  {
    "name": "sensor2",
    ...
  },
  ...
]}
```

And since we have this mechanism in place, we can let the JSON object have data of objects of various types, as well as other information about what the server is doing (Listing 3-17).

Listing 3-17. JSON object describing components of different types

```json
{
  "sensors": [
  ...
  ],
  "motors": [
    {
      "name": "motor1",
      "speed": 30
    },
    ...
  ],
  "measuring": true
}
```

This is a powerful way of communicating the machine's state to the dashboard. It allows for the same protocol to be used for a change in a single component as well as the entire state of the machine. Dumping all the data the machine has is specifically useful when the dashboard loads and needs to be populated. Until now we had to either rely on template rendering or wait for each sensor to report to the dashboard. The latter is problematic in terms of reliability engineering: a sensor would not even appear on our dashboard until a measurement is taken. However, if a sensor failed and had stopped reporting, there would be nothing in the dashboard to imply that, and we would be left to rely on our memory to tell us that a particular sensor is missing from the dashboard. Therefore, it is a good idea to give to the dashboard, as soon as it's ready, all the data regarding the machine and use that data to populate the DOM. We'll add that feature to our code in the following sections.

JSON Message Structuring

How do we actually encode these JSON objects? So far, when we constructed a JSON object to represent a sensor, we used the simplest methods we could find. In JavaScript we used JSON.stringify() directly on the object, which made a JSON object from all data members of the object, ignoring any functions. The result of that was the inclusion of some data members we were not interested in, such as the I2C bus object in our Si7021Temp class. This is even worse in Python: json.dumps() doesn't know how to ignore functions and throws an exception, so we had to laboriously build our own dictionary to pass to json.dumps().

There are ways to get around these problems: for JavaScript, JSON.stringify() can take a *replacer* as argument. The replacer can be a function that is being called for every key-value pair in the object and determines how, if at all, it will be represented in the JSON object. Alternatively, the replacer can be an array whose values represent the only keys allowed in the JSON object. The code in Listing 3-18 shows both ways the replacer argument can be used to create a JSON object that has only the name, measurement, and units keys.

Listing 3-18. Using the replacer argument with JSON.stringify()

```
function replacerFunction(key, value) {
  let allowedKeys = ['name', 'measurement', 'units'];
  if (allowedKeys.includes(key)) {
    return value;
  } else {
    returned undefined; // key will not be included
  }
}

var replacerArray = ['name', 'measurement', 'units'];
```

```
// both of these will work
JSON.stringify(someSensor, replacerFunction);
JSON.stringify(someSensor, replacerArray);
```

Yet another way includes only specific members of an object when encoding it to JSON is to completely override the encoding process by implementing a toJSON() method in that object. If we introduce such a method to our Sensor superclass, all of its subclasses will render to JSON the same way, and we will never have to remember to use replacer argument (see Listing 3-19).

Listing 3-19. Customizing JSON encoding with toJSON()

```
class Sensor {
  // ...
  toJSON() {
    return {
      name: this.name,
      measurement: this.measurement,
      units: this.units
    };
  }
  // ...
```

If we follow the guidelines that we set earlier for structuring JSON messages, we should remember to change the way the measuring loop sends out data to the dashboard. Let's also add code to dump the state of the machine to the dashboard once it's ready. We'll completely rewrite the measuring loop and the connection event handler of the WebSockets server (Listing 3-20).

Listing 3-20. JavaScript measuring loop and connection event
handling rewritten

```javascript
setInterval(() => {
  if (isMeasuring) {
    for (sensor of sensorList) {
      sensor.measure()
      wsServer.broadcast(
        JSON.stringify({sensors: [sensor]}));
    }
  }
}, 5000);

wsServer.on('connection', function connection(ws) {
  wsServer.broadcast(JSON.stringify({
    sensors: sensorList
  }));
  ws.on('message', function incoming(data) {
    // handle incoming data here
  });
});
```

Note that we're sending the data about a sensor immediately after it
performs a measurement rather than waiting for the loop to finish and all
sensors to take their measurements. Doing the latter is just fine and might
be very suitable for an application where the data takes a very short amount
to read. For other applications, however, where different components of the
system generate data at less predictable times, it makes sense to send data
specifically for that new datapoint. The point is to remember to conform
to the protocol, which in this case is having the encoded sensor data as an
item in a list, and that list being the value of a key named `"sensors"`.

For our Python code, we should find a better solution than the one
we have – constructing a dictionary from scratch every time we want to

send a message. One of the problems we were trying to solve was that the object we were encoding had functions, which json.dumps() can't handle. In Python, to make sure json.dumps() doesn't hit a function, an object's __dict__ field can be passed instead of the object itself, like so:

```
json.dumps(some_sensor.__dict__)
```

But this doesn't solve the exclusion of unwanted members, such as the I2C bus in our example. We can build a custom encoder, and unlike JavaScript, we'll have to remember to use it as an argument whenever we want to encode our objects (see Listing 3-21).

Listing 3-21. Custom JSON encoder for the Sensor class

```
class SensorEncoder(json.JSONEncoder):
  def default(self, obj):
    if isinstance(obj, Sensor):
      return {
        "name": obj.name,
        "measurement": obj.measurement,
        "units": obj.units
      }
    return json.JSONEncoder.default(self, obj)
```

Our custom encoder extends the json built-in module's JSONEncoder. It overrides its default() function, which decides how the object is encoded. Note how the new function checks for the class of the object: as our code evolves, this approach will allow us to add more tests and code that specifies how to encode instances of other classes as well. If the object to be encoded is not a Sensor (or any of the other classes we can check for), we assume that the object can be encoded by the original default() function.

As we did with the JavaScript server code, let's plug in the new encoder into the measuring loop. While we're at it, we'll update the WebSockets connection handler so that all the data is dumped to the dashboard upon connection, as we did with the JavaScript implementation (Listing 3-22).

Listing 3-22. Python measuring loop and connection event handling rewritten

```python
def measuring_loop():
  global ws_event_loop
  while True:
    for sensor in sensor_list:
      sensor.measure()
      msg = json.dumps(
        {'sensors' : [sensor]},
        cls=SensorEncoder)
      asyncio.run_coroutine_threadsafe(
        send_to_all(msg), loop=ws_event_loop)
    time.sleep(5)

async def client_handler(socket, data_handler):
  client_set.add(socket)
  await socket.send(json.dumps(
    {"sensors": sensor_list},
    cls=SensorEncoder))
# ...
```

JSON Message Parsing

Examine Listing 3-23, which replaces the ws.onmessage() event handler in the dashboard code from Listing 3-12. It demonstrates how JSON objects can be decoded and handled in the dashboard's JavaScript code.

Listing 3-23. Decoding JSON messages

```
ws.onmessage = function (ev) {
  data = JSON.parse(ev.data);
  for (let key in data) {
    switch (key) {
      case 'sensors':
        for (let sensor of data.sensors) {
          if (!document
            .getElementById(sensor.name)) {
            let newLine =
              document.createElement('li');
            newLine.setAttribute('id', sensor.name);
            document.getElementById('sensor-list')
              .appendChild(newLine);
          }
          document.getElementById(sensor.name)
            .innerHTML =
            `${sensor.name}: \
            ${sensor.measurement} \
            ${sensor.units}`;
        }
    }
  }
}
```

Note   The `switch` block has only one `case`: this is to allow for other cases to be implemented later, for example, motors or system stats.

We've created a handler that is able to use incoming data from the server to both dynamically generate the DOM and update it in real time. This implementation makes the template rendering unnecessary, which reduces the number of ways the server and the dashboard communicate, and thus eliminates some potential confusion. This comes with a price, though: as can be seen from the code in Listing 3-23, the code that generates DOM can get very verbose. Using template rendering to merely create the DOM and then WebSockets to populate the data both on loading and in real time is a good strategy to pursue, especially when the dashboard's layout is complex. This is a technique we'll explore in the next chapter.

WHAT'S IN AN OBJECT?

Now is an opportunity to address a very common bug when decoding JSON messages: looping through the keys and using the `switch` statement on each of them is one way to traverse the message and handle all the keys. Another good way would have been to check for the existence of every key:

```
if ('sensors' in data) {
  //...
```

But in that case, note that we check the existence of a key with the `in` operator and not like this:

```
if (data.sensors) {
  //...
```

What is the difference? Both tests will fail, as wanted, when the `sensors` key is not present in the JSON message. However, the latter will also fail if the value of `data.sensors` does exist but it is 0 or `false`. Sure, there is no good reason for this to happen in our example, but if we conduct the same test for fields that do have a good reason to have 0 as a value, such as the speed of a motor or the position of a joystick, we risk ignoring the actual data and assuming the key doesn't exist. This is why it's good practice to always use the `in` operator to test the existence of a JSON key.

Note that the `hasOwnProperty()` method does pretty much the same thing as the `in` operator in this case. There are differences in behavior when performed on an inherited class instance, but for simple objects the brevity and readability of the `in` operator has an advantage.

Summary

In this chapter we looked into two methods of communicating back and forth between the project's main program and a web Dashboard: HTTP requests and WebSockets. Using HTTP requests is simple and uses the infrastructure that we already put in place to allow the program to serve a web page. However, this technique requires the web page to constantly request for updates, making the communication inefficient and not as timely as it could be, as it is not driven by changes in the project's state. WebSockets address this exact problem, allowing updates to be triggered by the server code, reducing data traffic to a minimum. WebSockets come with a price, though: they require additional infrastructure and extra care for connectivity.

We discussed some best practices to use when working with WebSockets. We saw the advantages of the server code sending new data to the dashboard as the data is ready and also dumping all the information to the dashboard as soon as a new client connects; we learned how constructing an update message as a dictionary of arrays helps keep the code compact and organized; we also showed how having the dashboard's DOM relies more heavily on classes rather than ids helps keeping the HTML file cleaner and the accompanying client-side JavaScript coherent.

In the following chapter, we will focus on the dashboard itself. We will see how to take advantage of our frequent updates in terms of the web dashboard's visual design. Also, as promised, we'll learn how to effectively combine the advantages of template rendering and WebSockets.

CHAPTER 4

Dashboard Design

So far, our dashboard was completely text based. Adding graphic design
elements to it will not only make it more pleasant to look at, but it will
also help us navigate the different sections of the dashboard, see the
data in context, and quickly identify issues that need to be addressed.
In this chapter we will go through some tools and techniques for data
visualization that will add both functionality and pizzazz to our dashboard.
For this purpose, we will examine the dashboard's design both in terms of
software and appearance.

Strategizing

The key to successfully programming any web page is keeping a separation
between the document's structure, content, and design. When these
three elements are decoupled, it is easier to make changes to one of them
without having to change the others, or at least keeping the adaptations
needed to minimum. This also allows for large-scale changes to be made
with very minor modifications to the code and generally keeps the code
more organized.

In terms of structure and design, the separation is achieved by
restricting the design specification to a CSS file while leaving the HTML
to describe the structure and hierarchy of the different elements. We have
seen that the relation between structure, content, and design is established
by assigning classes and ids to DOM elements that JavaScript and CSS can
relate to.

© Eyal Shahar 2019
E. Shahar, *Project Reliability Engineering*, https://doi.org/10.1007/978-1-4842-5019-8_4

In the previous chapter, we showed different strategies for using HTTP requests and WebSockets. Moving forward, the strategy we will take is to use a combination of the two. To generate the structure of the dashboard, we will use template rendering. This will allow us to write very little code, even if we are monitoring many components. Moreover, if the system has good design, the template itself doesn't need to be modified if components are added, removed, or changed. For updating the dashboard, we will continue to use WebSockets, but we will drastically change the way these updates are presented in the dashboard by modifying the front-end code and introducing some CSS rules.

Beefing Up the Project

To make this exploration effective, we will add a little bit more meat to our project. Let's have two temperature sensors installed and add two fans that will be controlled by two GPIO pins. Each fan will be paired with one of the temperature sensors and will be turned on if the temperature measured by that sensor crosses a given threshold. We will implement this project on a Raspberry Pi and choose GPIO20 and GPIO21 for the pins that control the fans. Sure, this is not a very exciting project, but it gets us enough components to display on the dashboard. See Listing 4-1 for the code that gets added to the main program: for simplicity, only the JavaScript implementation is considered here.

Listing 4-1. Adding fans to the weather station project

```
var gpio = require('rpi-gpio');

gpio.setMode(gpio.MODE_BCM);
class Fan {
  constructor(name, pin) {
    this.name = name;
```

```
    this.pin = pin;
    gpio.setup(this.pin, gpio.DIR_OUT);
  }

  set(state) {
    this.state = state;
    gpio.write(this.pin, this.state);
    wsServer.broadcast(JSON.stringify({
      fans: [this]
    }));
  }
}

var threshold = 24; // arbitrary value, celsius
var fanList = [];
fanList.push(new Fan('left', 20));
fanList.push(new Fan('right', 21));

setInterval(() => {
  fanList[0]
    .set(sensorList[0].measurement > threshold);
  fanList[1]
    .set(sensorList[1].measurement > threshold);
}, 5000);
```

Serving Static Files

As our dashboard is getting more complex, it might be a good idea to
remove JavaScript and CSS from the HTML file and put them in separate
files. We often refer to such files as *static files*, as they are not rendered by
the templating engine. Static files can be accessed directly by their route,
as long as we tell the Flask or Node what folder all static files are located.

Traditionally, that will be a folder called "public" or "static" that is located inside the project's folder. For a Node.js project, we would use the command

```
app.use(express.static('static'));
```

Within the static folder, the convention is to have a "scripts" folder for JavaScript files and a "styles" folder for CSS files. In the HTML file, we'll then link to a CSS file within the <head> tag, files like this:

```
<link rel="stylesheet" type="text/css"
    href="styles/style.css">
```

JavaScript files are included like this:

```
<script src="scripts/script.js"></script>
```

If a JavaScript file contains code that executes immediately after loading and this code relies on DOM elements, the <script> tag should come after these elements. Otherwise, the elements will not yet be there for the code to refer to. Another way to do this, considered by some as healthier, is to put the <script> tag inside the <head> tag, and everything that should execute right after the page loads should be called by window.onload() or document.onload().

In the simplest implementation, Flask looks for these files in a folder called static by default. Using them from the HTML files is the same as shown before; however, the path should be preceded by static/.

Creating a Template

Since we are working with the JavaScript implementation of the project, we will write a template for the Pug templating engine. A good way to have all of the data nicely organized is to put each sensor in a row of a table (Listing 4-2).

Listing 4-2. Using Pug to put each sensor in a table row

```
h1 weather station
div (id='dashboard-sections-container')
  div (id='sensors')
    table
      caption sensor data
      tr
        th name
        th time
        th measurement
        th units
      each sensor in sensors
        tr (class='sensor' id=sensor.name)
          td= sensor.name
          td (class='time')
          td (class='measurement')
          td= sensor.units
  div (id='fans')
    table
      caption fans
      tr
        th name
        th state
      each fan in fans
        tr (class='fan' id=fan.name)
          td= fan.name
          td (class='state')
```

A few words about tables: an HTML table starts with the `<table>` tag, followed by an optional `<caption>` tag. A table consists of rows, indicated by `<tr>` tags, and each row has either header cells, indicated by `<th>` tags, or regular cells, indicated by `<td>` tags. It is possible to surround header and body rows with a <thead> and a <tbody> tag, respectively. This can help browsers with scrolling through bigger tables, but we don't need that in our case.

Data Updates

As you can see, some of the cells in each row get rendered along with the page: the sensor's name and the units of the measurements. The content of these cells will not change as updates come in. The other cells – the time of the last measurement and its value – are left empty, and they rely on the live updates to fill them with content. We should modify the JavaScript code we wrote in Listing 3-23 that handles incoming updates. See Listing 4-3 for the updated code.

Listing 4-3. The updating function modified to the new template-rendered dashboard

```
function updateDashboard(data) {
  for (key in data) {
    switch(key) {
      case 'sensors':
        for (let sensor of data.sensors) {
          let sensorElement =
            document.getElementById(sensor.name);
          sensorElement
            .getElementsByClassName(
              'time')[0].innerHTML = sensor.time;
          sensorElement
            .getElementsByClassName(
              'measurement')[0].innerHTML =
                sensor.'measurement'.toFixed(3);
        break;
```

```
case 'fans':
  for (let fan of data.fans) {
    let fanElement =
      document.getElementById(fan.name);
    if ('state' in fan) {
      if (fan.state){
        fanElement.classList.add('on');
        fanElement.classList.remove('off');
      } else {
        fanElement.classList.add('off');
        fanElement.classList.remove('on');
      }
    }
  }
  break;
  }
 }
}
```

Looking at the lines of code that deal with the temperature sensor updates, it's obvious that this code now shrunk considerably. We no longer need to build this part of the DOM with JavaScript code, as this is taken care of by the template. Note how we follow the protocol that we formulated in Chapter 3: we check for the existence of a sensors key in the incoming data JSON object, and if it exists, we interpret it as an array of sensors and process their data.

We also extended this function to deal with incoming updates for the fan's state. In response to each fan's state, we set a class to the DOM element that represents the fan to either on or off. In this case, this element and entire <tr> table row, and not just the state cell. This is all we need to do, as we will soon use some CSS to do the rest.

Scrutinizing the Code

There are a couple of things we should talk about in terms of programming: first, before probing the state of the fan, we test to see whether the state field is even present in the incoming JSON object. We have talked about the importance of this before, but this is a good opportunity to reiterate. We tested using the line

```
if ("state" in fan):
```

Consider the alternatives: evaluating the test if(fan.state) would result in false both if state is actually false and also if the state field is not even included, leading us to think that the fan is off regardless of its state. We might be tempted to be more specific and try something like if (fan.state == true), but that will actually throw an exception if the state field is not present, preventing the function from resuming execution. Making sure first that the field actually exists is the safest and most reliable way to read data in a JSON object.

Then there's the matter of toggling the on and off classes. The way it's presented in Listing 4-3 might seem a little verbose. One might prefer to use the *conditional operator*, as shown in Listing 4-4.

Listing 4-4. Using the conditional operator to add and remove classes

```
if ('state' in fan) {
  fanElement.classList.add(
    fan.state ? 'on' : 'off');
  fanElement.classList.remove(
    fan.state ? 'off' : 'on');
}
```

This compresses seven lines of code into two, but not without a price: first, this is slightly less readable than the previous example, as using the conditional operator often is; second, any type of conditional, be it an if-then, the conditional operator, or a loop termination condition, are all computationally costly. By using the syntax shown in Listing 4-3, the program uses two conditionals rather than one, so although the code is shorter, it's actually less efficient. In our program, these updates happen relatively infrequently. If this function was invoked many times every second, then efficiency would be a thing to worry about. In conclusion, with readability and efficiency on one side of the ring, and brevity on the other, the former wins.

As our web page gets more intricate, the mechanisms which we use to locate DOM elements should also be re-evaluated: getElementById() and getElementsByClassName() could be replaced by the newer querySelector()[1] and querySelectorAll()[2] that take CSS selectors as an argument, similarly to the jQuery library API. By using CSS selectors, one query can be used to select a very specific element or a set of elements. However, since a CSS selector needs to be formulated, the code for each query can be slightly harder to read: in our example, we could end up with something like

```
querySelector(`#${sensor.name} .time`) = //...
```

Also, querySelector() and querySelectorAll() are a little more computationally expensive for the browser, although that is usually insignificant. Just as in the case of toggling the on and off classes, I chose code that is more verbose, but also more readable and more efficient.

Due to my own background in digital signal processing, I tend to pay attention to efficiency, probably more than necessary. However, I do feel that being mindful of these considerations even when it's not critical helps me write more efficient code at times when it is. At the end of the day, it is a

---

[1] https://developer.mozilla.org/en-US/docs/Web/API/ParentNode/querySelector

[2] https://developer.mozilla.org/en-US/docs/Web/API/ParentNode/querySelectorAll

matter of coding style, and your preferences may differ. The main purpose of this discussion is to shed light on the various courses of action and the type of inner discussion a programmer should have when formulating any piece of code.

Basic CSS

Now that we have laid out our elements and gave them ids and classes, we can use CSS to style the dashboard so that it is easy to navigate and is aesthetically pleasing. When we're done, our dashboard will look like Figure 4-1.

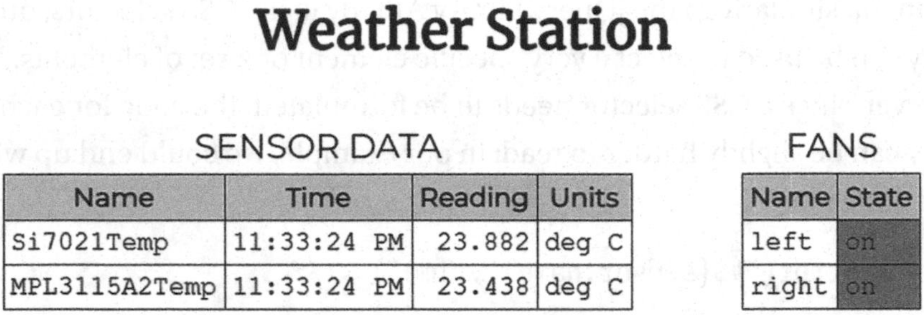

Figure 4-1. *Our weather station's dashboard after some styling*

Tables

Putting borders on the tables makes it easier to differentiate between the cells even when they're in close proximity. It also helps in understanding which value belongs to each line. *Collapsing* the borders means that instead of each cell having its own borders, neighboring cells share a border. This saves on space while keeping a cleaner design. Last, adding background color to the header line cells, especially in a page with multiple tables, helps to create separation between the tables and establish hierarchy (see Listing 4-5).

Listing 4-5. CSS file for general dashboard layout

```
table, th, td {
    border: 1px solid black;
    border-collapse: collapse;
}

th {
  background-color: lightblue;
}
```

Recall from Table 2-3 that the syntax table, th, td means that this CSS style is applied to elements of these three tags.

Text

The next sub-sections discuss a few guidelines that I find useful when styling text elements.

Capitalization

Instead of capitalizing text in the HTML file, it can be useful to enter the text in lowercase in the file and specify the capitalizing style in the text-transform CSS property. The capitalize and uppercase values are useful options for this property, mostly for headers, and using CSS instead of introducing capitalization to the text itself means that it's easier to make changes to the design. Another option for headers is to use the font-variant property with the small-caps value. Figure 4-2 shows the effect of these different settings.

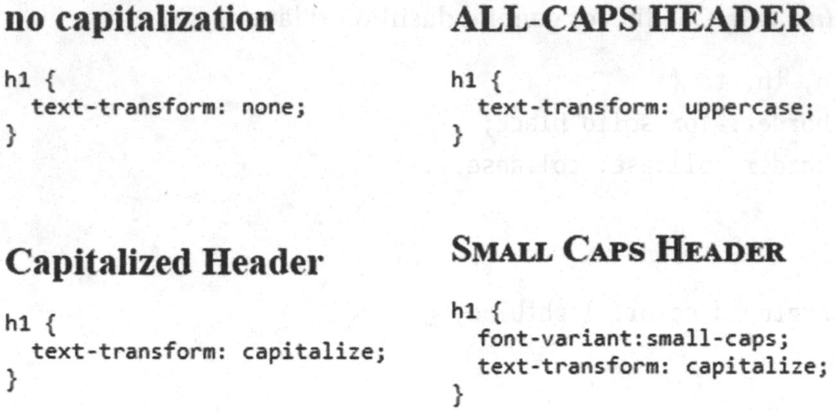

no capitalization

```
h1 {
  text-transform: none;
}
```

ALL-CAPS HEADER

```
h1 {
  text-transform: uppercase;
}
```

Capitalized Header

```
h1 {
  text-transform: capitalize;
}
```

Small Caps Header

```
h1 {
  font-variant:small-caps;
  text-transform: capitalize;
}
```

Figure 4-2. *Text capitalization in CSS*

Numerical Columns

For a table column that contains updating numerical values, it's a good idea to set the font to a monospace one. In monospace fonts all the characters have the same width in pixels. Then, we can also set the text to be right-justified and make sure that the column is wider than what we expect the content to be. In our example, the CSS code will look like Listing 4-6.

Listing 4-6. Styling a numerical table column

```
.sensor .measurement {
  font-family: monospace;
  text-align: right;
  width: 5em;
}
```

Recall from Table 2-3 that the CSS selector .sensor .measurement means "all elements of the class measurement that are contained in an element of the class sensor". Using em³ units, which are equal to the effective font size, and setting the width to more ems than the number of characters expected, makes sure that the content of the table cell will always have room.

These settings, in conjunction with the toFixed() JavaScript function, make sure that our real-time updating data does not cause the table size to keep changing and also that all the numerical data is aligned in terms of the decimal point, which are two features that increase readability.

Fonts

Unless you are designing signs for a rustic style wedding in the San Francisco Bay Area, I would recommend refraining from using too many fonts in one document. A good rule of thumb is to stick to two fonts – one Serif and one Sans Serif, with the addition of a monospace variant for numerical data. A safe choice is to use the Serif font for more text-heavy parts like headers and the Sans Serif font for the data. For a dashboard, try not to go too exotic with your selection of fonts, and pick ones that relate to one another and share a similar atmosphere. Obviously, fonts such as Comic Sans and Fantasy should never ever be used. By anyone.

Layout

Positioning HTML elements using CSS can be extremely frustrating, and this is often due to confusion regarding what the participating CSS properties, display and position, actually **do**.

---

[3]To learn more ems and other CSS sizing units, see Mozilla's guide: https:// developer.mozilla.org/en-US/docs/Learn/CSS/Introduction_to_CSS/ Values_and_units

The display Property

The display property determines how an element behaves within the context of its surrounding elements and how its children are placed. This addresses, for instance, whether elements appear in the same line or one below the other, how they are spaced, and how they are affected by width and height properties that are assigned to them. Table 4-1 details a few of the more common values that the display property can accept.

Table 4-1. *Some common display values*

Value	Description
inline	Appears in the same line as the surrounding elements
block	The element starts at a new line and takes the width of its parent
inline-block	Appears in the same line as its surrounding elements, but its width and height can be set
none	The element is not displayed and does not affect the document's layout
grid	Appears as a container of a grid system for its children
flex	Appears as a container for a row or column of child elements

While inline, block, and inline-block are easier to grasp, the newer grid and flex are more complex but are significantly more powerful, especially if an element has multiple children that relate to each other in a specific way. We are going to spend some time specifically on flex, since it's perfect for our use case: we need a clean design that works well for both desktops and mobile devices, but we don't want to spend too much time on making it – the dashboard is not the project itself, but rather just a tool, and it is only going to be used by us.

In our example, we have two `<div>` elements that are direct children of the `dashboard-sections-container` `<div>` element. A `<div>` element, by default, has its `display` property set to `block`. This means that unless we change it, each of these sections will start on a new line and will be as wide as its parent. On a desktop screen, this is inefficient, since we can squeeze several of these sections side by side. A *flexbox*, which is a `<div>` element that has its display property set to `flex`, does just that. We can set the style of the container as shown in Listing 4-7.

Listing 4-7. Using a flexbox for laying out the sections

```
#dashboard-sections-container {
    display: flex;
    flex-direction: row;
    flex-wrap: wrap;
    justify-content : space-evenly;
}
```

A flexbox has its children spread out in a row or in a column, as determined by the `flex-direction` property. Setting the `flex-wrap` property to wrap lets children of the container be placed in a new row if they run out of space. Figure 4-3 shows a few flexbox properties and how they affect the layout. It is definitely not a comprehensive guide to all the flexbox properties and their available settings, but it's a good starting point and it does include some of the more useful features.[4]

Elaborate layouts can be achieved solely by using treating the document as a tree of flexboxes with both `row` and `column` directions. Figure 4-4 demonstrates how a dashboard might be structured this way.

---

[4]A good interactive guide to the different properties of the flexbox can be found here: `https://yoksel.github.io/flex-cheatsheet/#justify-content`

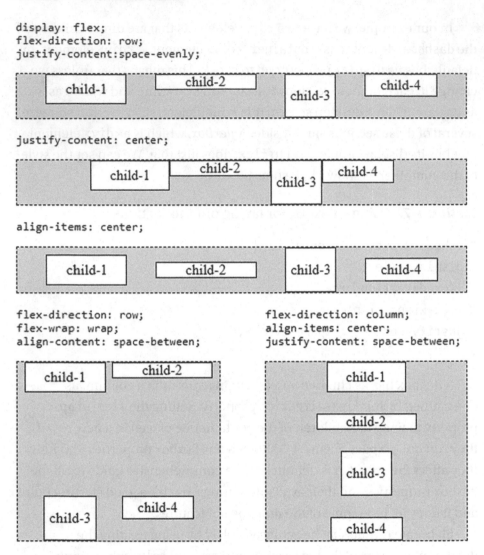

Figure 4-3. A few examples of flexbox properties. The CSS code before each example highlights only the featured properties for that example. These are applied to the flexbox container, which is the gray box with the dashed border. Find the code used to create these examples in the book's GitHub repository, /ch04/flex.html.

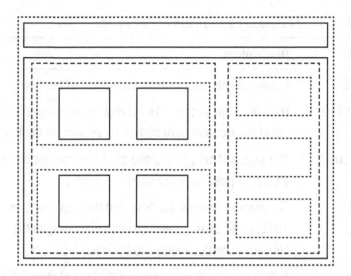

Figure 4-4. *A complex web page design can be relatively easily achieved using flexboxes. The HTML and CSS that generated this design can be found in the book's GitHub repository, /ch04/ flexdesign.html.*

The `position` Property

The combination of the `display` properties for all elements in the document creates what is often referred to as the *flow* of the document, as each element finds its place in the flow. This is when the `position` property comes into play: it determines how the element interprets its place in the flow. Table 4-2 summarizes the functionality of the possible values.

Table 4-2. *The position property's values*

Value	Description
static	Leaves the element in its natural place in the flow
relative	Uses the top, bottom, left, and right properties to offset the element from its natural position in the flow
absolute	The top, bottom, left, and right properties set the element's position in relation to its parent
fixed	The element ignores the flow, and the top, bottom, left, and right values are used to determine the element's position relative to the viewport
sticky	Acts like relative, unless scrolled out of view – then acts like fixed

Data-Driven CSS

The CSS we have used so far refers to the static layout of the HTML element and the overall design of the document. CSS, however, can be also used to convey information about the data and highlight elements that bear importance. It could be used, for instance, to highlight text that require attention, color an element in green or red to imply that certain things are on or off, and gray out control elements that are not currently functional.

Let's go back to the fan table in our dashboard. In Listing 4-2 we left a column for every fan to indicate its state. To demonstrate some principle of handling data with CSS, we can color the cells in this column green or red, depending on whether the fan is on or off, respectively. We can also fill the column with the actual words "on" or "off".

Unlike the values for the temperature sensor, when we receive fan data from the server, our client-side JavaScript code (Listing 4-3) does not change the properties of the cell that we want to eventually reflect the update, that is, the cell in the "state" column. Instead, the code changes the class of the entire row. The motivation behind this is that generally speaking, it's best if the JavaScript code knows as little as possible about the structure of the HTML documents. As we mentioned before, this compartmentalizes the various aspects of the program – layout and functionality – and makes it easier to debug and make changes. While we need to know to which table cell we insert the temperature value, we don't need that level of specificity in order to change the color of the status column. Examine the code in Listing 4-8.

Listing 4-8. Using color to convey the fan's state

```
.fan .state {
  color: white;
}
.fan.on .state {
  background-color: green;
}
.fan.off .state {
  background-color:   red;
}
```

The selector .fan.on .state means "elements of class 'state' that are contained in an element that is of both classes 'fan' and 'on'". This is the kind of logic we were building up to: while the JavaScript code only tells the HTML document "whatever you have going for this fan, just make sure you display in a way that conveys that it's on," it is the CSS that picks the exact child element and styles it. Furthermore, the CSS code is almost written in spoken English: "a fan that is on, its 'state' column's background color is green." This also allows us to use the class name "state" for other elements in the document, and either have common styles for all of them by using the simple CSS selector .state or have individual styles depending on the type of components by using more complex selectors, like we have just shown.

Let's wrap up this section with a cool trick: we can even use CSS to fill in the text inside the state column. Check out Listing 4-9.

Listing 4-9. Using the content CSS property to fill in text

```
.fan.on .state::before {
  content: "on";
}

.fan.off .state::before {
  content: "off";
}
```

This will put the actual "on" or "off" text inside the status table cells. Had there been already content in these cells, the text would have been added before it. However, since otherwise the cells are empty, it makes no difference whether we use the `::before` or `::after` selector. This trick is especially useful if different classes share this behavior, as it can all be handled with these two CSS rules rather than with JavaScript for every single class. This technique saves some lines of code and makes changes easier to make.

Responsive Design

The term *"responsive design"* refers to web pages designed in a way that displays well on both computers and mobile devices, through the use of HTML and CSS. The primary technique for achieving this is by applying different CSS rules depending on the device showing the page.

Media Queries

Obviously, the first step is to get a sense of what kind of device is displaying the content. This is most often done by examining the width of the screen.

In a CSS file, we can apply different rules based on the screen's width, as shown in Listing 4-10.

Listing 4-10. Selecting a CSS rule based on screen width

```css
@media screen and (max-width: 767px) {
  body {
    font-size: 15px;
  }
}

@media screen and (min-width: 767px) {
  body {
    font-size: 20px;
  }
}
```

CSS rules that start with the @ sign are called at-rules, and unlike other rules that apply to elements of specific tag, class, or id, at-rules define more general behavior. @media, also known as a *media query*, applies the rules it encompasses only for medias that match the query. In our case, the media has to be a screen – other options apply to printers and text-to-speech devices – and its width needs to comply with the minimum or maximum width requirement.

Note   Since competing CSS rules override each other, with those appearing later in the code winning, the code in Listing 4-10 would work the same even if the rules inside the first media query – the max-width one – had **not** been inside a media query. In that case, it would act as the default, and if the browser would decide to apply the min-width rules, these rules would override any other CSS rules that came before them.

Another way to do this is in the HTML files, selectively importing different CSS files based on the screen's width, as demonstrated in Listing 4-11.

Listing 4-11. Selecting a CSS stylesheet in an HTML file, based on screen width

```
<link rel="stylesheet"
  media="screen and (max-width: 767px)"
  href="mobile.css">
<link rel="stylesheet"
  media="screen and (min-width: 768px)"
  href="desktop.css">
```

We can have many different designs that accommodate different devices in different orientations. Table 4-3 shows a fairly economical system for classification of devices, and searching the Web would yield others, some being significantly more detailed. Personally, I tend to stick to the two shown earlier when it comes to designing a dashboard. After all, dashboards are only for the eyes of the people who operate the project and not the general public. If you are the only one who is going to see the dashboard and you do not own a tablet, adding a stylesheet for that specific form factor is probably an overkill.

Table 4-3. *Device classificaton based on display width*

Device Type	Minimum Width	Maximum Width
Desktops	992 px	-
Tablets in landscape	768 px	991 px
Tablets in portrait, phones in landscape	480 px	767 px
Phones in portrait	–	479 px

Element Sizing

When sizing elements in CSS, three sizing options are available that are preferable to px units when considering responsive design:

- Ephemeral units (em) are relative to the font size that is in effect for the element. If the font size is 10px, then 1em=10px.

- rem (root em) does the same, but is always relative to the font size of the root element.

- Percentages (%) allow elements to be sized in proportion to the size of their parents.

Using these units and avoiding px is considered good practice in web design, as it keeps the design and the code more uniform between devices and also keeps the number of rules that are chosen by media queries to a minimum.

Device Orientation

Most mobile devices scale the web page based on the device's orientation, an outcome that developers actually prefer to avoid. The solution to this problem is universal: almost all web pages include this line in their <head> section:

```
<meta name="viewport"
  content="width=device-width, initial-scale=1.0">
```

<meta> tags contain information about the document, and they are mostly used by search engines, but sometimes by the browser that is showing the document. For example, a <meta name="viewport"> tag gives the browser information about the page's size and scaling. The content attribute here tells the browser to set the page's width to the width of the device and also instructs it not to scale the content.

103

It's worth mentioning that we can use media queries to detect the **orientation** of the device, as shown in Listing 4-12.

Listing 4-12. Media queries for device orientation

```
@media (orientation: landscape) {
  /* some rules here */
}

@media (orientation: portrait) {
  /* other rules here */
}
```

This is useful when a single design for mobile devices just doesn't work for both orientations.

HTML Graphic Indicators

Before shopping around for libraries to help us create a more visually compelling dashboard, it's a good idea to see what options exist within the realm of plain HTML and CSS.

LEDs

In addition to plain text and colorizing the elements' backgrounds, LED-like indicators are yet another way to indicate status. Since these don't exist natively in HTML, a circle can be easily created by styling a `<div>` using CSS, as shown in Listing 4-13.

Listing 4-13. CSS code for LED-like indicators

```
.led-indicator {
  display: inline-block;
  height: 20px;
```

```
  width: 20px;
  border: 1px solid black;
  border-radius: 50%;
  background-color: lightgray;
}
.led-indicator.go {
  background-color: green;
}

.led-indicator.stop {
  background-color: red;
}
```

The trick lies in the border-radius property that curves the perimeter of the <div> element into a circle. Then, as we did with the table cells, we can apply different classes to the element using JavaScript to "light" the LED in different colors.[5]

Meters

The <meter> tag, which was introduced in HTML5, is a good way to visualize numerical values such as sensors, motor speeds, and system resources. The fact that meters are standard to the HTML specification is nice, although some older browsers do not support it, and each modern browser renders them differently with its own flavor. We'll focus on the behavior that is common to most modern browsers.

A meter element is controlled by its attributes. min and max determine the range of the meter, and value specifies the current value to be

---

[5]There are plenty of more elaborate techniques that colorize the LED in ways that really make it look like an electrical light, but that is beyond the scope of this book. See these links: www.hongkiat.com/blog/css3-on-off-button/ https://codepen.io/fskirschbaum/pen/MYJNaj

displayed. If these are the only attributes that are specified, the color of the meter will be green. Adding the attributes low and high causes the meter to show in yellow if value is outside of the low to high range.

By adding the optimum attribute and having its value set at either one of the side ranges, that is, between min and low or between high and max, the behavior changes: the meter is shown green if value is in the same range as optimum, yellow if it is in the middle range, and red if value is in the opposite range of optimum. Figure 4-5 offers a demonstration that is probably much easier to grasp than this explanation.

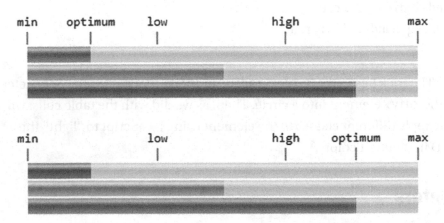

Figure 4-5. *The behavior of a meter element when the* optimum *attribute is used. The code that generated this figure can be found in the book's GitHub repository, /ch04/meter.html.*

Gradients

In addition to applying solid background colors to elements, it's possible to create color gradients with CSS. While gradient colors can be used to add depth and other design features, they can be also useful in data visualization. For example, in a project dashboard, a color gradient can visualize the state of a long LED strip. We'll explore exactly this example, and while there are several variants to the syntax that describes a gradient, we'll focus on syntax that serves this purpose best.

The classic way to do this is by having an empty `<div>` – we will give ours the id `#led-strip` – and using the color gradient as the background. The CSS syntax for such a color gradient would look something like this:

```
#led-strip {
  background: linear-gradient(direction, color1, color2, ...,);
);
```

direction can be a string defining the direction of the gradient, such as `to left` or `to top`, or an angle, that is, `90deg`. Color can be specified either by name, hex values, or, as we shall do in this example, RGB values.

Since we want to set the gradient programmatically, we can't rely on a CSS file, but rather we must change the `style` attribute of the `#led-strip` element. To represent the state of the LED strip, let's say that the server sends out a list where each item is one LED, represented as a list of the red, green, and blue values. It should look something like Listing 4-14.

Listing 4-14. An object that represents the state of an LED strip

```
[
    [0, 0, 127],
    [50, 50, 20],
    //...
}
```

Then the code in Listing 4-15 can be used to apply the corresponding color gradient to the `#led-strip` element.

Listing 4-15. Code for visualizing data as a color gradient

```
function rgbListToString(channelList) {
  return `rgb(${channelList.join(',')})`;
}

function dataToGradient(ledList) {
  let rgbStringList = ledList.map(rgbListToString);
  return `linear-gradient(to right,
    ${rgbStringList.join(',')})`;
};

// when data comes in from the
// server, this can be called:
document.getElementById("led-strip").style
  .background = dataToGradient(data.ledData);
```

rgbListToString() takes one color in the form of an [r,g, b] list and converts it into a string of the form "rgb(r, g, b)". The join() function is very useful for incidences where lists of data need to be converted to strings of values separated by commas, like when writing CSV files. We'll do that more later.

dataToGradient() puts it all together. First it takes the function's argument ledList and uses the map() function to create a new list from ledList's items, with every item going through rgbListToString(). Now, instead of a list of [r, g, b] colors, we have a list of "rgb(r, g, b)" strings. Isn't map() just awesome?

Finally, we use join() again to put all these together in one big string and plop it into a template. See Figure 4-6 for a comparison between an actual LED strip and its dashboard representation.

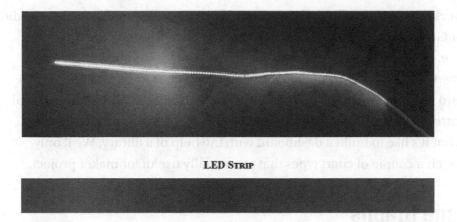

LED Strip

Figure 4-6. Top, an LED strip. Bottom, the LED strip's representation in a dashboard using a color gradient.

Google Charts

There is a large number of libraries out there that can help create fancy graphs and visualizations. *D3.js*[6] is probably the first name that pops to most programmers' mind. It's versatile and powerful but it has a steep learning curve, and it takes a considerable amount of code to even get a simple line graph off the ground. *Plotly*[7] offers some abstraction over D3.js which simplifies the process of adding graphs to web page but offers only a limited number of graph types. Other libraries may cost money, offer limited features, or just don't look that great.

Personally, I'm a sucker for *Google Charts.*[8] The graphs are pretty, the API is relatively simple, and it's free! The gallery offers graph types that are super useful for web dashboards, from line charts for showing data history, through maps that display connected users' location, to gauges that can display current sensor data and system resources usage. If you have ever

---

[6]https://d3js.org/
[7]https://plot.ly/javascript/
[8]https://developers.google.com/chart/

worked with any of Google's dashboards, such as YouTube's Creator Studio or Google Analytics, then you have already seen what Google Charts is like. Google Charts has a pretty extensive API that supports animation, event handling for user interaction, and even an SQL-like language built into it that supports data queries. This section will merely be a superficial introduction to Google Charts, and we will use it as a test case to show what it's like to build a dashboard with the help of a library. We'll only touch a couple of chart types that are actually useful for maker project.

Line Graphs

Let's start by looking at a line graph. These can be especially useful in plotting a history of measurements. In the following example (Listing 4-16), we'll assume that when the page fetches data from the endpoint sensor_ data, the JSON object received will be a list of measurements, each of them will be a list of two items: a timestamp and the measurement's value.

Listing 4-16. Drawing a line chart with Google Charts

```
<!DOCTYPE html>
<html>
<head>
  <script type="text/javascript"
    src="https://www.gstatic.com/charts/loader.js">
  </script>
  <script>
google.charts.load('current',
  {'packages':['corechart']});
google.charts.setOnLoadCallback(drawChart);

function drawChart() {
  let chart = new google.visualization.LineChart(
    document.getElementById('sensor-chart'));
```

```
  fetch('sensor_data')
    .then(function(response) {
      return response.json();
    })
    .then(function(jsonData) {
      let dataset = json.parse(jsonData);
      let data =
        new google.visualization.DataTable();
      data.addColumn('date', 'Date');
      data.addColumn('number', 'Value');
      data.addRows(dataset);
      chart.draw(data);
    });
}
  </head>
  <body>
    <div id="sensor-chart"></div>
  </body>
</html>
```

Let's slowly unpack this. That script we include in the very beginning
imports the *library loader*. This already brings to the discussion this
library's main drawback: it lives in the cloud and cannot be downloaded to
the project's machine. This means that the project must have access to the
Internet in order to use the dashboard. However, this is less and less of a
problem these days, and since we will most likely use this dashboard from
a remote device, assuming that the project's machine has access to the
Internet is only fair.

The loader's job is to load the required packages, which are the specific
parts of the library that provide the features we want to use. google.
charts.load() takes as arguments the version – using current will give us
the latest stable one – and the names of the packages we are interested in.

corechart is the package that handles the most basic graphs, such as histograms, pie charts, and of course line graphs.

Next, we define a callback function to be executed when the library is loaded. In the callback function, after we create a LineChart object in the sensor-chart element, we fetch() the data. Google Charts works with two closely related data structures: DataTable objects are used to construct the main body of data that the chart works with. They are two-dimensional arrays, with columns and rows. Columns can have various data types, such as string, number, or datetime. In a line chart, the first column is the x axis, and the remaining columns are data series. The other type of objects that charts can display is DataView, which is created from a DataTable object and is used to display subsets of the data.

In our code, once the data comes in, we create a new DataTable object, define the two columns, and since the data is already in the correct format – a two-dimensional array – we can just plop it into the DataTable object. All that is left is to tell the API to draw the chart.

Gauges

Gauges are a great means for visualization of real-time data, and Google Charts gauges are slick and easy to work with – as long as you understand the limitations. In our weather station example, they could be used to visualize the values of the sensors.

First, it is important to understand that the gauge chart can actually be a series of gauges: the gauge chart, like any other Google Charts, takes a DataTable object as an argument. The DataTable can have one of two formats: it can have two columns, and in that case every row is a gauge, with the first column being the gauge label and the second column being the value, or multiple columns and multiple rows. This case is a little weirder, since every column becomes a set of gauges, the first row is a label they all share and the next rows each of their values. We'll stick with the first case, where each row is one gauge.

Just like in the line chart, we draw the chart using the `draw()` function. This function takes a second optional `options` argument, which is a dictionary whose keys are specific to the chart type. For gauges, the options include `min` and `max` for the range of the gauge. This is where we encounter a limitation we need to consider: the values of `min` and `max` are common to all gauges within the chart. In our weather station, we explored both weather and pressure sensors, which use completely different ranges.

We could be creative. We could group the sensors into categories and create one chart for every **type** of sensors – one chart for all temperature sensors and another one for all pressure sensors. That would take care of the problem of the different ranges, for starters. Instead of using template rendering, we can send all the information we have on all the sensors immediately after the page loads via WebSockets, a technique we've explored earlier. Of course, if we went that route, there would need to be some information about how the sensors are grouped already on the server's side – either the JSON structure would need to have the sensors grouped by categories, or each sensor would need to have a data field identifying its type.

We are going to take a different approach. We are simply going to create one chart for every gauge, which means different `options` for each gauge. As a consequence, each chart will live in its own `<div>` container, so the `<div>` tag itself is the perfect place for the template rendering engine to plant information about the chart that it is going to contain. Of course, each sensor object on the server will have to have data members specifying its range.

So how can we store data in the `<div>` tag? When browsers interpret HTML into actual graphics, they ignore attributes that are irrelevant to that element. Programmers and libraries often take advantage of this little storage option to stash data specific to that element. By convention, these attributes start with the prefix `"data-"`. For us, this means each gauge's `<div>` will need to include a `data-label`, a `data-min`, and a `data-max` attribute. When the library loads, we can invoke these data attributes and use them to generate the charts. A Pug snippet would look something like Listing 4-17.

Listing 4-17. An example of how a Pug template can be used to prepare containers for gauges

```
script(
  src='https://www.gstatic.com/charts/loader.js')

div(id='gauges')
each sensor in sensors
  div(
    id=sensor.name
    class='gauge-container'
    data-label=sensor.name
    data-min=sensor.min
    data-max=sensor.max)
```

data attributes can then be accessed by JavaScript code using the element's dataset property, as demonstrated in Listing 4-18.

Listing 4-18. Drawing gauges in their containers

```
var gaugeChartDict = {};

google.charts.load('current',
  {'packages':['gauge']});
google.charts.setOnLoadCallback(drawGauges);

function drawGauges () {
  let gaugeContainerList =
    document
    .getElementsByClassName('gauge-container');
  for (let gaugeContainer of gaugeContainerList) {
    let chart =
      new google.visualization.Gauge(gaugeContainer);
    let options = {
```

```
    min: gaugeContainer.dataset.min,
    max: gaugeContainer.dataset.max
  };
  let data =
    google.visualization.arrayToDataTable([
      ['Label', 'Value'],
      [gaugeContainer.dataset.label, 0]
    ]);
  gaugeChartDict[gaugeContainer.dataset.label] = {
    chart: chart,
    options: options,
    data: data
  };
  chart.draw(data, options);
  }
}

function updateGauge(gaugeId, value) {
  let gauge = gaugeChartDict[gaugeId];
  if (gauge) {
    gauge.data.setValue(0, 1, value);
    gauge.chart.draw(gauge.data, gauge.options);
  }
}
```

There are three objects that we need to be able to access whenever we draw or refresh a chart: the chart object itself, the options object, and the data. Since we want to keep updating the charts as data comes in to the dashboard, we need a way to keep these objects and hold references to them. This is the purpose of gaugeChartDict. We create a dictionary with these three objects and use this dictionary as the value in key-value pair that we store in gaugeChartDict. The keys, of course, are the ids of the sensors. This way, when updates come in, we can call updateGauge();

115

pull up the chart `object`, `options`, and `data` objects; update the data object with the new value; and finally draw the chart.

Note how the data table is constructed: the first row is a header, and its cells are strings. This is how the chart knows each consecutive row is a gauge, in contrast to the alternative format we described previously. In fact, the actual strings in this case have no effect apart from that. Since we have only one gauge per chart, there's only one more row in `data`. However, when we update gauge's value in `updateGauge()`, we actually refer to row 0, since the header line is not actually a part of the table itself. As for the columns, the first column is the gauge's label, and the second is a value. Since indexes start at 0, we end up setting value of the cell in (0, 1) with the updated value.

The result can look something like Figure 4-7. Note that we skipped some modifications that should be made to the code responsible for getting the data updates through the WebSocket. The complete code for the weather station is in the book's code repository under the /ch04/weather-station folder, and it has separate endpoint for the gauge-centered dashboard.

Figure 4-7. *A gauge version of the weather station's dashboard*

Real-World Examples

Here are a few examples of dashboards I made for various projects. In fact, it is this type of work that drove me to write this book.

Tidal Memory

Tidal Memory[9] (Figure 4-8) is an Exploratorium exhibit developed by Charles Sowers[10] in 2013. Twenty-four clear tubes, each corresponding to 1 hour of the day, get filled with water at the same level as the current tide at that hour. It's a beautiful, yet technically complex exhibit, and therefore when it fails, the point of failure is not always immediately clear: the computer running the exhibit may fail to boot or the program may crash when the exhibit powers up in the morning; the data stream that the exhibit uses is provided by the National Oceanic and Atmospheric Administration (NOAA), and their machine could be down; the exhibit itself uses one air pressure sensor, one pump, a manifold, and a series of relays to constantly cycle over the tubes, sense the air pressure in a tank at the bottom of each tube, deduce the water level, and pump air to push the water and adjust the level. The pump, sensor, and relays are all possible points of failure – a potential each one of these components has fulfilled at one point or another.

Figure 4-8. *Tidal Memory in the Exploratorium's Living Systems gallery*

---

[9]www.exploratorium.edu/exhibits/tidal-memory
[10]http://charlessowers.com

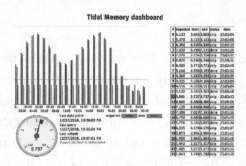

Figure 4-9. *Tidal Memory's web dashboard*

The dashboard we integrated into the exhibit (see Figure 4-9) was built to help us detect the source of problems if and when they happen. We used a Google Column Chart to visualize the state of the exhibit – for each tube in the exhibit there are three bars – one for the tide data it is supposed to present, one for the water level inside the tube as calculated from the measured air pressure, and one for the state of an LED at the top of each tube. If there's a problem at the data flow, it is immediately apparent in this graph, as all tide data columns will be flat. If there's a problem that is specific to one of the tubes, such as a failed relay or a leak, that is reflected in the graph as well.

We also use a Google Charts gauge to visualize the water level in the tube that is currently being evaluated by the sensor and adjusted by the pump. The gauge, along with the column chart, is getting updated in real time. This is not only visually compelling but also very informative. If the pump is having issues getting the water to the right level, watching the gauge can give some hints as to what is going on. Finally, there's a table that shows all the data, including the reason that the relay array switched from one tube and moved to the next one: it could be due to the water reaching the correct level, the tube already being at the right level, or failing to reach the desired level after a preset time window.

Wired Pier

The Exploratorium is home to an array of instruments measuring the conditions of the atmosphere and water around its campus in piers 15 and 17 on the San Francisco Embarcadero. *Wired Pier* is the amalgamation of these instruments, along with a group of exhibits that visualize the data they produce, a public facing web site,[11] and the infrastructure that makes all of that work. Needless to say, every now and again things don't work, and examining the dashboard we made for the Wired Pier network (see Figure 4-10) has become an essential step in figuring out why.

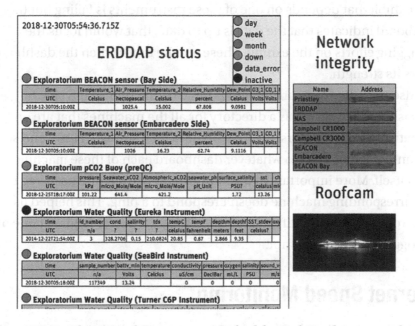

Figure 4-10. *The Wired Pier network dashboard. In the network integrity section, the IP addresses of the machines have been blurred for security.*

---

[11]www.exploratorium.edu/environmental-field-station

119

Although this dashboard is fairly busy, it doesn't do much: each table shows the last measurement taken by one of the instruments, but that's not the useful part. The LED indicator that precedes the name of each instrument gives a quick indication to the time that has passed since this instrument last took a measurement. For most of these, if the last measurement was taken more than a few minutes ago, that would indicate a problem. For others, 1 or even 2 days is reasonable. The black indicators are used for instruments that are no longer active.

If an indicator shows that the last measurement is over a week old, that means that it's time to write some emails and run some tests. However, if an exhibit that depends on one of these instruments is failing but the dashboard indicates that the data is up to date, that would focus the debugging efforts on the exhibit. These are the times when the dashboard shows its strength.

Also note the "Network integrity" table on the right-hand side of the dashboard. It serves as a directory for all the machines that are on the network – data loggers, the network-attached storage (NAS), and so on – and provides links to whatever dashboard each of these machines offers itself. More importantly, the background of each line turns red if the corresponding machine doesn't respond to a ping. This helped us numerous times in identifying a crashed server, a power failure at one of the loggers, or a faulty script.

Internet Speed Monitoring

This last example is a dashboard I built to monitor the Internet connection speed at my house (see Figure 4-11). I built this to make sure I had solid and continuous data while I was working with my ISP to fix my slow connection. This dashboard features a Google Line Chart, and it proved itself as instrumental evidence every time I had to call the ISP and stress that the problem has not been fully fixed. The chart clearly shows their first failed attempt at fixing the problem on August 13, which made the situation worse; a second attempt that made things better, but then something failing again on August 30; and their last fix on September 7 which finally resolved the issue.

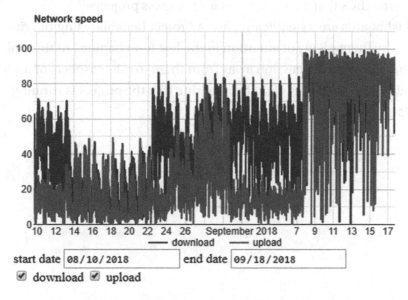

Figure 4-11. *A dashboard for monitoring Internet speed*

Summary

Dashboards shine when projects fail. A well-designed dashboard can turn a painful process of debugging into a matter of a few seconds. What makes a dashboard one that is visually well-designed is clean and clear layout, logical visualization of data, and easy accessibility from devices with various screen sizes. In terms of software, a good design is one that decouples layout, style, and functionality as much as possible.

Web dashboards are useful not just for debugging and controlling projects as we've shown here – they can be used as the actual interface for projects as well. The advantage in doing so is that the project and its interface become decoupled. The user interface is written in a suite of languages designed for the job – HTML, CSS, and JavaScript – while the project is written in whatever language that does the job best. Finally, this decoupling allows the project to be interacted with from any device, which is great for SBCs that are configured for headless projects.[12]

Dashboards are a significant part of Project Reliability Engineering, so we gave them plenty of attention in the last few chapters. At this point we are steering the discussion away from them to other aspects of project reliability, and we'll start with the machine that the project is running on and its configuration.

---

[12]A machine is considered "headless" when it is configured to run without the use of a keyboard, a mouse, and a monitor.

CHAPTER 5

Project Configuration

In previous chapters, we emphasized the importance of separating
functionality, structure, and style. Another important separation that we
haven't touched upon is the separation of code and configuration. Once
the project's configuration becomes a separate component, new questions
start to arise, such as what file format to use, what should be treated as
configuration vs. what should be hard-coded, how to temporarily override
the configuration, and more.

Being mindful about how the project's configuration is handled is
an essential step toward making the project robust, resilient to changes,
scalable, and easy to debug.

Motivation

In all the code examples we have been discussing, we have violated
a pillar of good software design: we have been using *magic numbers*.
Magic numbers are numbers that are hard-coded in the program, and
it is considered bad practice to use them. Instead, it is always better
that constants, or if they are not supported by the language – variables,
are used.[1]

---

[1]Python, for example, does not have constants. By convention, variables that are
supposed to act as constants have all caps names.

© Eyal Shahar 2019
E. Shahar, *Project Reliability Engineering*, https://doi.org/10.1007/978-1-4842-5019-8_5

There are good reasons for magic numbers to be considered an abomination. First, they are detrimental to the readability of the code. If you read a piece of code and encounter a line that raises pin 4 high, unless there is a comment that says what pin 4 is connected to, it will take some guesswork for you to figure out what the purpose of that line is. The same goes for delay times, array sizes, and so forth. The second reason is that when such a value appears multiple times in the code, writing and modifying the code becomes significantly harder if the value is hard-coded in each and every occurrence. Last, constant numerical values can appear anywhere in the code, so when the need arises to change a value, finding it can take some time.

Now that it is clear why magic numbers are a bad idea, the same notion can be extended to strings, IP address, and even entire objects: we have shown previously that by using interfaces and inheritance we can make it easier to swap one implementation of a class with another, for instance, various types of temperature sensors. But when we actually need to do the swap, is this something we'd want to do by changing the hard-coded program, or would we prefer having the type of temperature sensor to be used specified in the project's configuration?

In addition, there is the issue of debugging. There are a number of things we might want the project to do differently when we develop or debug it than when it's up and running: we might want to use more rigorous logging, use simulated components rather than the actual physical ones, or completely ignore, bypass, or disable some of the program's functionality. Again, hard-coding these decisions in the program makes the process of turning them on and off laborious and error-prone.

Using a configuration file, or multiple configuration files, is a good way to keep all of the settings in one place and out of the code. In the following sections, we will discuss different options for file formats, practices for formulating configuration files, what can be considered as configuration data, and more.

File Formats

A configuration file can be saved in various formats, and while it's possible for programmers to choose any format available or even design their own, we will explore three common formats: XML, JSON, and YAML. It is highly recommended that you get yourself acquainted with them and use the one that is best suited for the task at hand.[2]

XML

XML[3] (Extensible Markup Language) is the most veteran of these three. It is a close relative of HTML and has a very similar format: data is arranged in elements, indicated by an opening tag and a closing tag. An element can have attributes, included in the opening tag, and content, which is placed between the opening and the closing tag. The content can be either a value or child element. If an element does not have content, it can be represented by one, self-closing tag.

Consider the two fans from our weather station, and see Listing 5-1 for three options for including their configuration in an XML configuration file.

Listing 5-1. Configuration XML file, using attributes and child elements

```
<!-- Example 1: using attributes -->
<fans>
  <fan name="fan1" pin="20" />
  <fan name="fan2" pin="21" />
</fans>
```

---

[2]Other formats that are not reviewed here but are worth mentioning are TOML, CSON, and .ini files.

[3]www.w3.org/XML/

```
<!-- Example 2: using child elements -->
<fans>
  <fan>
    <name>fan1</name>
    <pin>20</pin>
  </fan>
  <fan>
    <name>fan2</name>
    <pin>21</pin>
  </fan>
</fans>

<!—Example 3: using both -->
<fans>
  <fan name="fan1">
    <pin>20</pin>
  </fan>
  <fan name="fan2">
    <pin>21</pin>
  </fan>
</fans>
```

There are no real rules regarding when a property of an element should be an attribute or a child element. Sometimes it is obvious that child elements should be used, for example, if there are several properties of the same type. In Listing 5-1, <fans> has two <fan> elements in it. This can only be implemented with child elements, as there cannot be more than one attribute with the same name in an element. Also, each <fan> has its own properties, and attributes can only have a simple value, such as a number or a string, but not multiple values, for instance, both a name and a GPIO pin, as we have in our example.

Otherwise, attributes are more economical than child elements in terms of the number of lines, but they are slightly harder to read. Once again, it ends up being a matter of personal preference.

XML is used more often to transfer data between machines over the Internet than to store configuration data, and even in that arena it has been losing popularity to JSON. It is more verbose than the other two formats reviewed here with its closing tags and its child elements vs. attributes dilemmas, but it's far from being dead. It's still very much present and can be found in many places such as SVG files, podcast streams definition, and Google Earth data. Furthermore, its similarity to the familiar HTML syntax still makes a compelling argument for programmers to use it not only for transmitting data online but also for storing configuration data.

JSON

JSON[4] (JavaScript Object Notation) is a popular choice for storing configuration data for two main reasons: first, the format is ubiquitous. It is used, like XML, to transmit data between machines over the Internet, it is based on the way objects are represented in JavaScript, and JSON objects are very similar to Python objects. Second, it is compact and highly readable, especially when compared to XML. The format is mature, and stable libraries for it that are well maintained exist for most popular programming languages.

There are three types of entities in JSON: at the lowest level, there are *literals*. These are numbers, strings, boolean values (true and false), and null. Then there are *dictionaries*, made of key-value pairs, and *lists*, which are ordered collections of values. When we say "value" in the context of dictionaries, these can be literals, or they can be nested dictionaries and lists themselves.

Our fans' configuration might look in JSON something like Listing 5-2.

---

[4]www.json.org/

Listing 5-2. Example of a configuration JSON file

```
{
  "fans": [
    {
      "name": "fan1",
      "pin": 20
    },
    {
      "name": "fan2",
      "pin": 21
    }
  ]
}
```

For JavaScript, decoding JSON does not require using any additional libraries. Projects that are written in other languages that involve some sort of network communication will most likely already make use of a library that can decode JSON. There are, however, some drawbacks for using JSON for configuration files. The biggest one is that JSON does not allow for comments, which means that you can't include documentation in the file to explain what the different settings are. Some might hack their way around it, like including "pseudo-properties," as in Listing 5-3.

Listing 5-3. Using pseudo-properties for JSON documentation. Note that the comment at the end denotes the rest of the code, and not an actual comment, as these are not allowed in JSON

```
{
  "_fans": "Documentation for fan list goes here",
  "fans":[  // ...
```

But obviously, this solution is suboptimal. Also, JSON requires a lot of punctuation, and a well-formatted file will include many newlines – both of these contribute to files that are not always easy to read.

YAML

YAML[5] (recursive acronym for "YAML Ain't Markup Language", and originally "Yet Another Markup Language") was designed specifically for the purpose of *data serialization* – capturing the state of objects in a way that can be stored or transmitted and then reconstructed from that data. It puts great emphasis on human readability, as it supports comments and makes little use of punctuation, relying on indentation for determining hierarchy within the data. YAML has quite a range for how complex it could be, and the same data can be represented in several ways. We are going to cover only the most basic form of it. Once again, we'll start by looking at what our fan's configuration might look like in YAML (Listing 5-4).

Listing 5-4. Example of a configuration YAML file

```
# Fan configuration
fans:
- name: fan1
  pin: 20
- name: fan2
  pin: 21
```

Just like JSON, YAML has three types of *nodes*: *scalars*, which are strings or numbers; *sequences,* which are similar to JSON's lists and are ordered lists of nodes; *and mappings*, which are key-value pairs, just like JSON's dictionaries.

---

[5]https://yaml.org/

Nodes in a sequence are denoted by a prefix of a hyphen and a white space preceding them. These prefixes must have the same indentation for all nodes in the sequence. In our example, each fan is represented by a mapping, which is denoted by the format key: value, and once again, all pairs in the mapping share the same indentation. Comments, like in Python, start with the number sign (#).

As you can see, YAML's main advantages are its compactness, high readability, and support of comments. The main drawback in YAML is that it relies on indentation and other fragile syntax rules.

Parsing a YAML file can be done using the PyYAML[6] library for Python. Listing 5-5 demonstrated how the configuration described earlier can be read.

Listing 5-5. Reading a YAML configuration file

```
import yaml
with open('config.yaml', 'r') as f:
  config = yaml.full_load(f)
for fan in config['fans']:
  print('{} uses pin {}'
    .format(fan['name'], fan['pin']))

# The output of this program should be:
# fan1 uses pin 20
# fan2 uses pin 21
```

For Javascript, js-yaml[7] will produce similar results.

---

[6]https://pyyaml.org/
[7]www.npmjs.com/package/js-yaml

Code

Finally, the configuration can be described simply by code that is separate from the program's code. In Python, for example, we can write a file called config.py, which will contain the configuration data (see Listing 5-6).

Listing 5-6. config.py, configuration in code

```
cfg = {'fans': [
  {
    'name': 'fan1',
    'pin': 21
  },
  {
    'name': 'fan2',
    'pin': 20
  }
]}
```

And then the project's main code can import cfg from this file (Listing 5-7).

Listing 5-7. Using config.py in the main code

```
from config import cfg
for fan_cfg in cfg['fans']:
  print('{} uses pin {}').format(
    fan_cfg['name'], fan_cfg[pin])
# output:
# fan1 uses pin 20
# fan2 uses pin 21
```

To do the same in JavaScript, we can start by writing the configuration file (Listing 5-8).

131

Listing 5-8. Using config.js in the main code

```
const cfg = {
  fans: [{
    name: 'fan1',
    pin: 20
  },
  {
    name: 'fan2',
    pin: 21
  }
]};

module.exports = {
  cfg: cfg
};
```

And import the configuration as shown in Listing 5-9.

Listing 5-9. Using config.js in the main code

```
const cfg = require('./config').cfg;

for (let fan of cfg.fans) {
  console.log(`${fan.name} uses pin ${fan.pin}`);
}
// output:
// fan1 uses pin 20
// fan2 uses pin 21
```

Interpreting the Configuration
The Constructor's Argument

The next step is to interpret the configuration file as the program starts up. The original constructor for our Fan class (Listing 4-1) took two arguments: the fan's name and the GPIO pin number. We should consider changing the constructor so that it takes a configuration dictionary, so that the constructor can accept an item from the configuration file's fans list. See Listing 5-10 for the modified constructor.

Listing 5-10. Modifying the Fan constructor to accept a configuration dictionary

```
class Fan {
  constructor(fanConfig) {
    Object.assign(this, fanConfig)
    gpio.setup(this.pinNumber, gpio.DIR_OUT);
  }
// ...
```

This one argument replaces the list of arguments that we previously had for the constructor. This does not only simplify the process of passing the parameters from the configuration file to the new object, it also makes it easier to make changes to the object if the development process requires that. If later on we would like to add an argument to the constructor, we would just need to make sure to include it in the configuration file and have the constructor do whatever it needs with that field, but the definition of the constructor and the way it is called would stay the same. This comes with a price: it is no longer evident from the constructor's *signature* – its argument list – what kind of data it needs in order to initialize.

Note the `Object.assign()` function: it copies all the properties of the object that is the second argument to the object that is the first argument. In our case, this copies all the properties of the configuration object to the Fan object.

Dynamic Instantiation

When dealing with the `Fan` classes, the configuration was pretty straightforward, since we only instantiated objects of a single type of class. It's not uncommon for a project to be able to generate objects of different classes to carry a certain task. Our temperature sensors are a good example: in the previous chapter, we had two of them filling similar roles and adhering to the same interface. Because of that, the two types of sensors are interchangeable, and their arrangement can also be defined in the configuration file: we can include information in the configuration file that will help the program determine which class it should instantiate for each role. Listing 5-11 shows what a portion of a YAML configuring the temperature sensors might look like.

Listing 5-11. Configuration file segment for the temperature sensors

```
# Sensors configuration
sensors:
- name: temperature_east
  type: Si7021Temp
  i2cBusId: 1
  units: "deg C"
- name: temperature_west
  type: MPL3115A2Temp
  i2cBusId: 1
  units: "deg C"
```

Now, when we instantiate those sensor objects, a JavaScript code may look like Listing 5-12.

Listing 5-12. Instantiating classes based on a configuration file

```javascript
const fs = require('fs');
const path = require('path');
const yaml = require('js-yaml');

const fileName =
  path.join(__dirname, 'config.yaml');
var fileContent =
  fs.readFileSync(fileName, 'utf8');
var config = yaml.load(fileContent);

var sensorList = [];
for (let sensorCfg of config.sensors) {
  switch (sensorCfg.type) {
    case 'Si7021Temp':
      sensorList.push(
        new Si7021Temp(sensorCfg));
      break;
    case 'MPL3115A2Temp':
      sensorList.push(
        new MPL3115A2Temp(sensorCfg));
      break;
  }
}
```

The loop iterates through the list of sensors, and it checks for its type field for each sensor. The program then instantiates an object, based on the value of the type field, and pushes it into sensorList.

Command-Line Arguments

Introduction

Another way to affect the project's configuration is through the *command-line arguments*. These are the additional text fields that are entered after the program's name in the command line. For example, copying a file using the terminal can be done by the command

```
cp filename.src filename.dst
```

The names of the source and destination file names are command-line arguments. There are several types of command-line arguments, and while the terminology has several variations, we will stick with the following:

- *Positional arguments* are mandatory, and their role is determined by their position in the command. In the command

  ```
  cp filename.src filename.dst
  ```

  the two arguments are positional arguments.

- *Subcommands*, as the name suggests, instruct the program to perform a specific task. In the command

  ```
  npm install express
  ```

  the argument install is a subcommand, and express is an argument for that subcommand.

- *Options* affect the behavior of the command. Sometimes they take their own arguments. When they don't, they are known as *flags*. In the command

  ```
  python -v -m SimpleHTTPServer
  ```

  -m is an option, SimpleHTTPServer is its argument, and -v is a flag.

In the Linux convention, command-line options are denoted by either a dash followed by a letter or two dashes followed by a word. Sometimes there are both a letter and a word version of the same option. For example, typing either node -v or node --version will cause node to print its version number.

There are many useful things we can tell the program to do through the command line: we can instruct it to run in "verbose" mode, where the program meticulously prints to the screen everything it does; we can run it in "simulation" mode, where perhaps physical sensors and actuators are replaced by software-simulated one; we could instruct the program to initialize with a different configuration file than the one it usually uses; and so on.

In Python, the command-line arguments can be read with the **argv** property of the sys module. It is an array of **all** the strings in the command, as shown in Listing 5-13.

Listing 5-13. Reading the command-line arguments using the sys module

```
import sys

print('There are {} arguments:', len(sys.argv))
for arg in sys.argv:
  print(arg)
# for the command:
# > python project.py --conf-file alt-cfg.yaml
# the output will be:
# > There are 4 arguments:
# > python
# > project.py
# > --conf-file
# > alt-cfg.yaml
```

It might already be evident that making sense of the command-line arguments is not a trivial task. We need to distinguish between positional arguments, subcommands, options, and the arguments that belong to those options.

Parsing

Fortunately, Python has a built-in module called `argparse`[8] that helps significantly with this task. Not only does it store all the arguments and options in a nicely organized structure, it also helps with setting defaults for the options, managing optional vs. required options, and providing special case options, most notable is the help option. `argparse`, being a powerful, built-in module, is the most common way to deal with command-line arguments in Python. It has been ported to JavaScript,[9] but it's worth mentioning that there are quite a few modules for JavaScript that are more popular, such as yargs,[10] commander,[11] and minimist.[12]

To get started with `argparse`, we need to import it into the program and create an instance of an `ArgumentParser` (Listing 5-14).

Listing 5-14. Instantiating an `ArgumentParser` object

```
import argparse
parser = argparse.ArgumentParser(
  description="Weather station project")
```

---

[8]https://docs.python.org/3/library/argparse.html
[9]https://github.com/nodeca/argparse
[10]https://github.com/yargs/yargs
[11]https://github.com/tj/commander.js
[12]https://github.com/substack/minimist

Then it's a matter of adding the various command-line options to the parser and finally parsing the command line. For example (Listing 5-15):

Listing 5-15. Adding arguments to the argument parser

```
#...
parser.add_argument('--interval', type=int,
                    dest='loop_interval')
parser.add_argument('--conf-file',
                    default=['config.yaml'],
                    nargs=1)
parser.add_argument('--fan-pin',
                    nargs=2,
                    type=int,
                    action='append')
parser.add_argument('-v', '--verbose',
                    action='store_true')

args = parser.parse_args()
```

Let's start from the end: the last line is the one actually performing the parsing, storing the various options in an `argparse.Namespace` object. This type of object doesn't do much other than store the arguments as its properties. For example, to know whether it should run in verbose mode, the program would need to invoke the value of `args.verbose`. The name of the property can be automatically determined by `argparse` or manually set by adding a `dest` parameter to the `add_argument()` function as demonstrated for the `--interval` option.

The examples in Listing 5-15 are loosely based on our weather station project. The first option we added sets the measuring interval, and as a default, options take one argument.

By default, `argparse` treats option arguments as strings. That can be changed using the `type` parameter that tells `argparse` what type this argument is, which in this case is `int`.

If the default interval is stored in a variable called INTERVAL, we could change the measuring loop we wrote in Listing 1-2 so that the interval could be overridden by the interval option, if the option is specified in the command (Listing 5-16).

Listing 5-16. Getting an integer from the command-line options

```
INTERVAL = 5
def measuring_loop():
  while True:
    #...
    time.sleep(args.loop_interval or INTERVAL)
```

The second option we added, --conf-file, is the same as we described in Listing 5-13: it tells the program to load an alternate configuration file. It is not unusual for options to have names that consist of two words, and by convention, these are separated by a hyphen. However, argparse converts hyphens in option names to underscores, so in this case the value will be stored in args.conf_file.

The narg parameter tells argparse how many additional arguments an option consumes – in this case it's 1, the file name. If nargs is not specified, the option will consume one argument **if provided**, which is stored as a value in the Namespace object. However, if nargs is specified, the option's arguments will be stored as a list rather than as a value, even if nargs=1.

Note that we specified here a default value – this ensures that args. conf_file exists and has a valid value, even if not specified in the command line. This a more graceful way to specify default value than the way we did it for the measuring loop interval. As we mentioned, if this option is included in the command, its argument will be stored in a list. This is why we set the default value to also be a list. We can then load the configuration file, whether it was specified in the command line or not, by calling

```
with open(args.conf_file[0], 'r') as f:
  config = yaml.full_load(f)
```

The next argument is the option `--fan-pin`. This option changes the GPIO pin that controls one of the fans. Therefore, this option will require two arguments: the fan index and the GPIO pin number. However, note that we used `action='append'` this time. This means that the option can appear multiple times in the command, and each occurrence is added to a list. Using both the `append` action and defining `nargs` results in a list of lists. If this last paragraph was a little confusing, the following example will help clarify. Let's say we execute the command

```
python project.py --fan-pin 0 19 --fan-pin 1 17
```

If we added `print(args)` to the end of the Python code, the output would be

```
Namespace(conf_file='config.yaml', fan_pin=[['0', '19'],
['1', '17']], loop_interval=None, verbose=False)
```

To apply this option, we can start by loading the configuration file, then overriding fan configurations with whatever is specified in the command-line option, and finally instantiating the fans. Listing 5-17 demonstrates how this can be done.

Listing 5-17. Creating Fan objects using the configuration from the command line

```
#...
if args.fan_pin:
  for fan_option in args.fan_pin:
    fan_index = fan_option[0]
    new_fan_pin = fan_option[1]
    config['fans'][fan_index]['pin'] = new_fan_pin

fan_list = (Fan(f) for f in config['fans'])
```

The last line uses list comprehension to generate a list of Fan objects. It's equivalent to this:

```
fan_list = []
for f in config['fans']:
  fan_list.append(Fan(f))
```

The last option added in Listing 5-15 tells the program to run in verbose mode. Notice that here we specified two ways to enable this option: -v and --verbose. Also, this option doesn't expect any additional arguments, but using the store_true action, we instruct argparse to give the verbose option the value True if the flag is present and False if it is not. Of course, the action store_false also exists, and naturally, it does the exact opposite.

Getting Help

By default, argparse creates option flags, -h and --help, that cause the program to show a help message rather than run normally. Running

```
python project.py -h
```

will produce the output in Listing 5-18.

Listing 5-18. Default help message produced by argparse

```
usage: project.py [-h] [--interval INTERVAL]
                  [--fan-pin FAN_PIN FAN_PIN]
                  [--conf-file CONF_FILE] [-v]
Weather station project

optional arguments:
  -h, --help          show this help message and exit
  --interval INTERVAL
  --fan-pin FAN_PIN FAN_PIN
```

```
--conf-file CONF_FILE
-v, --verbose
```

This is really not that bad for a start, but this help message can use some of our own help. We can add some parameters to the options to make the help message more legible. Consider the --fan-pin option: argparse gave both arguments it consumes the names FAN_PIN. To clarify what each argument does, we can use the metavar parameter. It can be a string for options that consume one argument or a tuple of strings if there are more. We can also add the help parameter to add text after each option that describes exactly what it does. If we add these parameters to the options, as shown in Listing 5-19.

Listing 5-19. Revised command-line option parameters supporting the help message produced by argparse

```python
parser.add_argument(
  '--interval', type=int,
  help='set measuring loop interval',
  metavar='time_sec')

parser.add_argument(
  '--fan-pin', nargs=2, type=int, action="append",
  help='override fan GPIO pin number',
  metavar=('idx', 'pin'))

parser.add_argument(
  '--conf-file', nargs=1, type=str,
  default=['config.yaml'], metavar='filename',
  help='set configuration file')

parser.add_argument(
  '-v', '--verbose', help='verbose',
  action="store_true", default=False)
```

The help message will be as shown in Listing 5-20.

Listing 5-20. Help message after adding help-related parameters to the command-line options

```
usage: project.py [-h] [--interval time_sec]
                  [--fan-pin idx pin]
                  [--conf-file filename] [-v]

Weather station project

optional arguments:
  -h, --help            show this help message and exit
  --interval time_sec   set measuring loop interval
  --fan-pin idx pin     override fan GPIO pin number
  --conf-file filename  set configuration file
  -v, --verbose         verbose
```

This is significantly clearer and more helpful.

Configuring an Arduino Project

We've been discussing the configuration of programs through configuration files and command-line arguments, suggesting that we have easy access to these, as is the case with SBCs. When using microcontroller boards, such as Arduinos, the situation is very different. Most often, Arduino projects are configured either through one or more .h files or in the code itself. There is a better option, though.

The Arduino's EEPROM

The Arduino Uno, one of the most popular boards around, features the ATmega328P. This microcontroller has *EEPROM* (*Electrically Erasable Programmable Read-Only Memory*). This memory acts like *ROM*

(*Read-Only Memory*) in the sense that it is non-volatile, meaning that the data stored on it persists when power is turned off. Also, EEPROM is not meant to be constantly read and written like *RAM* (*Random-Access Memory*) – it's much slower and has a more limited lifespan. It is, however, perfect for storing configuration data.

First, we need a way to get the configuration into the EEPROM in the first place, and the whole point is to design this in a way that frees us from having reprogram the Arduino every time we want to change the configuration. One way to do this is through the serial port, and if we re-examine the formats we discussed earlier, we can see that JSON is a good candidate: it is fairly compact, and it doesn't rely on indentation.

With respect to storing the configuration on the EEPROM, there are two strategies we can take: we can either store a JSON encoding of the configuration or store the configuration in an object, and let the EEPROM library encode that object for storing.

In the following example, we'll have two things that need to be configured: the measuring interval and the pins to which fans are connected. The program will expect to get a string that looks like this:

```
{"interval":6,"fans":[2,6]}
```

so that the number of fans will also be determined by the length of the array.

Storing Configuration as JSON

Let's start with writing a JSON string. First, we need to do some setting up and get the data from the serial port (Listing 5-21).

Listing 5-21. Arduino code for reading and writing JSON configuration on the EEPROM

```
#include <EEPROM.h>
#include <ArduinoJson.h>
```

```
enum ParseResult {
  PARSE_SUCCESS,
  PARSE_ERROR
};

const int configAddress = 0;
char incomingMsg[256];
char charBuff[256];
StaticJsonDocument<256> jsonDoc;
int msgIndex = 0;

int * fanPins = 0;
int numFans = 0;
int interval = 20; // default value

void setup() {
  Serial.begin(9600);
  msgIndex = 0;
  loadConfig();
}

void loop() {
  while (Serial.available()) {
    char c = Serial.read();
    if (c == '\r' || c == '\n') {
      charBuff[msgIndex++] = '\n';
      charBuff[msgIndex++] = '\0';
      if (PARSE_SUCCESS == parseJson(charBuff)) {
        dumpConfig();
        printConfig();
      }
      msgIndex = 0;
    }
```

```
  else {
    charBuff[msgIndex++] = c;
  }
 }
 // Attend to the rest of the project
}
```

There are a few interesting points here that we should unpack. Notice how we read from the serial port: we don't wait for data to be available, and when it is, we don't wait until the data is ready at the serial port or until it's all there, so that the Arduino can continue running its stuff. Instead, if serial data is available, we add it to a char[] buffer. When a newline character ('\n') or a carriage return ('\r') comes in, that represents the end of the JSON string. I discovered that ArduinoJson is buggy if the string that it's parsing doesn't end with a newline, so we add that at the end of the string and mark the end of the string in the buffer with a null character ('\0'). Then the buffer is passed for parsing with parseJSON(), and if the parsing works, the new configuration is written to the EEPROM with dumpConfig(). We will write these functions next, starting with parseJson() (Listing 5-22).

Listing 5-22. Using JSON-encoded data for configuration

```
ParseResult parseJson(const char *s) {
  DeserializationError error =
    deserializeJson(jsonDoc, s);
  if (error) {
    Serial.println("parsing failed");
    Serial.println(error.c_str());
    return PARSE_ERROR;
  }
```

```
JsonArray fansConfig = jsonDoc["fans"];
if (!fansConfig.isNull())
{
  if (fanPins) {
    delete[] fanPins;
  }
  numFans = fansConfig.size();
  fanPins = new int[numFans];
  for (int i = 0; i < numFans; ++i) {
    fanPins[i] = fansConfig[i];
  }
}

if (jsonDoc.containsKey("interval"))
{
  interval = jsonDoc["interval"];
}
return PARSE_SUCCESS;
}
```

First, notice how the function returns PARSE_ERROR or PARSE_SUCCESS, values of the ParseResult enum that we declared earlier. It's much easier and readable this way than returning a numerical value. Otherwise, everything else should look familiar, besides the lines that allocate memory for the fan's array. This is not necessarily the best way to do this on an Arduino – Arduinos are not great for dynamic data structures. Another way would be to set a fixed size array, with its size being the maximum possible number of fans. Then, we could keep a variable that says what the actual number of fans is and use only that number of array cells.

Also notice the two different ways to check for a key in the JSON object: for the fans array, since it's not translated directly to a configuration variable, we read the key without knowing if it exists.

148

To verify, we call the result's isNull() method and decide how to proceed. For the interval, we check for the key existence first using the containsKey() method. If the key exists, we can read directly into the variable. Next, the dumpConfig() function, which encodes the configuration to JSON and writes it to the EEPROM (Listing 5-23).

Listing 5-23. dumpConfig() encodes the configuration to JSON and writes it to the EEPROM

```
void dumpConfig() {
  JsonObject root = jsonDoc.to<JsonObject>();
  root["interval"] = interval;
  JsonArray fanConfig = root.createNestedArray("fans");
  for (int i = 0; i < numFans; ++i) {
    fanConfig.add(fanPins[i]);
  }
  serializeJson(jsonDoc, charBuff);
  EEPROM.put(configAddress, charBuff);
}
```

Notice that receiving the incoming configuration JSON strings, parsing them, and encoding the data to JSON for storage are completely decoupled. This guarantees that the entire configuration will stay intact even if incoming configuration strings include only partial information. For example, if only the interval time is specified in the string, the fan information will not be changed – not in the running project and not on the EEPROM. Also, this allows us to use parseJSON() to parse the data from the EEPROM on startup. We have called loadConfig() in setup() but have not yet implemented it. Now is the time (Listing 5-24).

Listing 5-24. Implementing loadConfig()

```
void loadConfig() {
  char s[256];
  EEPROM.get(configAddress, s);
  parseJson(s);
}
```

Configuration Object Serialization

The EEPROM.put() method can take any object, not just char[] arrays, and *serialize* it. Serializing an object means encoding it in a way that can be stored or transmitted and then reconstructed back from that representation. We've been doing similar things when transmitting data back and forth between the project's program and the dashboard, but I chose not to use the term "serialization," since we never really reconstructed objects from their representation. This case is different: if we incorporate all configuration parameters in one struct and read and write that struct to the EEPROM, that would be considered "serialization." This will be our configuration object (Listing 5-25).

Listing 5-25. The configuration struct

```
struct Configuration {
  int interval = 20; // default value
  int fanPins[MAX_NUM_FANS];
  int numFans = 0;
} cfg;
```

We can't dynamically allocate the fanPins array in this case. If we did, the thing that would actually be written when serializing this object would be the address of the memory block allocated for the array, but the values in that array would not be serialized. The solution is for the configuration

150

struct to have an array that can hold MAX_NUM_FANS fans and specify with numFans how many of the items in the array are used.

We will need to modify parseJSON() to store data from incoming messages in the configuration struct (see Listing 5-26).

Listing 5-26. Modified parseJSON() that uses the configuration object

```
ParseResult parseJSON(const char* s) {

  // ...
  JsonArray fansConfig = jsonDoc["fans"];
  if (!fansConfig.isNull()) {
    cfg.numFans = fansConfig.size();
    for (int i = 0; i < cfg.numFans; ++i) {
     cfg.fanPins[i] = fansConfig[i];
    }
  }

  if (jsonDoc.containsKey("interval")) {
    cfg.interval = jsonDoc["interval"];
  }
  return PARSE_SUCCESS;
}
```

Then, the matter of writing and reading from the EEPROM becomes really simple, as shown in Listing 5-27.

Listing 5-27. Modified loadConfig() and dumpConfig() that use the configuration object

```
void loadConfig() {
  EEPROM.get(configAddress, cfg);
}
```

```
void dumpConfig() {
  EEPROM.put(configAddress, cfg);
}
```

Storing on an SD Card

Another way to store the project's configuration is on an SD card. The SD
library doesn't offer a way to serialize complex objects like EEPROM.put()
does, so we have two options: either stick to storing the data as a JSON
string or write our own serialization system, which will probably more
compact. While SD cards can hold more data than the EEPROM, that is
not necessarily an advantage we should rely on, since if we read a JSON
string from the SD card, we still load the whole thing into the Arduino's
RAM. Having said that, the main advantage of working with an SD card
is that we can remove them from the project setup, stick them into a
computer, and edit the configuration file manually, where working with
JSON (or some other human-readable format, or that matter) is necessary.
If the JSON configuration file becomes too big for the Arduino to load, it
can always be broken into several files, each responsible for configuring a
different aspect of the project.

In our example, one file is enough. The only changes that need
to be made to the code presented in the previous section are in the
loadConfig(), dumpConfig(), and setup() functions. See Listing 5-28 for
the modified code.

Listing 5-28. Modified code to read and write configuration from an
SD card

```
#include <SD.h>
const int sdChipSelect = 4;
// ...
```

```
void setup() {
  SD.begin(sdChipSelect);
  // ...
}

void loadConfig() {
  File configFile = SD.open("config.jsn");
  char s[512];
  configFile.read(s, 512);
  configFile.close();
  parseJson(s);
}

void dumpConfig() {
  // ...
  SD.remove("config.jsn");
  File configFile = SD.open(
    "config.jsn", FILE_WRITE);
  configFile.println(s);
  configFile.close();
}
```

We named the file "config.jsn" instead of using a .json extension. The SD library expects files to have file names with no more than eight characters and extensions with no more than three characters. Note that before writing the file, we remove it. Otherwise, writing to an existing file using the SD library **appends** data to the file. We need to remove the file first if we want to rewrite it.

It's also important to note that there are two points of possible failure that we are not managing: the SD card may not be present when we call SD.begin(), and the file may not be missing or corrupt when we call SD. open(). We will discuss that next.

Handling Configuration Errors

Introducing configuration files to a project needs to happen with care. The program needs to be able to decide how to proceed if the configuration file is missing or if it's ill-formatted; it has to have a plan in case some of the values are missing; and as mentioned, if the configuration file is on external hardware, an SD card, for instance, it needs to know what to do if the media can't be mounted.

There is really no single course of action here, but the first thing to decide upon is whether the program should proceed or not. If we choose to proceed with execution, we should make sure that the program has another set of values it can use for its configuration. If we recall Listing 5-21, we'll see that the configuration values numFans, fanPins, and interval were declared with default values. All we need to do is to make sure these are not touched if the configuration file is missing or the SD card cannot be accessed. Here (Listing 5-29) is a modified loadConfig() function.

Listing 5-29. Modified loadConfig() deals with a missing configuration file

```
void loadConfig() {
  File configFile = SD.open("config.jsn");
  if (!File) {
    return;
  }
  /...
}
```

Even in projects that are built for public places, running the program at all cost is not always the right decision, and when debugging a project having it gracefully recover ill-formatted can actually be detrimental to the debugging efforts: in a project I worked on, one computer, let's call it Machine A, was supposed to send data to Machine B. When I made a change to Machine A's program configuration file, Machine B's program stopped responding. Now, that was odd, because the change I made had nothing to do with the communication, and both programs seemed to be running. It turned out that I accidentally entered another character somewhere else in that file, which was a JSON file. That caused the program to treat the file as ill-formatted and resort to defaults. The default IP address to which the program sent data was, of course, 127.0.0.1, which always means "this machine." This meant that Machine A was sending messages to itself, and not Machine B.

The point, once again, is to be mindful and make strategic decisions: whether the program should continue or not, how default values are applied and which values make sense, and what additional steps should be taken.

Configuring with Hardware

Sometimes it makes sense to change a project's configuration using hardware. This can be the case when dealing with projects that are not connected to a network, Arduino projects, and projects that don't have a lot of parameters to expose. The inputs on most SBCs are strictly digital and not plentiful, so we should be very mindful of what parameters we expose and how.

Jumpers

Jumpers simply connect one point in the circuit to another. Jumper caps (Figure 5-1) do exactly that, connecting two adjacent header pins on circuit. A jumper cap's presence or absence acts as a switch that can be used to change a program's configuration (Figure 5-2).

Figure 5-1. *Jumper caps are simple way to change the configuration of a project*

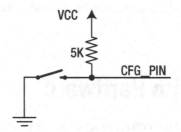

Figure 5-2. *A configuration jumper can be treated as a switch and should be used with a pull-up (or pull-down) resistor*

In the circuit depicted in Figure 5-2, the configuration appears as a switch. If the switch is closed, that is, the jumper is present, the voltage on the pin is pulled to ground. The resistor, called a pull-up resistor, makes sure that when the switch is open, a known voltage (V_{CC}) is applied to the pin, so that the state is known. Many SBCs, the Raspberry Pi included, have pull-up and/or pull-down resistor that can be engaged using software.

Due to the binary nature of the jumper, the way it affects the project must also be binary. Perhaps it selects between two values, or between the content of a configuration file and program defaults. Perhaps it just selects between two possible values, as shown in Listing 5-30 (we'll stay in Arduino land for this).

Listing 5-30. Changing configuration using a jumper

```
#define INTERVAL_PIN
int interval;

void setup() {
  pinMode(INTERVAL_PIN, INPUT_PULLUP);
  interval = digitalRead(INTERVAL_PIN) ? 1000 : 5000;
)
```

DIP Switches

DIP switches usually come as eight tiny switches bundled together in a through-hole packaging (Figure 5-3).

Figure 5-3. DIP switches

Having multiple switches doesn't mean that every switch has to control a different parameter. Using two switches for one parameter gives us four options rather than two, as demonstrated in Listing 5-31.

Listing 5-31. Using multiple pins to configure one parameter

```
#define INTERVAL_PIN_0 5
#define INTERVAL_PIN_1 6
```

```
int interval;

void setup() {
  int intervalOptions[] = {30, 60, 90, 120};
  pinMode(INTERVAL_PIN_0, INPUT_PULLUP);
  pinMode(INTERVAL_PIN_1, INPUT_PULLUP);

  int intervalConfig =
    digitalRead(INTERVAL_PIN_0) +
    digitalRead(INTERVAL_PIN_1) << 1;

  interval = intervalOptions[intervalConfig];
)
```

We are treating the switches as digits in a binary number, which is why we bit-shift the result of `digitalRead(INTERVAL_PIN_1)` to the left. This two-digit binary number has four possible values, which we then use as an index in an array of options.

Summary

We have reviewed various aspects of configuration in this chapter: reading files of different formats, getting instructions from the command line, recovery from missing configuration information, configuring an Arduino project, and configuration using hardware.

There's a significant amount of effort that goes into setting up a well-organized configuration setup, and it's very tempting to just throw magic numbers into the code. But it's worth it, and that is apparent the second serious debugging needs to be done or when changes need to be made on the spot, which is why it's good to incorporate a configuration setup early on before the code gets too complex and hard to control.

CHAPTER 6

Machine Setup

For a project to run smoothly, it needs the right environment. In this chapter we'll discuss how to configure the machine on which the project is running. For the sake of simplicity, we'll assume the machine is a Raspberry Pi with Raspbian Stretch Lite as the operating system, but most of the topics and examples that we'll discuss in this chapter translate readily to other single-board computers with different flavors of Linux.

User Setup

In a Linux system, every process runs under a user: the user may run the process by entering a command in the terminal, or it may run automatically by the system at times set by the programmer in advance. This means two things: First, the user must have permission[1] to execute the program. Second, the user must have the permissions to access the hardware required by the program, such as the GPIO pins or the I2C buses. Notice that I referred to the user as "it" – a user account doesn't have to be tied to a person. Very often users are tied to a certain role the machine has to play. The root user is a good example for this. Other examples are the mysql user on machines that run MySQL, or www-data on machines running Apache.

---

[1]Learn more about permissions and the Linux file system here:Molloy, Derek. Exploring Raspberry Pi: *Interfacing to the Real World with Embedded Linux*. Indianapolis, IN: John Wiley & Sons, 2016. pp 70–78.

© Eyal Shahar 2019
E. Shahar, *Project Reliability Engineering*, https://doi.org/10.1007/978-1-4842-5019-8_6

To run our weather station, we need to access the I2C bus and the GPIO pins. As we have established, root has permissions to do whatever it wants, and pi, another user that your Pi came with, also has permissions to access all of the Raspberry Pi's peripherals. The reason pi can do this is because it is a part of all the Pi's hardware groups. Being a part of the i2c group allows a user to use the I2C bus, and groups like gpio and spi have similar roles.

This purpose of introduction was to lead to the main question of this section: under which user should our program be running? It seems like we have a few options.

We can run it under root, but that is considered bad practice. The power that root possesses can cause serious damage to the system, since there is nothing to stop it if a piece of code accidently tries to do something that is bad for the system. Moreover, if the program is intended to be run by root, tending to the program often has to be done by the programmer as root, and while it's fine to log in as root every now and again, doing it too often can lead to disasters. It takes just that one time when you delete your entire machine or block yourself out of it to acknowledge that.

We can run it as pi. That's a perfectly valid option, though not my personal favorite. Although it's much harder for pi to cause actual damage, it still has way more power than needed to run most projects. Since it's so common in Raspberry Pi machines, it's a common target for online attacks, and last, it lacks personality. I'm not just being cute, although this is a part of my argument.

We can run it under our own user. Since we'll still need the permissions for that, we can sudo the command. That works just fine from the command line, but since we are about to automate the execution of our program and sudoing will require an explicit inclusion of our password in the configuration file, that doesn't sound like a good idea. Actually, having your personal password in a file is never a good idea. The proper thing to do would be to just give us the right permissions by adding our user to the relevant groups.

But that's still not giving personality to the user – the weather station is not **us**. It is a program that has its own agenda, doing its own thing. Moreover, if we choose to run other programs on the same computer, it may be a good idea to separate them, so each one of them has its own permissions and its own files.

Let's review the process of adding the new user. We'll name the user weatheruser. We start with the useradd command

```
sudo adduser weatheruser
```

This also creates a folder for the user in the /home folder. In our case, the folder /home/weatheruser is created. We'll be asked for a password, which we should enter, and some information about the user, such as the user's name and phone number – we can leave these blank by hitting enter. Next, we need to add the user to the groups it needs to be in in order to run the project. Again, we use the adduser command, but since the user already exists, adduser knows it's being used to add the user to a group. To add weatheruser to the gpio, we enter the following command:

```
sudo adduser weatheruser gpio
```

Where Should the Code Live?

The Linux file system can be a little confusing, and it doesn't help that maker-type projects don't usually fall under a well-established convention. To avoid the file system's clutter and for keeping things simple, I prefer having the code for a project reside in the project's user home folder. In the weather station's case, I'd make the folder /home/weatheruser/ weatherstation/ where the code for the project will be saved.

Network Configuration

When most machines are connected to the network, by default, they are configured to get their network settings from the router using a protocol called *DHCP (Dynamic Host Configuration Protocol)*. This includes assigning IP addresses to the various machines on the network. While most of the time a router will remember the various machines that it worked with and will assign the same IP address to a machine if it came off and on the network, there is no guarantee to that. To be sure we can always log into a machine, access its dashboard, and include it in projects that incorporate more than one machine, it is crucial that the IP address is set manually. This requires us to configure all the network settings. Sadly, there are too many ways to set the network configuration, and they work differently on the various Linux distributions and machines. We'll first review what the different settings mean and what we should set them to and then discuss some common methods.

The Settings
Default Gateway

The *default gateway* is the machine that is used to send and receive data from external networks. In most cases, this is a router, and in home networks, its address is almost always 192.168.1.1.[2] If you don't know the IP address of your router, you're in trouble, because this means that you've probably never changed the password for your network, and the Admin password to your router, which leaves you extremely exposed to threats. Find the manual for your router, make sure to change both the Wi-Fi and Admin passwords, and familiarize yourself with the Admin interface. We'll need it to proceed.

---

[2]192.168.0.1 is also a very common address, but we'll proceed with 192.168.1.1.

IP Address

We need to give the machine an address we know is not taken by any other device, and never will be. First, it's a good idea to limit the range of addresses that the router can assign to devices using DHCP, like your laptop, phone, and your family and friend's devices. This can be done in the router's Admin dashboard – here's a screenshot of mine (Figure 6-1).

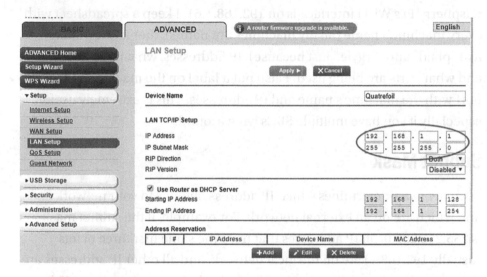

Figure 6-1. *Section of a router's Admin dashboard for setting DHCP address range*

Most people don't use advanced settings such as this, so it's not uncommon for them to be buried in submenus. My router is set so that addresses between 192.168.1.128 and 192.168.1.254 are free for dynamic assignment with DHCP. When I manually assign an IP address to a device, it's between 192.168.1.2 and 192.168.1.127.

It's also a good idea to check that the address we're about to use is free. We can ping the address we choose, but not all machine responds to pings. The safest way to know that an address is free is to look in the router's Admin dashboard. There's usually an "Attached Devices" screen, or something similar. Now that we know which addresses are free, we can choose one and make a note.

Personally, I have a system. Since I don't have more than 12 machines at a time that need static IP addresses, I use addresses in increments of 10. For example, my main server uses 192.168.1.10, and the Raspberry Pi that I use for writing the code in this book is on 192.168.1.60. If a machine uses Wi-Fi, that interface has an address that is an increment of 1, so my Raspberry Pi's Wi-Fi interface is on 192.168.1.61. I keep a spreadsheet with every machine's name (all my machines are named after fabric patterns, like "plaid" and "argyle," just because), IP addresses, what projects run it, and what ports are being used. I also put a label on the machine's Ethernet port with the machine's name and IP addresses. This is extremely useful, especially if you have multiple SBCs lying around.

Subnet Mask

A *subnet mask* determines which IP address belongs to your network and which are on an external network. For example, if the subnet mask is 255.255.255.0, all IP addresses that have the same first three octets (usually 192.168.1) are on the local network, and all other IP addresses are to be found on external networks. Networks that have more than 255 hosts will need a different subnet mask, but that's beyond the scope of this book. For our purposes, 255.255.255.0 is what we need.

Broadcast

Sometimes, your machine needs to send data to all other machines in your network, for example, to know which other machines are out there. The *broadcast* address determines which address range should be covered when this happens. This address should be just calculated from your network: in our case, the network is 192.168.1.x. To create the broadcast address, just fill that x with binary 1s, which gives a broadcast address of 192.168.1.255.

DNS Servers

The *DNS (Domain Name System) servers*, also called *name servers*, are machines that hold databases that map URLs to IP addresses. If they can't find the URL in their databases, they will query another name server and return the result. The name servers that your network is using are probably maintained by your ISP provider. Most machines will be configured to know the addresses of two name servers: a primary and a secondary that is used as a backup. When a machine is configured through DHCP, the router is responsible for providing these addresses to your machine. However, since we are configuring the network settings manually, we need to know what these addresses are. There are a few ways to obtain them:

- While the machine is still using DHCP, type in the command line

  `cat /etc/resolv.conf`

- Look for it in the router's Admin dashboard.

- Check with your ISP provider.

- You can use alternative, public DNS servers, such as Google's 8.8.8.8 and 8.8.4.4. However, unless you feel there's something wrong with the performance you're getting, I recommend using your ISP's servers.

- Some routers appear to couple as a name server. If they do, you can use their address, which is probably 192.168.1.1. Behind the scenes, they get the name servers' addresses from your ISP and forward requests to them.

Applying Network Configuration

Once we know what our settings should be, we can apply them to the machine. Before we get started though, we need to know how the operating system identifies the networking interface. If we are using an Ethernet cable, the interface's name is probably eth0. If it's wireless, it's probably wlan0. To make sure, check the output of ifconfig.

Ubuntu

In Ubuntu, the network configuration is set by the file /etc/network/ interfaces. Find the part that configures the interface of interest and change it to match Listing 6-1.

Listing 6-1. Network settings for a static IP address

```
auto wlan0
iface wlan0 inet static
  address 192.168.1.60
  netmask 255.255.255.0
  gateway 192.168.1.1
  dns-nameservers 192.168.1.1 8.8.8.8
  wpa-ssid NetworkName
  wpa-psk NetworkPassword
```

The auto keyword tells the operating system to try to start the connection on that interface when the machine turns on. Naturally, if a wired interface is being configured and not a wireless one, the two last lines can be omitted. Otherwise, replace NetworkName and NetworkPassword with your network's SSID and password.

Raspbian

Although it is possible to configure the network connection by editing the interfaces file, the recommended method for Raspbian is to edit a different file, /etc/dhcpcd.conf. Listing 6-2 shows the lines that we need to add to this file in order to give the machine a static IP address.

Listing 6-2. Setting a static IP address in /etc/dhcpcd.conf

```
interface wlan0
static ip_address=192.168.1.60/24
static routers=192.168.1.1
static domain_name_servers=192.168.1.1
```

Instead of specifying the subnet mask, the IP address is given in *CIDR* (Classless Inter-Domain Routing) *notation*. The number after that slash indicates the number of 1s in the binary representation of the subnet mask. Our subnet mask is 255.255.255.0, which in binary is 111111111111 1111111111100000000, or 24 1s and 8 0s.

If we want the machine to connect to a wireless network, we need to specify which network we want to connect to and provide the password. Instead of specifying the network SSID and password in a file, the easiest way to do this is by entering sudo raspi-config in the command and follow the menus "Network Options" and then "Wi-Fi," where the user is asked to enter the SSID and password.

Accessing Remotely

Static IP address

At this point, our machine is only visible to other devices within the local network – the one governed by our router. If we try to use a mobile phone's browser to navigate to 192.168.1.60 from anywhere outside the local network in which the machine lives – a friend's house, a coffee shop, or on the street using the cellular network – we will either get connected to a different device that has that address in **that** network or, more likely, get an error message stating that no device on the network has that address.

To be able to connect to the project from outside the network it's in, you first need to know what the public IP address of your router is. While for devices on the local network its address is 192.168.1.1 (or one of the other variants mentioned earlier), it has a different, unique address for the rest of the world. That address is given to the router by your ISP, and unfortunately, it is not guaranteed to be permanent. Call your ISP and ask – some ISPs will give you a static IP address for a monthly fee. Some might just give you a static address for free.

This address, however, is not the address of the machine running the project, but rather the address of the router. In order to actually communicate with the machine from outside the network, we need to set up *port forwarding* (sometimes called *port mapping*) in the router. Figure 6-2 shows a screenshot of my router's interface that is used to add a new port forwarding service.

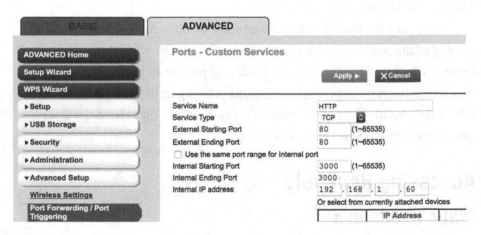

Figure 6-2. *Section of a router's Admin dashboard for setting port mapping*

This causes any communication addressed to my router at port 80 to be forwarded to my Raspberry Pi that has the address 192.168.1.60, at port 3000. Port 80 is the default HTTP port, and whenever you don't include a port when you navigate your browser to a web site, it actually addresses port 80. Routers will usually let you set as many services as you want. You could, for instance, use different ports as a way to address different machines. You can also map incoming communication on port 22 to your machine's port 22: that's the default port for SSH, and adding this mapping will allow you to SSH remotely.

Using a Domain Name

If you just have a static IP address, you need to remember it whenever you want to access the project remotely. Moreover, if the project serves a page that should be visible to the public, giving people just an IP address can be a little awkward. At that point, you'd probably want to own a domain name to point to the project. Once you have bought a domain, your domain registrar will provide you with an online management dashboard. In that dashboard you can set the *DNS resource records*. The type of resource record we care about is called an *A record*, which is the record that determines the IP address associated with your domain. Figure 6-3 shows a screenshot of the dashboard Google provides for their domain registration service.[3]

Figure 6-3. *Section of the Google Domains dashboard for setting DNS resource records*

Dynamic DNS

There is an alternative to the static IP address route: *Dynamic DNS* (*DDNS*). There are several companies offering DDNS services, most of them work on a freemium model, so you can definitely get started with a

---

[3]https://domains.google.com

pretty good service for free.[4] These services will provide you with a software that you would install on your machine. This software will constantly monitor your public IP address that is given to you by your ISP. If it changes, it will notify the service, which in turn will update the DNS resource records. The main advantage of using DDNS is that the entire setup can be done for free, if you're comfortable with the selection of free domain names these services offer. The main disadvantage is that changes to the DNS resource record take time to propagate through the entire Domain Name System – sometimes minutes, sometimes hours. If that can be a problem to your project, perhaps DDNS is not the route for you.

Note   Some routers have the software for popular DDNS services installed on them, eliminating the need to install any software on your machine.

Launching on Startup

When deploying a project, we want to make sure that the program starts automatically after reboot. We also want the program to restart if it crashes for some reason. In this section we'll explore a few strategies to achieve these goals.

Running as a cron Job

cron is a Linux utility that is used for scheduling tasks. Some common uses for cron are making backups, cleaning up log files, checking the machine's resources, and generating reports. For the purposes discussed in this chapter, we can use cron to launch our project on boot. Every user on the

---

[4]I recommend starting with No-IP, one of the key players in the field: www.noip.com

machine has its own `crontab` file, which tells cron what jobs should be executed in the name of the user and when it should execute them.

To edit the `crontab` file, type `crontab -e` in the terminal. The file contains some comments explaining, very superficially, how to add tasks, but we'll try to do a better job here.

Every line in the file describes a task and the schedule in which it should execute. The line starts with the schedule, represented by five space-separated fields: minute, hour, day of the month, month, and day of the week. After these numbers comes the task itself, which is simply written as a shell command.

The schedule fields follow these rules:

- A plain number indicates a specific value. For example, if the hour field has the value of 14, it implies 2PM. A value of 2 in the "day of the week" field means the job will execute on Tuesday (0 being Sunday).

- An asterisk (*) means "any." For example, if the minute field is 0 and the hour field is *, the job will execute every hour on the hour.

- The format */x means "in steps of x" or "every x." To run a task every half an hour, the minute field should be */30, and all the other fields should have an asterisk (*).

So, for example, the line

```
0 8 */15 * * /usr/bin/python3 ~/script.py
```

will cause the command `/usr/bin/python3 ~/script.py` to execute on 8 o'clock in the morning on the 1st and 16th of every month.

Launching on Boot

cron can also execute commands on boot. This can be done by substituting the schedule fields with @reboot, like this:

```
@reboot /usr/bin/python3 ~/project/main.py
```

Notice the command itself: we can't just call Python like we do from the command line, but rather we have to specify Python's full path. When as user logs into a terminal session, Linux loads the user's *environment variables*. These determine various aspects of the session, such as the user's home directory and the colors to be used during the session. One of these variables is PATH, which is a list of locations where the system looks for executable commands. This is how the operating system knows where to find the Python interpreter when we type python3 in the command line, for example. However, cron doesn't run under a terminal session and has a different, fairly minimal, set of environment variables.

Note   To see the difference between the two environments, try this: type printenv in the command line to see the terminal session's environment variables. Then, add this to the crontab file:

```
*/1 * * * * printenv > ~/env.log.
```

This will output the cron's session environment variables into a file, env. log, in the user's home folder, every minute. Wait 1 minute and examine the file's contents by typing cat ~/env.log. Remember to remove the added line from crontab when you're done with this experiment.

Long story short, we must include the full path when we run a program, whether it's Node, Python, or a shell script. Alternatively, we can change the PATH variable as soon as cron starts, as shown in Listing 6-3. This is especially useful if cron has to run several programs from the same location.

Listing 6-3. Adding node's path to cron's environment variables

```
PATH=/usr/bin/
@reboot python3 ~/project/main.py
```

> **Note** python3 is usually in /usr/bin/, and node is usually in /usr/local/bin/. To make sure, type whereis python3 or whereis node in the command line.

One more thing to consider is the working directory upon execution. cron's working directory is the user's home folder. If the program looks for a file with a relative path, it will be relative to the user's home folder and not the folder where the main program is in, and this can often lead to errors. We can make sure that the program itself never relies on the working directory: in Python, for example, we can use the __file__ constant to determine the location of the main file, and in Node.js we can use the __dirname constant. However, it's also fine to assume that the program's working directory is the one in which the main file is located, as long as we change the working directory before running. cron can run multiple commands in one line, so we can cd into the file's location and only then execute the command

```
@reboot cd ~/project; python3 main.py
```

> **Note** The semicolon (;) will cause the second command to execute after the first one, regardless of the success of the first command. Another option is the && operator: if used, the second command will execute only if the first one returned an exit status of zero, implying successful execution.

Sometimes it might be preferable to leave prep work, such as changing the working directory, to a shell script that is located in the same folder as the main program. Such a script can also make sure the program restarts if it crashes. Consider the script in Listing 6-4.

Listing 6-4. Shell script executing the main program

```
#!/bin/bash
cd $(dirname $0)
while true
do
  python3 main.py
done
```

The first line is called a *shebang*. It is used in executable files to tell the operating system what interpreter to use for the program. The default is the shell interpreter, so it can be omitted for shell scripts.

The second line changes the working directory to the one that the script is located in. The dollar sign ($) is used for several kinds of *expansions*, and in this line, we see two of them: *parameter expansion* expands a parameter into its value. When a command is executed, the command-line arguments are stored in numbered parameters, and as we've learned in the previous chapter, the one that will be stored in parameter 0 is the command itself, which is probably something like `~/project/project.sh`.

`dirname` is a command that takes in a string representing a path to a file or a folder and returns the folder in which it is located – in our case, this would be `~/project/`. However, we need to actually generate this string or, in other words, evaluate the expression `dirname $0` before we hand it over to the `cd` command. This is where that other dollar sign kicks in. In this case, it acts an expansion called *command substitution*, which executes the command and replaces it with its output. In our case, what ends up being executed after both expansions take place is just `cd ~/project/`, which is exactly what we need.

Of course, we could have just wrote that, literally, in the shell script, but there are two main advantages of doing it the way we did: first, if we ever move the project or rename the folder it's in, this command will still cd into the correct directory; second, this tiny script can be reused for other projects.

Crash Recovery

cron schedules only the execution of program; it doesn't care, however, what happens when they terminate. If we use cron, it is up to us to make sure that the program relaunches if it crashes.

Python

For programs written in Python, one technique is to wrap the entire main code in a try-except block and wrap that block in an infinite loop. If the main code crashes, an exception is thrown, the except block can then take some post-crash measures, such as send an alert or log the exception, and then the loop just starts all over again (see Listing 6-5).

Listing 6-5. Restarting a Python program after crash. The main code is wrapped in a try-except block that is wrapped in an infinite loop.

```
if __name__ == "__main__":
while True:
  try:
    # main code goes here
  except:
    # take post-crash actions
```

forever.js

Node.js programs, on the other hand, often don't have a main loop, but rather wait for events. Fortunately, there are some libraries that can come to our assistance and actually simplify the whole process. We'll mention two: forever.js and pm2. *forever.js*[5] is a lightweight library that is primarily aimed at Node.js projects. forever.js needs to be installed globally (npm install forever -g), and then, to run a program forever, one should cd into the project's directory and run forever start app.js.

In fact, forever.js is not limited to running Node.js projects: using the -c (command) option, it can run anything runnable, including Python programs:

```
forever start -c python3 app.py
```

If we use this line in the crontab file, we'd be all set with both launching on reboot, and relaunching in case of a failure. We must, as you may recall, use full paths in crontab:

```
PATH=/usr/local/bin/;/usr/share/
@reboot forever start -c python3 main.py
```

pm2

Another popular library is *pm2*.[6] It can be used in a similar way to forever.js: cd into the project folder and run pm2 start app.js. It knows to use the system's default Python interpreter if the file's extension is .py. Most SBCs today have Python 2.7 as their default interpreter, so to use Python3 we can specify the interpreter with the command

```
pm2 start app.py --interpreter=python3
```

---

[5]https://github.com/foreverjs
[6]http://pm2.keymetrics.io/

pm2 can also automatically launch the program on boot. Entering pm2 startup in the command line will cause pm2 to detect the operating system and how services are run in it. Then, it will respond with its recommendation of how the startup script should actually be initialized. It's usually a good idea to just copy and paste the recommendation – this is what I got:

```
sudo env PATH=$PATH:/usr/local/bin /usr/local/lib/node_modules/
pm2/bin/pm2 startup systemd -u weatheruser --hp /home/weatheruser
```

The env command at the beginning will cause the next command, modules/pm2/bin/pm2 startup (startup being the subcommand) to run in a temporary, alternative environment to the one we're currently in. This means, for example, that the changes made to PATH will not persist once the command finishes executing. The -u option sets the user, and the --hp option specifies the user's home folder.

Next, we can make sure that all the programs we want to run during startup are running. Last, we need to tell pm2 that the current running processes are the ones it should run on startup by entering pm2 save.

pm2 is fancier than forever.js as it has more features. For instance, you can use pm2 monit to launch a dashboard that monitors all processes currently running under pm2.

Running As a System Service

Another option for launching a project is running it as a system service. Services are programs that run in the background, either waiting to handle various events or carrying all sorts of important tasks. cron itself, for example, is a service, and so are SSH, databases like MySQL and MongoDB, and web servers like Apache. There are some nice perks that come with running a program as service, such as restarting after failure and setting the working directory.

systemd is the program that manages the services running in the system, and it uses files called *unit files* that define the various services available. These are located in /etc/systemd/system/ and have a .service extension. If we want to run our program as a system service, we must create one of those files. Listing 6-6 shows what a unit configuration file for our weather station might look like.

Listing 6-6. Unit configuration file for running the weather station project as a service

```
[Unit]
Description=Weather station project
After=network.target

[Service]
ExecStart=/usr/bin/python3 weatherstation.py
WorkingDirectory=/home/weatheruser/weatherstation/
User=weatheruser
Restart=always
RestartSec=1
ExecStopPost=/bin/bash /home/weatheruser/weatherstation/fail.sh

[Install]
WantedBy=multi-user.target
```

There are quite a few parameters that can be set when configuring a service, and each of them has many options. We'll discuss only the ones that are useful to us.

Before we dive into the various settings, it's important to mention that services are only one type of units. Other types are sockets, timers, and mounting points, to name a few. Unit files resemble .ini files in their format: they have sections that are denoted by their bracket-enclosed titles, and each section consists of key-value pairs. Service unit files have three sections: [Unit], [Service], and [Install]. The [Unit] section describes the unit itself and its dependency on other units. We used the Description field, which gives the service a human-readable description. Entering the command systemctl in the command line, for instance, prints out a list of all services available for systemd, along with their description. The second parameter we set is After, which helps systemd determine the order in which units are started if started together. A *target unit* groups together several other units, or indicates a synchronization point – network.target, for example, is a unit managed by the system that indicates that the network is ready. It's a good idea to run services that have network capabilities after this target.[7]

The [Service] section contains parameters that are only applicable to services. ExecStart is the actual command to be executed. Notice, as in the crontab file, that full paths must be used. WorkingDirectory sets, obviously, the working directory. This is easier than the cron scenario where we had to change the directory before executing the command. User determines which user the job would run under.

It is the following few parameters that make the use of service extremely compelling: ExecStopPost specifies a command to execute when the service exits, Restart tells systemd to relaunch the service if it exits, and RestartSec determines how long systemd should wait before relaunching it. This allows for a seamless restart in case of a failure while giving the opportunity to take actions such as cleanup, logging the restart, and notifying the people maintaining the system. Notice that although the command is a shell script, we still had to tell systemd that it must use bash to interpret it.

Last, the [Install] section determines how units that are being started at boot should be enabled. Setting WantedBy to multi-user.target tells the operating systemd to start the service when a multi-user system

---

[7]To learn about other targets managed by the system, type man systemd.special in the command line.

is ready. This target loads a bunch of other services, so it is common for services that are manually installed, such as ours, to be loaded at this stage.

Once the unit file is ready and saved in the /etc/systemd/system/ folder – let's say under the name weatherstation.service – we need to tell systemd to rescan the folder. systemctl is the command that controls system, and rescanning is done by using the daemon-reload subcommand

```
sudo systemctl daemon-reload
```

Then we need to tell systemd to include the service in the boot sequence by using the enable subcommand

```
sudo systemctl enable weatherstation
```

The service will start upon reboot. It can also be started, stopped, and restarted manually by using the start, stop, and restart subcommands.

Setup Documentation

Just as the software and hardware of the project are important to document, so is the machine's setup. It's not unlikely that coming back to a machine after a while you will not remember what its IP address is, what the project that it's running is called, under which username it's running, and how it is managed. We've mentioned putting a sticker on machines and keeping a spreadsheet. I also recommend leaving setup documentation on the machine itself.

In addition to the project's username, I have my own user set on all my SBCs. This way, no matter which SBC I pick up (assuming that it's mine, of course), I know I can log into it. There, in my home folder, I can keep a README.txt file with all the information about this machine. In projects where multiple people have access to the machine, I use a fancier trick: the file /etc/motd (motd stands for "message of the day") is a text file containing the message users see when they log in. That's a perfect place to put a message such as the one in Listing 6-7.

Listing 6-7. Content of /etc/motd for a machine running the weather station project. This is presented to users when logging in.

```
Project: Weather Station
This project runs under the username "weatheruser".
The code is in /home/weatheruser/weatherstation/
The project runs as a service managed by systemd.
```

When I feel even more adventurous, I use the /etc/update-motd.d/ folder. It contains executable files whose names start with double-digit numbers. When a user logs in, they are executed in the order of these numbers. This means that dynamic information can be presented to the user. For example, to display the machine's IP address, the script /etc/update-motd.d/20-ipaddress can be created (Listing 6-8).

Listing 6-8. Content of /etc/update-motd.d/20-ipaddress showing the IP address of the machine upon logging in

```
#!/bin/sh
echo "This machine's IP address is $(hostname -I)"
```

The hostname command can show and set the machine's host name. The –I option causes the command to display the IP addresses of the device, excluding the local host address (127.0.0.1). Notice how, again, command substitution is used inside the string that echo is supposed to print.

The files in /etc/update-motd.d/ don't have to be shell scripts – they can be any executable file. Just make sure they have a valid shebang and that they have execution permissions. Adding execution permissions to a file can be achieved with the chmod command. In our example, that would be

```
sudo chmod +x /etc/update-motd.d/20-ipaddress
```

Summary

Setting up the environment in which the project lives plays an important part in the project's stability. For some, including myself, setting up the machine is far from being the favorite part of the working on a project: it can feel mundane and removed from the original, exciting reasons that gave birth to the project in the first place. Remember that tiny script that changed the working directory to the once the script is in? That's the kind of code many makers will find on the Internet, copy and paste it without understanding **why** it works the way it does, and move on to more fun things. I hope that in this chapter we managed to make the machine setup part somewhat more interesting and transparent.

Making sure that the project keeps running after crashes may solve one problem – the project being down – but it actually creates a new problem: not only something went wrong with the project, but unless we actively do something, we may never know what the issue was. In the next chapter, we will explore logging, a key tool that can help us investigate the circumstances that lead to projects failing.

CHAPTER 7

Logging

In previous chapters we put a lot of emphasis on dashboards. Looking at the system in real time as it reacts to commands or internal changes is extremely beneficial, but it's only one way to observe a system. Often, the things that we want to observe either happen when we're not looking or just happen too fast. This is why logging – keeping a record of what the system did or tried to do but failed – is just as important.

In this chapter we'll discuss some key aspects of logging: we'll discuss what can be done with log messages, how to prevent log files from clogging the hard drive, and how to configure the loggers in code, in configuration files, and through the command line. Logging can be as simple or as sophisticated as the programmer wishes, and this chapter (along with the following chapter) does not take the easy route. As with any other chapter in this book, I encourage you to pick and choose from the techniques reviewed here based on your comfort level and project needs. We will explore these concepts by focusing on Python's built-in logging module, but the same concepts appear in the many logging libraries that are available for JavaScript and other languages.

The Good Old `Print`

Printing information to the console is the quickest and simplest way of logging. Using `console.log()` in JavaScript or `print()` in Python requires no additional setup and, in many cases, can help quickly solve crippling bugs.

© Eyal Shahar 2019
E. Shahar, *Project Reliability Engineering*, https://doi.org/10.1007/978-1-4842-5019-8_7

When using console printing to solve a bug, it's really important to remove the console-printing code as soon as the bug is resolved and definitely to clean up all unnecessary console printing before the program is finished and deployed. First, printing to the console is a surprisingly heavy operation in terms of computational power, so leaving unnecessary printing commands can severely slow down the execution of the program. Second, once those prints stay in the code and others get added, clutter is inevitable, and debugging becomes more difficult.

stdout and stderr

For every process that runs under Linux, the operating system holds a table of *file descriptors*. These are non-negative integers that are used to index all files referenced by that process. Of course, every process needs different files, but every process's file descriptor table is automatically populated with these three: file descriptor 0 refers to the standard input stream, called stdin. In a shell session, this stream takes its input from the keyboard; file descriptor 1 refers to the standard output stream, called stdout, which in a shell session has its output printed to the screen. When a Python program executes a print() command, the output doesn't go straight to the screen: it actually goes to stdout, and by default, that leads to the output being presented on the screen. Same goes for console.log() in JavaScript; file descriptor 2 is the standard error stream, called stderr. Like stdout, its output is presented on the screen by default. However, things that end up going through the stderr are different. First, there are errors generated by the operating system. Then there are error messages generated by the interpreter, be it Node.js or Python, in response to errors that occur during execution of the code. Last, there are messages generated by the code itself. In Node.js, console.error() sends its output to stderr. In Python, in order to print to stderr, one must be more explicit:

```
import sys
print("error message", file=sys.stderr)
```

We can generate log files by simply redirecting the output and error streams to files. Redirecting stdout and stderr to files can be done using the shell's redirection operators. It's possible to create a file every time the process started and redirecting the output of stdout to it using the ">" operator:

```
node app.js > out.log
```

However, this will override the file every time this command is executed. If something is causing our program to crash and we set a mechanism to restart the program, we are bound to lose any helpful log messages that the program generated as it approached the crash. A second option is to use the ">>" operator, which opens a new file if one doesn't exist, but appends to an existing file:

```
node app.js >> out.log
```

Both of these are actually shorthand. The second option, for instance, is shorthand for this:

```
node app.js 1>>out.log
```

which means that the output of stdout, or file descriptor 1, is redirected to the file log.out. Consequently, output to stderr will not be written to the file. We can, however, explicitly send the output of stderr to a different file:

```
node app.js >> out.log 2>>err.log
```

This tells the operating system to redirect the standard output of app.js to out.log, and the output of its file descriptor 2 to err.log. Alternatively, if we just prefer using the same file for both streams, we can redirect the output of stderr to stdout:

```
node app.js >> out.log 2>&1
```

The ampersand (&) is there to make sure that the "1" is not interpreted as a file name, but rather as the file descriptor for stdout.

If we chose to launch the program with a line in crontab or a shell script, we can use redirection there. In crontab, for example, we can write this line:

```
@reboot /usr/bin/python3 ~/project/main.py >> /tmp/out.log 2>&1
```

In the previous chapter, we mentioned two libraries, forever.js and pm2, that can be used to launch projects and restart them when they crash. When forever.js is used to launch a program, instead of printing output to the console, forever.js writes printed messages to files. By default, every time the program restarts, a new file with a random name is opened in the folder ~/.forever, and all messages are written to it. It's possible, instead, to specify the name and path of three log files to which messages are written, using command-line options. The -l option specifies the files to which messages produced by forever.js itself, while the -o and -e options specify the files for the stdout and stderr, respectively. For example, the command

```
forever app.js -l /tmp/out.log -o /tmp/out.log -e /tmp/err.log
```

will cause forever.js log messages to be written out.log, output messages to out.log as well, and error messages to err.log, all in the /tmp/ folder.

pm2 operates in a similar way, however the default behavior is slightly different: for every process, two files are used under ~/.pm2/logs/, one being the standard output log file and the other the error log file. They are named as the name of the process, with –out and –err suffixes and have a .log extension. For example, for a program called app.py, we can expect to find the ~/.pm2/logs/app-out.log log files. To use a different set of files, it is possible, just as in forever.js, to use the -o and -e command-line options.

Where Do Logs Go?

Log files can be written anywhere on the hard drive that makes sense to the programmer. However, there are a few places that make more sense than others.

One popular choice is just to create a `logs` directory inside the project's folder. This keeps the log files close to the project itself and out of the way of system files. It's good to remember, in that case, to make the proper accommodations for this folder and not to treat it as part of the code. For example, if the code is under Git version control, the line

```
logs/
```

should probably be added to the `.gitignore` file to prevent from committing the log files to the repository[1].

A second option is to write log files to the `/tmp/` folder. This folder gets deleted every time the machine reboots, so machines that are supposed to be rebooted daily can benefit from such a setup: instead of putting mechanisms in place to clean up the logs, they get deleted on every reboot. However, if a machine shuts down or reboots unpredictably, the logs are deleted and will not be able to provide insights into what went wrong. This method is generally not recommended and should be used only when the circumstances are right.

Last, there's the `/var/log/` folder. The purpose of the `/var/` folder itself is to hold variable files – files which are created, modified, and deleted as programs across the system do their business. `/var/log/` is specifically designated for log files, but usually the writing permissions for that folder are restricted to the system. Of course, permissions can be changed, but usually it is advised not to add write permissions to folders where only the system has them. What can be done, however, is to open a project-specific log folder under `/var/log/` and give **that** folder adequate permissions: the owner and group could be the project's user. The owner, group, and others should all have reading permissions as well as execution (which for folders just means the ability to open the folder). Only the owner, and perhaps the group (it doesn't really matter in this case), should have writing permissions for this folder.

---

[1]We'll talk more about Git and the .gitignore files in Chapter 9.

Understanding Log Levels

Many programs and logging libraries support the concept of *log levels*. When log levels are implemented, every log message is assigned a *severity level*. Lower severity levels are usually used for debugging and record keeping, imply normal program operation, require no immediate human intervention, and tend to occur more frequently. On the other hand, when log messages with higher levels of severity are produced, that means something is very wrong. These messages require a response – perhaps a bug fixed or even the machine rebooted. The higher the severity, the less we expect to see these messages in our logs.

This system has two compelling features. First, it eliminates the clutter that comes with detailed logging: we can set, at the program level, what is the minimal level that we wish to record in our logs without changing the code. Once the log files are there, we can get over the clutter by filtering for the messages of the severity level that we care about. We can even direct different levels of severity to different files.

The second compelling feature of this system is the possibility to automate the type of action the system takes based on the severity level: for lower levels, perhaps nothing should be done. For higher levels, maybe somebody should be notified via email. For the highest levels, perhaps the sprinklers should be turned on...

There is no one standard system for the naming and ordering of severity levels. Some systems may have as few as two levels, some may have ten different ones. Having said that, most systems use similar terms. In the next section, we will discuss Python's logging library, which has a very typical naming system, as described in Table 7-1.

Table 7-1. *Log levels in Python's logging module*

Level	Uses and Implications	Value
DEBUG	Verbose information that is useful for debugging the program. This can be anything from a variable's value to announcing the invocation of a function	10
INFO	Important information about the normal operation of the program. Some examples are initialization of components, connection to services or clients, and task completion	20
WARNING	An event has occurred that could potentially lead to an error or indicate that something is wrong. For example, a missing configuration file or a bad reading from a sensor	30
ERROR	An error has occurred. The program may continue running, but functionality may be limited or not as expected. Inability to connect or loss of connection to are some examples	40
CRITICAL	A serious error has occurred which forces the program to shut down. Human intervention is required immediately	50

Assigning numerical values to the different levels makes it possible to programmatically put various thresholds, for example, to what actually gets logged. This specific threshold is usually called the *logging level*. Different logging levels are adequate for different scenarios. A WARNING logging level is usually desired for normal program operation, while a DEBUG logging level is more useful during development and, as the name suggests, debugging.

We can split these levels into two groups: on the lower end of severity, DEBUG and INFO messages imply normal program operation. If the logger is using the standard streams for its output, these messages get directed to STDOUT. On the higher end of severity, WARNING, ERROR, and CRITICAL messages imply that something is wrong and needs attention. Usually, loggers direct these messages to STDERR.

DEBUG and INFO Messages

The lifespan of lines of code issuing a DEBUG message, as a general rule, should be kept to minimum. They should be written in order to help diagnose a bug and removed once the problem is solved. Because of their usage, DEBUG logs tend to pile up otherwise, often to a point where the log files become unintelligible. A second reason to keep these lines temporary is due to the program's efficiency: writing to the console or to the screen takes time and computational power, and even if the logging level is above the DEBUG level, there is some computational power that goes into comparing the level of the message to that logging level to decide whether the message should be recorded on file or not.

On the other hand, lines that use the INFO level for logging are expected to be a part of the finished code. They are usually used for logging normal, yet important events that happened during the execution of the program, such as steps in an initialization sequence, or connections made to online servers.

WARNING, ERROR, and CRITICAL Messages

WARNING messages don't necessarily imply that the program is broken. You may have seen warnings generated by an interpreter or a library when using a deprecated feature: everything is still working, but these WARNING messages should be addressed at some point.

The distinction between ERROR messages and CRITICAL[2] is also subject to interpretation, and this is the place to reiterate: it is up to the programmer to decide how to rank each log message. Some programmers and organizations assert that a CRITICAL message should imply that an error has occurred of which the system cannot recover on its own. Others couple the severity with the urgency of the action that should be taken.

---

[2]Some naming systems use FATAL instead of CRITICAL.

In the weird space of maker projects, severity of events may not align with what is common in the more traditional software industry. A server going down due to a power outage, for example, is something big software companies never really have to deal with: their servers are often "in the cloud," meaning that there are many servers in multiple locations, always ready to cover for any servers that are unable to fulfill their tasks. If a company's service is rendered completely unavailable, that is definitely a situation that falls under the CRITICAL category.

But in the context of maker projects, the situation may be different: is a power outage of a maker project really a critical situation? If an exhibit in a museum freezes, should the programmer immediately come back from a vacation? At the Exploratorium, for example, if an exhibit needs to be power cycled a couple of times a week, we consider that good enough.

Logging Libraries
Python's logging

Python comes with its own logging module, called, conveniently, *logging*. Once the logging module is imported, its most basic logging functions can be called, and their output will be printed to the console through stderr (see Listing 7-1).

Listing 7-1. Logging to the screen with basic usage of the logging module

```
import logging

logging.debug('Debug message')
logging.info('Info message')
logging.warning('Warning message')
logging.error('Error message')
logging.critical('Critical message')
```

The different methods shown in Listing 7-1 are all equivariant to
logging.log(level, msg), with the level argument being one of the
constants logging.DEBUG, logging.INFO, logging.WARNING, logging.
ERROR, and logging.CRITICAL. These constants have the numerical
values described in Table 7-1. The msg argument is the message that
needs to be logged.

By default, the logging level for the logging module is WARNING. This
means that DEBUG and INFO messages will not yield output. Therefore, for
the program in Listing 7-1, we can expect the following output (Listing 7-2).

Listing 7-2. Output for Listing 7-1

```
WARNING:root:Warning message
ERROR:root:Info message
CRITICAL:root:Critical message
```

This is the default behavior of the library's default logger. The output
format includes the level of the message, the logger's name which is root,
and the message itself. Also, as mentioned earlier, the default destination
of the log messages is stderr. However, we can change this behavior. We
can also have more loggers.

Logger Configuration

To change the behavior of the default logger, we can use the logging.
basicConfig() function, with any of the optional keyword arguments
shown in Table 7-2.[3]

---

[3]As with any other library this book explores, the list of arguments presented here
only covers some of the options. For more advanced features and options we have
not covered, the reader is advised to consult the library's online documentation:
https://docs.python.org/3/library/logging.html

Table 7-2. *Partial list of optional keyword arguments for the* `basicConfig()` *method*

Argument	Description
filename	The name of the file to which log messages are written. If not specified, messages are sent to `stderr`
filemode	Mode of opening the file. 'w' for write, 'a' for append (default)
format	String format to be used (see Table 7-3)
style	Style of formatting, if format is specified: '%': `printf`-style formatting (default) '{': `str.format()` style formatting '$': `string.Template` style formatting
datefmt	If date/time is included, use this format (see Table 7-4)
level	Sets the logger level

The `format` argument lets you programmatically embed data in the log message. As we saw earlier, the default format includes the logger's name (`root`) and the message's severity. Table 7-3 lists some of the more useful fields that can be used.

Table 7-3. *Partial list of log message attributes that can be used for message formatting*

Attribute	Type	Description
asctime	String	Time when the message was generated, in human-readable format
filename	String	Name of the file that generated the message
funcName	String	Name of the function that generated the message
levelName	String	Message severity, in text
message	String	The message to be logged

(*continued*)

Table 7-3. (*continued*)

Attribute	Type	Description
lineno	Number	Number of the line that generated the message in the source code
module	String	The name of the module that generated the message
name	String	The name of the logger that was used to generate the message
msecs	Number	Millisecond portion of the timestamp for the generated message

The default formatting style for log messages is the printf style. In this style, attributes which are strings, for instance, asctime, are denoted like this: %(asctime)s, where the s stands for "string." Attributes that are numbers are denoted like so: %(lineno)d. The newer str.format() is a little cleaner and more consistent with the way we have been treating strings so far. In this style, all that needs to be done is to surround the attribute with curly brackets, like so: {asctime}. To use this format, make sure to set the style keyword argument to '{' when using logging. basicConfig().

Based on the complexity of the project and what it is that you are trying to achieve with logging, you may want different attributes included in the log. I find that including the time is extremely useful. First, when debugging a project, I often run it again and again with minor modifications. In these cases, the logging output is often repetitive, and seeing the timestamp is useful to know that the program indeed executed, and the output really hasn't changed.

Including the severity level's name can help filter or search the log for specific levels. The most useful use case for this is finding the first occurrence of an ERROR or a CRITICAL message and tracing the log back from that point in an attempt to track down the chain of events that led to that message.

Including the file name (or module name) along with the function name and line number can prove to be very efficient when debugging and when the log gets cluttered. With these attributes included in the log, finding the piece of source code that generated a log file line becomes a significantly faster task.

This is a good point to pause for a quick example that demonstrates a pretty detailed log format as well as the use of logging.basicConfig() (Listing 7-3).

Listing 7-3. Logging format and logging.basicConfig() example

```
import logging

FORMAT = '[{asctime}] {levelname}: {message} \
  ({filename}:{funcName}:{lineno})'

logging.basicConfig(
  filename='app.log',
  filemode='w',
  level=logging.INFO,
  style='{',
  format=FORMAT)

def test_logging():
  logging.info('Info message')

test_logging()
```

After running this program, the contents of the file app.log should look something like this:

```
[2019-03-17 22:51:00,432] INFO: Info message (formatting.
py:test_logging:14)
```

Notice that in this example, we surround the time with square brackets and the location of the logging code (file, function, and code line number) in parenthesis: in my personal experience, using these symbols contributes to the log's readability.

The format of the date and time can be changed by setting the `datefmt` argument when using `logging.basicConfig()`. Formatting is done in the same way as when using the function `time.strftime()`: providing a string that includes *directives*. These are then replaced by the data based on the current time. A list of the available directives is given in Table 7-4.

Table 7-4. *Selected directives for formatting date/time with* `datefmt`

Directive	Description
%Y	Year with century as a decimal number (e.g., 2019)
%m	Month as a decimal number, between 01 and 12
%d	Day of the month, between 01 and 31
%H	Hour, between 00 and 23
%M	Minute, between 00 and 59
%S	Second, between 00 and 61[4]

There are quite a few directives that we did not include in Table 7-4, and this is because they are useless to us. We want to avoid any text representations, such as names of months and weekdays, since we want to make it easy for both us and a machine to be able to quickly compare, navigate, and sort the timestamps. This is also why we move left to right, from largest scale fields to the smallest: the year field is first, and the seconds is last. We use only directives that maintain a constant number of

---

[4]Yes, 61. Every few years a leap second is introduced to synchronize the clock to the Earth's rotation. However, this explains only the value of 60. The 61 value is supported for historical reasons.

characters. As a result, comparing to timestamps as strings is the same as comparing their actual date and time values. Again, this doesn't mean that we actually need to sort the log files – but this does make the log file easier to search and navigate, both manually and programmatically.

You may notice that there is no directive for higher time resolution, namely, microseconds. There is, however, the msecs attribute we can use in the format string. To manually reconstruct the output by using the default date and time formatting, we can revise the code with the lines in Listing 7-4.

Listing 7-4. Manually formatting the log message's timestamp

```
FORMAT = '[{asctime},{msecs:0>3.0f}] {levelname}: \
    {message} ({filename}:{funcName}:{lineno})'

DATEFMT = '%Y-%m-%d %H:%M:%S'

logging.basicConfig(
    filename='app.log',
    filemode='w',
    level=logging.INFO,
    style='{',
    format=FORMAT,
    datefmt=DATEFMT)
```

msecs return the millisecond portion of the timestamp with precision of 13 decimal places. We're probably good with just the integer part of that value. We also want to make sure that this value produces exactly three characters and is zero-padded if needed. For example, if msecs returns 13.3039583485845, what we actually want to see is 013. This is what the {msecs:0>3.0f} means. It reads, from left to right, that msecs should be zero-padded, be aligned to the right, and have three digits for the integer part and no decimal places.

197

Adding Loggers

As mentioned, we can add more Logger objects. These have the advantage of forming a hierarchy between log messages based on their origins and also provide different ways for handing messages.

A new Logger object can be created either by calling logging.getLogger() for a top-level logger or by getting a child object of an existing logger using the .getChild() method. Both of these functions are called with the desired logger name as an argument. For example:

```
app_logger = logging.getLogger('app')
```

In our weather station project, we might want a child logger to handle specifically with the operation of the fans:

```
fans_logger = app_logger.getChild('fans')
```

The name of a child logger gets its parent's name as a prefix, separated by a dot. In the preceding example, the fans' logger will be called app.fans. The nice thing about the Python logger library is that if you call getLogger() with the same logger name from multiple modules, you get the same logger object. So, for instance, if we had our fans controlled by a different module and would still like their logger to be a child of the app logger, all we'd have to do is

```
fans_logger =
  logging.getLogger('app').getChild('fans')
```

We never instantiate a logger ourselves – we always tell the library to get the logger object for us. If it exists, the library will return the correct object. If it doesn't, the library will first instantiate it for us. In computer science, this is known as the *singleton design pattern*.[5] By doing this, the library

---

[5]Design patterns are common techniques, or recipes, that are used to solve common programming problems. This is a classic book on the topic:Gamma, Erich, Richard Helm, Ralph E. Johnson, and John Vlissides. *Design Patterns: Elements of Reusable Object-oriented Software*. New Delhi: Pearson Education, 2015.

makes sure there's no more than one logger with the same name, that many modules can use the same logger, and that using the logger is thread-safe.

Just like the default logger, Logger objects also have the .debug(), .info(), .warning(), .error(), and .critical() methods, as well as the .log() method.

Logger objects don't have one method that sets everything up like the default logger's basicConfig(), and everything needs to be meticulosity configured. To set the logging level of the logger, the .setLevel() method should be used. By default, child loggers propagate the messages they log to their parent, who logs them as well. To prevent this behavior, the Logger object's .propagate property can be set to False. If this is done, however, the log messages don't actually go anywhere. To determine the way a Logger object handles its messages, we need to add to it some *handlers*, which deserve their own section.

Using Handlers

We've discussed logging to a stream and logging to a file. For a Logger object, the destination of the log messages is determined with *handlers*: StreamHandler objects send messages to streams such as stdout and stderr, while FileHandler objects send messages to a file. There are many more types of handlers that send the messages over email, as an HTTP request, over a TCP socket, and more. We will discuss a few of these more exotic handlers later, but for the purpose of demonstrating the basic concept of handlers, we'll stick with a simple FileHandler object. Consider the example in Listing 7-5.

Listing 7-5. Adding a handler to a Logger object

```
formatter = logging.Formatter(
  fmt='[{asctime}] {levelname}: {message}',
  style='{'
  )
```

```
handler = logging.FileHandler('fans.log')
handler.setFormatter(formatter)
logger = logging.getLogger('app').getChild('fans')
logger.addHandler(handler)
```

First, we instantiate a Formatter object. We need one if we want to change the default formatting, and we probably do: for a Handler object, the default formatting is just the message itself. As you can see, the Formatter object takes the format as the fmt argument, which is the same as the format argument for logging.basicConfig(). It also takes the formatting style and date format with the style and datefmt arguments, just as logging. basicConfig() (datefmt is not used in Listing 7-5). Once the formatter is ready, we can create a FileHandler object, set its formatter to the formatter we created, then create a logger, and add the handler we just created.

Note   As an aside, note how we created the logger as a child of another logger: if this code was in a module that we import to the main program and the app logger was an object defined in the main program, this module would not have had direct access to the app logger object. However, since we let the logging module manage our Logger objects, and these are singletons, logging. getLogger('app') returns the correct object.

Usually, when we see an object's methods that start with the word "set" and take another object as an argument, it means that the first object holds only one object that fills the function of the argument object. Instead of reading this sentence again, just consider this: a Handler object can have (and only needs) one formatter, and the method .setFormatter() is a hint to that. Conversely, methods that start with the word "add" imply that the object can have many objects that fill that function. The name of the method .addHandler() implies that a logger can have many handlers, each writing the messages to a different place and having a different logging level. This can be useful for many applications, specifically for setting up some sort of an alerting mechanism – but more on that in the next chapter.

Logging in JavaScript
The Console Object

We have mentioned briefly using console.log() and console.error() as the JavaScript equivalent to Python Print(). However, the Console object is quite complex and is packed with interesting features. In addition to .log() and .error(), there are also .debug() and .info() that write to stdout, and .warn() that, along with .error(), write to stderr. Just using this set of methods, along with stream redirection, can be considered a decent logging system.

Some other cool methods of console include .assert(), which takes a condition as a first argument and outputs the second argument, preceded by the text "Assertion failed," as an error if the condition fails. So, the line

```
console.assert(a==1, "a is not 1")
```

is equivalent to

```
if (!(a==1)) {
  console.error("Assertion failed: a is not 1");
}
```

You can set named counters. Calling console.count("hits") will create a counter named "hits" if one does not yet exist and set to 1. If it does exist, it will increment the counter by 1. Then, it will write the result to stdout. Executing console.countReset("hits") will reset the counter to zero.

Console even has timers. console.time("lap") will reset a timer called "lap", and console.timeEnd("lap") will write to stdout the time that has elapsed.

Testing for conditions, counting events, and timing the execution of a block of code are often things programmers log, so it's nice that console has these features built in. console has some other cool features, but we will not touch on them as they are directed more toward debugging programs that run in the browser.

Winston

Of the many JavaScript logging libraries, Winston[6] is probably the most prevalent and comprehensive one at the time of writing this book. It is packed with features and is extremely customizable. Since we went through many general principles of logging in the previous sections, I just want to show the general gist of what working with Winston looks like. Examine the code in Listing 7-6.

Listing 7-6. Example of using Winston logging library for JavaScript

```javascript
const winston = require('winston');

const logger = winston.createLogger({
  format:  winston.format.combine(
    winston.format.timestamp(),
    winston.format.printf((info) => {
      return `[${info.timestamp}]` +
        `${info.level.toUpperCase()}:` +
        `${info.message}`;
    })
  ),
  transports: [
    new winston.transports.File(
      {filename: 'error.log', level: 'error'}
```

---

[6]https://github.com/winstonjs/winston

202

```
  ),
  new winston.transports.Console({level: 'info'})
 ]
});

logger.info("This is an info message");
logger.warn("This is a warning");
logger.error("This is an error message");
```

Among the parameters that a logger can be initialized with are format and transports. Transports are Winston's equivalent to Python logger handlers: they describe a destination for the log messages. In the preceding example, we included two transports: one that writes messages to a file and one that prints them to the screen. Notice that each transport has its own logging level, just like with the Python logging module. However, in Winston, all transports that belong to a logger use the same formatter.

When the logger formats the message, it passes an info object to a *formatter,* and in the preceding example, we use a combination of two formatters: timestamp and printf. An info object has at least two fields, level and message; both are fairly self-explanatory. Some formatters access these fields to create a final message. Other formatters can actually change the info object. Also, as we see here, formatters can work together on a message to create one big formatter using winston. format.combine(). In the preceding example, we combine the timestamp formatter that adds the timestamp to the info object with the printf formatter. The printf formatter passes the info object to a function that can manipulate that object as it wishes. We've created a pretty generic format here, with the timestamp (which was added by the timestamp formatter) in brackets, and we also converted the level to uppercase.

Winston's core transports and the ones contributed by the community span HTTP requests, MongoDB, email, and rotating log files (more on that later in this chapter), and the list goes on and on. You can even use

Winston for things such as profiling[7] and exception handling and write your own transports and formatters. It's a powerful beast, but there are some simpler ones out there, such as debug[8] and log4js.[9] We are not going to dive deeper into these libraries or Winston's more advanced features – all we needed is to get a feel of what logging in JavaScript looks like.

Roll Your Own

As with many other features your software requires, you might find that writing your own logging library might be a better solution than using an off-the-shelf one. At this point, you should know what the common features of a logger are. For simple projects, logging can be as simple as redirecting the output of print commands to files, as we've seen earlier in the chapter, or slightly more involved, like writing directly to a file. In a more complicated setup, you'd create a logger class of which you'd need to get an instance. This is where things can get more delicate, especially when different modules and thread want access to the same logger. As we mentioned before, logging libraries take care of this by making sure that a logger object is a singleton, so if two calls are made to instantiate the same logger, only one object is actually created, and both calls return a reference to that same object. If you do make your own logging library, this will probably be the trickiest pitfall.

Log Rotation

All these messages being logged can pose a serious danger of the hard drive to becoming clogged.[10] This can be a problem in any type of

---

[7]*Profiling* refers to dynamic analysis of a program. During profiling, measurements are taken for the amount of time that the program spends in various functions, how often functions are called, how much memory is used, and so on.

[8]https://github.com/visionmedia/debug

[9]https://log4js-node.github.io/log4js-node/

[10]Unfortunately, the word "clog" is **not** an abbreviation of "congesting log."

machine, but it definitely poses a more immediate threat to SBCs, where hard drive space is significantly scarcer.

The most common technique for keeping the log files under a manageable size is *log rotation*. In this method, a log file's lifespan can be viewed as having three stages: first, the file serves as the active log file to which log messages are being written. Next, after a certain amount of time or after the file reaches a pre-determined size, a rotation happens: the file gets renamed – usually it gets a .1 postfix – and is put away for archiving, while a new file is created in its place and becomes the active log file. The file that previously had the .1 postfix also gets renamed, and its postfix gets changed to .2, and so forth. Only a limited number of archived log files are kept on the hard drive, and if that number is reached, the last file in the rotation moves to its last phase, which is to be deleted from the hard drive.

Linux's logrotate

For its own system logs, Linux uses a program called logrotate to handle log rotation. logrotate looks at the /etc/logrotate.conf file and the files under /etc/logrotate.d/ to determine what files should be rotated and how.

A logrotate configuration file consists of several blocks. Each block starts with a list of files that share the same rotation configuration. Next is a list of directives which determine how these files are rotated. For example, Listing 7-7 could be the block that handles two log files for the weather station example.

Listing 7-7. Example of a logrotate configuration block

```
/home/weatheruser/weatherapp/fans.log
/home/weatheruser/weatherapp/app.log {
  daily
  rotate 7
```

```
compress
create 644 weatheruser weatheruser
}
```

The first directive we see is `daily` that tells `logrotate` that the rotation should happen, well, daily. Other options are `weekly` and `monthly`. The option `hourly` is also available, but by default, `logrotate` is activated once a day by `cron.daily`, so it would run once a day anyway. To run `logrotate` hourly, one needs to use the hourly directive and move `logrotate` from `cron.daily` to `cron.hourly`.

The next directive we see is `rotate`. This directive determines how many rotations a file goes through before it is deleted from the hard drive. Alternatively, logs can rotate only once they reach a certain size using the `size` directive, for example, `size 50k`.

The `compress` directive tells `logrotate` to compress the log file on its first rotation using `gzip`. Other directives add features to the compression of logs, such as `compresscmd`, with which it's possible to specify a different program for the compression.

The `create` directive is slightly more involved. It states how the new log files are created: under which user, group, and permissions. Obviously, the program writing the log file must have writing permissions for the file. In our example, we enabled that by having log files created with `weatheruser` as the owner and the `weatheruser` group as the file group. As for permissions, we let anybody read the file, but only `weatheruser` can write to it.

File Watching

Let's say that the project's program is running, a log file is open, and the program is writing log messages into it, and at some moment it is time for `logrotate` to do its thing. `logrotate` will rename the active log file and create a new one in its place, but the project will not write to the new log file – rather, it will still write to the old file, even though it was renamed. This is because once a program opens a file, the handle it keeps for it has no longer anything to do with its name, but rather, it holds the file descriptor, and that doesn't change when a file is renamed.

The solution to this is to keep an eye on the log file, and before writing to it, make sure that its name has not changed. If it has, the file should be closed and the new one should be opened for writing. The Python logging module has this feature built in: instead of using a regular `FileHandler`, we can simply use a `WatchedFileHandler`.

Note   The three basic handlers, `StreamHandler`, `FileHandler`, and `NullHandler` (that does nothing), are located in `logging`. All other handlers are in `logging.handlers`.

In-Program Log Rotation

It's possible to perform log rotation from within the program, instead of relying on `logrotate`. Some libraries provide that feature, and again, we turn to Python's logging module for an example.

Python's logging module has two handlers that can be used instead of the basic `FileHandler` in order to enable log rotation: `RotatingFileHandler` rotates the log once it reaches a certain size, and `TimedRotatingFileHandler` rotates the log after a certain amount of time. Their initializer functions take as arguments the desired file name and several optional keyword arguments. Table 7-5 describes a few of those arguments.

Table 7-5. *Keyword arguments for* `RotatingFileHandler` *and* `TimedRotatingFileHandler`'s *initialization*

Argument	Description
`backupCount`	Number of backups saved
For RotatingFileHandler:	
`maxBytes`	Maximum file size, in bytes
For TimedRotatingFileHandler:	
`when`	Units for rotation intervals: `'S'`: Seconds `'M'`: Minutes `'H'`: Hours `'D'`: Days `'W0'`-`'W6'`: Weekday (0 is Monday) `'midnight'`: At midnight
`interval`	Number of units between rotations

For example, a handler that rotates the log file once it reaches 1kb and keeps seven log files in the rotation can be initialized this way:

```
handler = logging.handlers.RotatingFileHandler(
  'out.log', backupCount=7, maxBytes=1024)
```

And a handler that rotates the logs once a day at midnight can be initialized like this:

```
handler = logging.handlers.TimedRotatingFileHandler(
  'out.log', backupCount=7, when='midnight')
```

Logging Configuration

In Chapter 5 we discussed the importance of keeping the configuration of a project out of the code, and the logging configuration – the logging level, location of the log files, and whether the messages appear on the screen – is no exception. I highly recommend adding a logging section in the configuration file that specifies the logging level and the path of the log files.

Many Linux programs can run in "verbose" mode, often by applying the -v command-line option. This usually does two things: it forces debug messages to stdout, and it overrides the logging level to be the lowest available. In some programs, this would be the default behavior if no argument is provided to the -v option, but an optional argument can set the logging level. See how this can be implemented in Listing 7-8.

Listing 7-8. Overriding debug configuration with a command-line argument

```python
import argparse
import logging
import sys
import yaml

parser = argparse.ArgumentParser()
parser.add_argument(
    '-v', dest='verbose', nargs='?', const='DEBUG')

args = parser.parse_args()

with open("config.yaml", 'r') as stream:
    config = yaml.load(stream, Loader=yaml.Loader)

logger = logging.getLogger('app')
file_handler = logging.handlers.WatchedFileHandler(
    config['logging']['file'])
logger.addHandler(file_handler)

if args.verbose:
    config['logging']['level'] = args.verbose
    verbose_handler = logging.StreamHandler(sys.stdout)
    logger.addHandler(verbose_handler)

logger.setLevel(config['logging']['level'])
```

There are a few things worth unpacking here: first, let's see how `argparse` parses the -v option. If the -v option is not used, then the option's destination variable, `args.verbose`, will be None. This will effectively leave the logging level as specified by the configuration file. If the -v option is used, the destination variable will have a valid value, but what is it? `nargs` is '?', which means that there might be an additional argument. If there is one, that will be used as the value. If not, the value will be as specified by the `const` argument, which is DEBUG.

The way we designed it in this example is that if the -v option is used, regardless of the specified logging level, we add another handler that outputs the messages to the console. Both handlers, the file handler and the new stream handler, use the same logging level – the one specified in the command-line argument. Therefore, if the -v option is used, we override the `config` structure with this logging level setting and set the logging level of the logger, but not the handlers. Since the levels of the handlers have not been set, they will both use the level of the logger. Remember that these are all design decisions that are pretty arbitrary, and they are just as good as any other setup.

What to Log

We've been talking all this time about **how** to log, but not really about **what** to log. For the most part, you probably know best what log messages matter to you. However, here are a few guidelines I believe are worth highlighting.

Exceptions

Many Python functions throw exceptions if they fail, for instance, opening a file that does not exist. The advantage of exceptions is that if caught, the program doesn't have to crash, but turn to alternative code that can mitigate the problem. Regardless of how we deal with the exception, it's usually a good idea to log that it happened (see Listing 7-9).

Listing 7-9. Logging Python exceptions

```python
try:
  with open('data.json') as data_file:
    data_file = data_file.read()
except:
  logger.error('data.json not found')
  # mitigate exception
```

Callback with Error Arguments

There are a couple of mechanisms in JavaScript that operate in a similar way: callbacks with error arguments and promises rejection. Recall Listing 1-15, where we implemented temperature reading from a Si7021 sensor. The method for reading a byte from the I2C bus had a callback with an error argument. When the error argument wasn't null, we had that reflected by the value of the measurement, but this is something we'd also want to log (Listing 7-10).

Listing 7-10. Logging a JavaScript callback with an error

```javascript
//...
this.i2cBus.i2cRead(0x40, 3, new Buffer(2),
                    (err, bytesRead, data) => {
  if(err) {
    logger.error(
      'Could not read data from Si7021: ' +
      JSON.stringify(err);
    );
    this.lastRead = -999;
    return;
  }
//...
```

Initialization Sequences

Many programs start with some sort of an initialization sequence, which is often failure-prone, since most of the program's dependencies are accessed there. Reading configuration files, importing libraries, initializing hardware, and establishing network connections are some examples of processes that happen during startup and have the potential to fail. It can be beneficial to log before attempting each of these phases, perhaps at the INFO level, a message such as "Initializing temperature sensor." If the program fails during the initialization process, it's extremely helpful to know which phase the culprit is.

Entering and Leaving Functions

It's a very common debugging practice to add log messages when entering and leaving a function, mostly to make sure that the function is not responsible for crashing or hanging or to observe the sequence in which functions are being called. This, however, can contribute to messy code and clogged logs. It's very tempting to add a log message saying "here!" just to make sure that the function is being called. Before you know it, however, there are ten more types of log messages conveying similarly obscure messages such as "made it!" or "function called." Here are some guidelines that I find useful:

- Be specific. Logs like "entering function" are not helpful. Make sure the logging command can be easily found when it's time for it to be removed.

- If the logging library offers an option to include the file name, line number, and function name, make use of it.

- Assign a DEBUG level to these log messages.

- Remove these logging lines as soon as it has been confirmed that the function is running correctly.

Parameters

Sometimes it's helpful to see that a parameter was initialized correctly, or to make sure that its value was not inadvertently changed by another part of the code. Once again, when logging parameter values, it's important to state what part of the code or what was the event that triggered the logging message ("Joystick activated, left motor now at 37%") and it's a good idea to keep the message at the DEBUG level.

Data

Continuous data is also useful to log – a robot's motor control and proximity measures, our weather station's sensor readings and fan's settings – these can shed light on the project's behavior and possible malfunctions. However, such data streams are usually better logged in dedicated numerical data files, for instance, CSV (comma-separated values) files, and not in a regular, text-based log file. CSV files can be read by any spreadsheet software or data visualization software and can be easily parsed by an automatic monitoring script to detect any trends or anomalies, as we will discuss in the next chapter.

Reading Log Files

We spent the entire chapter talking about how to write log files, but we should say a few words about reading them before we conclude. Log files are often very long – too long to be read by a code editor. There are two tools that I recommend using that are built into the Linux system and that for most cases are quite sufficient.

grep is a command for searching strings in files. The command

```
grep critical out.log
```

will cause all lines in the file out.log that contain the word "critical" to the screen.

The command less is an interactive tool for viewing files, as it allows for navigation within the document. Searching is done by hitting slash (/) and entering the search string. Hitting n will move forward to the next match, and N will take you back to the previous match. You can also apply a filter to view only lines that contain a certain string by hitting the ampersand sign (&) and the desired string.

Summary

In this chapter we covered some of fundamental principles and methodologies concerning logging: logging levels, a system to quantify the severity of log messages; output streams and how to redirect them to log files; handlers and formatters and how to use them under the Python logging library; log rotation, a common technique to keep log files' sizes under control; and logging configuration through a configuration file or a command-line argument; and we discussed how to make use of logging inside the program.

Some bugs are easy to find. Mismatched indentation in a Python file, a misspelled variable –these will crash the program exactly at the line where they appear. Other bugs are sneaky. They are lines of code that act as if everything is fine, but in fact create a problem for another piece of code somewhere else in the project; they are memory leaks, those incessant allocations of memory without releasing it; they are variables used to index an array that gets trampled somehow with a negative value – the list goes on and on. These sneaky bugs will start a chain of events that will crash your code in places you least expect them.

If I may be poetic about this, I'd say that these bugs have a story to tell, and in order to remove such a bug, its story must be first heard. Log files are the programmer's way of letting these bugs tell their story. It's like the movie *The Ring* (spoiler alert ahead), with the bugs being the creepy dead girl and log files acting as the video tapes.

This is why good logging practices are important. Healthy log files allow us to go back to the point where the program misbehaved and walk back from there until we find the event that set the unwanted chain of events in motion. But that's not all that logging is good for. When logging is done right, it's not only readable by humans, it's also readable by the machine itself. In the next chapter, we'll look at alerting, the various ways in which a system can let its operators know it needs attention. These occasions can happen not only when something critical, such as a crash, takes place but also when the system recognized concerning trends by monitoring its own logs.

CHAPTER 8

Advanced Logging, Monitoring, and Alerting

We've made dashboards we can use to observe the machine's behavior in real time, and we created logs that we can review retroactively and trace the origin of issues, if they arise. However, both of these tools require us to be proactive in order to know whether the machine needs our attention. Eventually, we don't want to babysit the project and wait for it to fail – instead, we want the machine itself to let us know that our attention is needed. *Alerting* is what happens when the machine lets you know it needs your intervention. For big companies, that's a huge topic, that covers questions such as what infrastructure should be built to decide when to send out alerts, what is the medium through which the alerts are sent, who to alert, what conditions should trigger an alert, and more. We'll start by talking more about how these companies approach some of these questions and then, as we've done so far, try to distill some of these ideas and bring them into the world of maker projects.

© Eyal Shahar 2019
E. Shahar, *Project Reliability Engineering*, https://doi.org/10.1007/978-1-4842-5019-8_8

How Big Tech Companies Do It

Before I move on to talk about how the big tech companies deal with monitoring, I should establish what exactly I mean by "big tech companies": I obviously don't mean all big tech companies. I am talking about companies that give real-time, around-the-clock services to a very large number of customers. These services don't run on one machine, but rather they run on many machines, deployed on multiple "server farms," and these machines may be maintained by the company itself or some third-party service provider (such as Amazon's AWS, Microsoft's Azure, or Google Cloud). Think of Google, Facebook, Twitter, Uber, and Etsy. They can't afford their service ever being down. When it is, you read about it in the news.

To understand how these big tech services deal with alerts, we need to talk about how they deal with logging and monitoring, and that starts with a company's state of mind. Because big services have many machines and program redundancy, they have to think in a way that is *scalable* – this means that the amount of human work put into the reliability of their service does not increase linearly as they serve more people or deploy more machines. For this reason, everything that can be automated is done by bots. Scalability also means that anecdotal failures don't really matter as long as machines and programs can recover automatically from failure. When such a failure does happen, this is an incident that should be documented in the log files, but no immediate human intervention needs to happen. However, if a process keeps restarting, a condition called *flapping*, then that's something the engineers want to know about.

So how this is done? For these services, the act of logging rarely means that code issuing the log message also writes the message to a hard drive. Rather, a logging service runs on its own machine, and the various processes send log messages to it. Then, other services do the monitoring – periodically reading the logs, extracting metrics, identifying trends, and, if necessary, triggering alerts. The engineers behind every process or feature have the ability to set these metrics and the threshold that trigger the alerts. Once an alert is set off, the *on-call* gets paged.

Who is this "on-call"? Typically, the alerts generated due to problems with mature features page the company's reliability team, while features that have been deployed more recently are monitored by the engineering team that develops them. Regardless, somebody from that team is always on-call, and they are the person that gets paged and are responsible for mitigating the issue.

Paging itself can happen in multiple ways – by a phone call, a text message, an email, or a push notification to an app on the on-call's mobile device, where some companies have their own app, and some use a third-party one. The alerts usually include information such as text explaining what happened, which is determined by the engineer who set the alerts, and a link to a *playbook* entry, which is a document that describes what are the first steps to take when dealing with such an alert, for example, where to find the relevant dashboards, what to look for in the log files, and what pieces of code are involved.

It's important to remember that the description I brought here is extremely general and is based only on what I personally know, not even from firsthand experience. I'm sure any engineer that has had on-call duties in a major tech company will have some reservations with my description based on their own personal experience. However, as I said, the importance of this description is to examine concepts from the world of SRE so that we can discuss how they can be translated to the world of SBC projects.

Email Alerts by Log Handlers

In the previous chapter, we looked at various types of log handlers (or *transports*, as they are called in Winston), and we mentioned that some handlers can send the log messages over email. *SMTP* (Simple Mail Transfer Protocol), as the name suggests, is the protocol used to send and receive email over the Internet, and in Python's logging module, SMTPHander is the handler used to send log messages directly to a desired mail address. There are two protocols used for encryption when sending email: SSL (Secure Sockets Layer) and TLS (Transport Layer Security). SSL is now considered deprecated, and probably for this reason SMTPHandler doesn't really support SSL, and if it does, I couldn't find any documented success, so moving forward we'll only discuss a setup that uses TLS.

The first thing we need is an email address to send the email from. While you could very well have the machine send email from your personal email account, I strongly recommend against it, for two reasons: first, it's much easier to accidentally ignore an email from yourself – some spam emails look like they were sent from your own address, and in different views of your mailbox, like the "sent emails" view, an alert can easily be missed in all the emails you sent to other people. Second, the password for the email account needs reside in the code (or in a configuration file). Putting your personal email's password in a piece of code is a serious security vulnerability, especially for maker projects that get deployed in art festivals and other public spaces. One solution is to open a dedicated email account for the project, or for multiple projects, as long as it's a different account from your own.

Once we have an email account for the project, we can set up the handler with it (see Listing 8-1).

Listing 8-1. Using the logging module's SMTP handler

```
mailhost = ('smtp.gmail.com', 587)
sender = PROJECT_EMAIL # replace or read from file
password = PROJECT_PWD # replace or read from file
receiver = YOUR_EMAIL # replace or read from file

subject = 'Alert: your project needs your attention!'
credentials = (sender, password)
```

```
mail_handler = logging.handlers.SMTPHandler(
  mailhost, sender, receiver, subject,
  credentials=credentials, secure=(),
  timeout=1.0
  )
```

```
mail_handler.setLevel(logging.CRITICAL)
logger.addHandler(mail_handler)
```

The handler is a little cumbersome to set up. For readability purposes, I am setting all the arguments first as variables and then using them to set up the handler. This way, the initializer's signature is still apparent in the code. Let's walk through these arguments one by one.

The first argument is the mail host. This refers to the server owned by the entity that gave you the email account that is responsible for sending the email alerts. This argument takes a tuple, made of the address of the server and the port it is using. It might take a little bit of digging around the Internet to figure out what these are. In our example, our account is a Gmail account. Gmail supports both SSL and TLS, but since we're using TLS, we'll work with port 587, which is the standard port for TLS encryption.

The next three arguments are self-explanatory: these are the address of the sender, which is the email address of the account we gave the project; the receiver, which when you work on your project should probably be your personal email address; and the subject, which is really up to you.

Next come a few keyword arguments. `credentials` is a tuple representing the account's credentials. This is a tuple whose items are the account's address and password. Up next is `secure`, which is a tuple with the names of a keyfile and a certificate file. Gmail does not require client authentication, so the tuple is empty. However, we must set this keyword argument to a tuple in order to enable TLS encryption. It's just the way it is. Last, the `timeout` keyword argument is also self-explanatory – it sets a timeout, in seconds, for the communication with the SMTP server, which means that if communication is not established within that period of time, an exception will be raised.

Logging As a Microservice

Microservices are a software architecture philosophy, in which applications are composed of a collection of independent programs that run independently, not even on the same machines, and communicate with each other over the network. This type of architecture is really hyped over recent years as it contributes to greater modularity and stability. Components can be restarted and even swapped without ever stopping the application, and when a component crashes, none of the other components are immediately affected. One of my favorite advantages is that since the application is made of several independent programs, each program can be written in a different language, allowing the programmer to choose the best fitting language for each component of the application.

Microservices need to interact with one another, and one approach is called *RPCs* (*Remote Procedure Calls*). Although there are some libraries that try to help formulate some sort of a protocol, RPCs, in general, are agnostic when it comes to format, protocols, and pretty much anything else.

In a maker project, implementing the logger as a microservice can be helpful especially if the project has multiple machines or processes that work closely together. One of these machines, or a dedicated one, can run a logging service, while all the other processes make RPCs to use this service for logging. This way, the programmer doesn't have to configure the logging mechanism for each and every machine and program. Also, the programmer can choose to consolidate the log messages from all the processes into one log file.

We are going to implement a logging microservice. This needs to happen in two stages: we need to implement the service itself, and we need to build a library such that each process that wants to use the logging service can use it. When a project consists of programs in several languages, there should be an implementation of the library in every language. In the name of brevity, we will keep everything written in Python.

The Service

Before we write anything, we need to decide how other programs will communicate with the server. One very popular route is through HTTP requests, but this is not my personal favorite. For small-scale projects, I prefer sending JSON messages over UDP.

UDP (*User Datagram Protocol*) is a network protocol that, in contrast with TCP (which HTTP uses), is not designed to be a reliable data transfer, so there is no error detection, packet numbering, acknowledgment upon receiving, and other features that ensure that the data sent is received correctly. It is, however, much faster and easier to use. For projects where the data transactions happen within a local network or in one computer, data errors are almost never a problem, which can make UDP a preferable method.[1] Since any sequence of bytes can be transferred over UDP, we can just format our log messages as JSON strings and send those to the logging service.

We will write the service in Python and base it on Python's logging library. This will allow us to focus only on the API part of the server. The server will expect to receive a JSON object with two fields: the log message's text and the severity level as a number. This will keep the server simple and will put the responsibility of formatting most of the message on the libraries used by the clients. See Listing 8-2 for the logging microservice's code.

---

[1]UDP is actually pretty popular with the creative coding community due to it being used as the underlying protocol for the OSC (Open Sound Control) protocol.

Listing 8-2. A Python logging service

```python
import socket
import logging
import json

UDP_IP_ADDRESS = '0.0.0.0'
UDP_PORT_NO = 3003

FORMAT='[{asctime}] {levelname}: {message}'

socket = socket.socket(
  socket.AF_INET, socket.SOCK_DGRAM)
socket.bind((UDP_IP_ADDRESS, UDP_PORT_NO))

formatter = logging.Formatter(FORMAT, style='{')
handler = logging.FileHandler('out.log')
handler.setFormatter(formatter)
logger = logging.getLogger('project-logger')
logger.addHandler(handler)
logger.setLevel(logging.DEBUG)

while True:
  data, client_addr = socket.recvfrom(4096)
  msg = json.loads(data.decode('utf-8'))
  logger.log(msg['levelno'], msg['text'])
```

As you can see, the formatter only adds the time and level to the original message. Also note that since all this code is doing is listening to the port and writing to file any log message that comes in, there is no need for multithreading. When writing other microservices that listen to ports for commands but do other things in the meantime, multithreading is necessary, as we saw when we incorporated dashboards in projects earlier in this book.

The Client Library

Python's logging module does have a DatagramHandler, which is designed to send log messages over UDP. However, the handler sends a pickled (Python's way of serializing and reserializing objects) version of the entire log record object. If this service is supposed to serve clients that are not written in Python, this can be a problem, since logging modules in other languages may have different fields for their log record object, and also pickling in a language that is not Python can be awkward. Instead we will have to write our own handler for clients to use. Listing 8-3 shows loglib.py, our logging service's Python client library.

Listing 8-3. loglib.py, a Python library for using the logging service

```python
import json
import socket
import logging
from io import StringIO

FORMAT='{message} (at {filename}:{lineno})'
DEFAULT_ADDRESS=('127.0.0.1', 3003)

class UDPHandler(logging.StreamHandler):
  def __init__(self, server_address=DEFAULT_ADDRESS):
    super(UDPHandler, self).__init__()
    self.server = server_address
    self.socket = socket.socket(
      socket.AF_INET, socket.SOCK_DGRAM)

  def emit(self, record):
    msg = {
      'text': self.format(record),
      'levelno': record.levelno
    }
```

```
    print(msg)
    self.socket.sendto(
        json.dumps(msg).encode('utf-8'), self.server)
def getLogger():
  formatter = logging.Formatter(FORMAT, style='{')
  handler = UDPHandler()
  handler.setFormatter(formatter)
  logger = logging.getLogger('service')
  logger.addHandler(handler)
  logger.setLevel(logging.DEBUG)
  return logger
```

We're basing our handler off the simplest handler available, StreamHandler, and we're overriding __init__() in order to store the server's address and port, and emit(), the method used to actually do something with the log message. emit() gets a record object that has all the fields describing the log message. Our emit() uses these fields to create our standard JSON object and send it over the UDP socket to the server. Now all that is left is to use this library in an actual client, as demonstrated in Listing 8-4.

Listing 8-4. Using the logging service's library in a Python client

```
import loglib

logger = loglib.getLogger()
logger.info('Log message goes here')
```

Monitoring

As mentioned before, for big tech services, monitoring usually means setting up processes that either periodically or continuously look at and log files and determine whether there are trends or recurring errors that require alerting an on-call engineer. Alerts are triggered not just for errors but also for various metrics being out of their normal range, such as the number of users that complete an interaction or the revenue from a certain feature, as this can also imply that something is wrong with the code.

For a maker project, it may be excessive to build a monitoring system. It may be enough to just take the path described earlier, in which the logging system is also responsible for sending alerts. Alerts will be sent for log messages with CRITICAL severity level, and that will dictate which log messages are classified as CRITICAL: those that require sending an alert. This approach, however, addresses individual events and not the rate at which events happen. It also doesn't take into account things that happen at the level above the running program, such as flapping: the program doesn't know how many times it had to be restarted in the past hour – that's where a monitoring mechanism can be useful.

A Simple Monitoring System

We can design a monitoring system in many ways. It can be, for instance, a cron job that runs every so often, scraping log files and CSV files, a server that listens to logging requests from other programs, or even embedded in the operating system's logging service.

This next example tries to stay simple, undertake both individual and recurring events, and stay out of both the main program and the logging system. We'll look at the last lines of log files, going back a certain time interval from the present, and count occurrences of strings, such as "ERROR" or "reboot." To each of those strings we'll assign a threshold of occurrences – once that threshold is passed, an alert will be triggered. We'll use a YAML file, such as the one in Listing 8-5, to configure the various alerts.

Listing 8-5. YAML configuration file for a monitoring system

```
# Check messages from the last x minutes
interval: 60
```

```
# Alert throttling, in minutes
throttle: 120

# Alerts types
alerts:
- string: ERROR
  threshold: 20
  message: Error rate
  playbook: https://tinyurl.com/pre-playbook01
- string: CRITICAL
  threshold: 1
  message: Critical errors rate
  playbook: https://tinyurl.com/pre-playbook02
- string: reboot
  threshold: 2
  message: Machine rebooted
  playbook: https://tinyurl.com/pre-playbook03
```

In this example, the interval is 60 minutes. The configuration states that we allow up to 20 occurrences of the string "ERROR", only 1 occurrence of the string "CRITICAL" and 2 occurrences of "reboot". The message field can be used for a descriptive text about the alert, and the playbook field can be used for including steps that should be taken to resolve the issue – more on that later. For now, check out Listing 8-6 for a Python implementation of the monitoring system.

Listing 8-6. A Python implementation of a simple monitoring system

```
from datetime import datetime, timedelta
import sys
import yaml

TIME_FORMAT = '[%Y-%m-%d %H:%M:%S.%f]'
TIME_SUBSTRING_LENGTH = 25
```

```
# Read configuration
with open('config.yaml', 'r') as f:
  config = yaml.load(f)
alerts = config['alerts']

# Add a counter field to each alert
for alert in alerts:
  alert['count'] = 0

# Messages before this time will be ignored
start_time = (datetime.now() -
  timedelta(minutes=config['time']))

# Count occurances
for line in sys.stdin:
  logtime_substring = line[0:TIME_SUBSTRING_LENGTH]
  logtime = datetime.strptime(
    logtime_str, TIME_FORMAT)
  if (logtime < start_time):
    continue
  for alert in alerts:
    if (line.find(alert['string']) > -1):
      alert['count'] += 1

# Check thresholds
for alert in alerts:
  if alert['count'] >= alert['threshold']:
    send_alert(alert)

def send_alert(alert):
  # Implement alerting here
```

Once we loaded the configuration, we have a list of all the different
types of alerts we want. We can utilize this list for counting occurrences –
we just need to add to each alert a count field and set it to zero.

Note that we are reading lines from `stdin` and not a file. This allows us to pipe log files into the monitoring script rather than reading the file from within the script. The advantage of that is we can do things like this:

```
tail -n 1000 out.log | python3 monitor.py
```

`tail` outputs the last n lines of a file – 1000 in our example. The pipe sign ('|') will take that output and make `monitor.py` use it as its input. With long log files, this can save the monitoring script a lot of work. We should make sure, however, that the number of lines we ask from `tail` to produce is big enough to capture all the log messages that occur within the desired time interval. The reading loop, as you can see, still discards any lines that are older than that. To do that, the script assumes every line starts with the timestamp, inside brackets, as expressed with `TIME_FORMAT`. It should look something like this:

```
[2019-05-02 23:45:14.687] ERROR: ...
```

The length of such a string is 25 characters, which is the length of the substring that we give `datetime.strptime()` to parse into an actual datetime object. After the counting is done, a comparison is done between the counted occurrences and the thresholds allowed, and alerts are sent accordingly.

We have another loop going through the different alerts, searching for the alert's string. When nesting loops this way there's always the question of efficiency and scalability – what if we go not through 1000 lines, but through 100,000 lines? What if we don't have just three types of alerts, but hundreds? For big tech services, this is a real concern. However, for our needs and the scale we're working in, nesting these two loops is fine. Once all the occurrences of the strings of interest have been counted, we compare them to the alert's threshold and issue an alert if necessary. I have omitted the code for actually sending the alert, as we have shown how this is done earlier in this chapter.

Alerts Throttling

We'd probably want run this script over and over, in some time interval using crontab. Note that this interval does not have to be the same as the interval, or time window, in which we inspect log messages. The time interval for running the script determines two things – how fast we would receive an alert from the moment a problem expresses itself in the log files and how often we would be alerted (or nagged) about it. On-call engineers in tech companies can acknowledge (or "ack") an alert: if the alert is sent via an app, then the app has a button for that. If the alert is sent by an automated phone call, the engineer can press a number to acknowledge the alert. The engineer can also reject the alert, in which case usually a secondary on-call engineer will receive the alert.

The point is including these features is probably excessive for a maker project, but we can take simple measures to reduce the number of actual alerts that get sent to us without reducing the rate in which we run the monitoring script, like employing some sort of a throttling mechanism. Examine Listing 8-7.

Listing 8-7. An alert throttling mechanism using a file

```
import os

TIME_FILE = '/tmp/lastalert'
MIN_ALERT_INTERVAL = 15 # or read from config file

def trigger_throttled_alert(alert):
  try:
    last_time = os.path.getctime(TIME_FILE)
    last_time = datetime.fromtimestamp(last_time)
    now = datetime.now()
    diff_minutes = (now - last_time).seconds / 60
  except:
    diff_minutes = MIN_ALERT_INTERVAL + 1
```

```
if (diff_minutes) > config['throttle']:
  with open(TIME_FILE, 'w'):
    pass
  send_alert(alert)
```

We'd also need to change the threshold-testing loop in Listing 8-6 to Listing 8-8.

Listing 8-8. Revised threshold-testing loop

```
# Check thresholds
for alert in alerts:
  if alert['count'] >= alert['threshold']:
    trigger_throttled_alert(alert)
```

In this example, we are using a file, /tmp/lastalert, just as means for timekeeping: we are looking at the time in which the file was created (getctime()), and if it was more than MIN_ALERT_INTERVAL minutes ago, we can send another alert. When we do that, we also open the file for writing and immediately close it. This basically re-creates the file, updating our timekeeping. Also note how we deal with the file being missing: we're just setting diff_minutes to a value larger than MIN_ALERT_INTERVAL, forcing the alert to be sent and the timekeeping file to be created. This would happen the first time the script has been activated since the machine was rebooted – you may recall that everything in /tmp/ gets deleted at startup.

Monitoring the Machine

We've talked about monitoring the program's log files, but it can be useful to monitor metrics of the machine itself. Primarily, it's a good idea to monitor the CPU utilization, the memory usage, and the available hard drive space. psutil is a Python library that makes it easy to access these

metrics, and it was also ported to JavaScript.[2] Again, there's a wide range
of things we can do with these metrics: for instance, we can log them
periodically and trigger alerts if we detect a trend, like the CPU usage
being high for a prolonged period of time. This can be implemented in
a way similar to the monitoring system from the previous section. In the
following example, however, we'll keep it simpler: we'll create a script
that writes the metrics to a CSV and trigger an alert if a metric exceeds a
given threshold. This script will be designed to be called by crontab and
the resulting CSV handled by logrotate. For this reason, we'll check for
the existence of the CSV file, and if it does not exist, perhaps because it
was rotated, we'll write the header line first. We'll start, of course, with a
configuration file (Listing 8-9).

Listing 8-9. YAML configuration file for system metrics monitoring

```
# sysmonitor.yaml
metrics:
- name: cpu
  threshold: 90
- name: mem
  threshold: 90
- name: hdd
  threshold: 75
```

We'll use this configuration file for both determining the order of metrics
in the final CSV file and determining the thresholds for triggering alerts. As
with our project monitoring system, we can add to this file fields such as
the text to be included in the alerts. The code in Listing 8-10 demonstrates
how to use the psutil library and also how to use the built-in CSV module
for writing the file. Remember that the metrics shown here represent only a
small portion of what is made available by the psutil library.

---

[2]https://github.com/christkv/node-psutil

Listing 8-10. Python code for a system metrics monitoring

```python
import csv
from datetime import datetime
import os.path
import psutil
import yaml

with open('sysmonitor.yaml', 'r') as f:
  config = yaml.load(f)
  metrics = config['metrics']

headers = ['time']
stats = [datetime.now().isoformat()]

for m in metrics:
  if m['name'] == 'cpu':
    data = psutil.cpu_percent(interval=1)
  elif m['name'] == 'mem':
    data = psutil.virtual_memory().percent
  elif m['name'] == 'hdd':
    data = psutil.disk_usage('/').percent

  if data > m['threshold']:
    print('Trigger alert for {}'.format(m['name']))

  headers.append(m['name'])
  stats.append(data)

if os.path.exists('sysmetrics.log'):
  with open('sysmetrics.log', 'a') as f:
    writer = csv.writer(f)
    writer.writerow(stats)
else:
  with open('sysmetrics.log', 'w') as f:
```

```
writer = csv.writer(f)
writer.writerow(headers)
writer.writerow(stats)
```

Note that the alerts are triggered when metrics instantaneously surpass a threshold. Of course, alerts can be triggered by looking at a time interval instead, calculating averages and trends or triggering an alert if metrics are consistently high, as we demonstrated in the simple monitoring we built in Listing 8-6.

The Playbook

A playbook is basically a troubleshooting guide. It is a collection of documents describing what actions should be taken when various problems manifest. A single document in this collection of documents is often called a *playbook entry*. The granularity of a single entry is really a function of the complexity of the project. At the Exploratorium, we use an internal wiki for all our documentation, and this includes our "Exhibit Pages." Typically, there's one page per exhibit, and besides information such as the identity of the developers, fabrication details, and periodic maintenance procedures, the page includes some troubleshooting information. For us, having one page per exhibit with all the known types of failures is usually enough. Tech services usually have a single playbook entry for every type of alert.

Playbook Content

Not everybody in our maintenance staff feels comfortable logging into a Linux machine, but often there are simple actions anybody can take to resolve, or at least help diagnose, the problem: tracing the power cables to make sure everything is powered, power cycling (turning off and on), using a browser to access a web dashboard, locating a projector's remote control to set the video input source, and looking at LED indicators on the project's circuit board, these are some examples of actions that we include in our exhibits' wiki pages for whomever is currently on maintenance duty.[3] The point is that sometimes projects are looked after by people who were not directly involved in the process of creating the project and have different skillsets than the ones the creators have – this can also be the case when projects are deployed as public art or as prototypes for products. In such cases, it's important that the playbook entry is written with these people's skillsets and knowledge of the insides of the project in mind.

Playbook Hosting

If your project already has a web dashboard with a static IP address, it can host the playbook as well. However, that's not necessarily a good idea. First, it's still a more involved process than some other solutions, and second, you need to be able to access the playbook when there are problems with your project, and a problem with your project can cause the playbook to not be accessible. This is why I strongly recommend on hosting the playbook on cloud services such as Google Docs or Dropbox: create the file, get a shareable link, use a service such as TinyURL[4] or Bitly[5] to create a shorter link, and include that link in the email or text message being sent.

If you're using GitHub, which we'll discuss in the next chapter, for version control, that can be an excellent place to host the playbook as well. You can author the entries as `.md` files and use the Markdown format and

---

[3]Fun fact: the Exploratorium does not have a dedicated maintenance team like other museums do. Rather, almost every staff member who works in the Exploratorium's shop is on maintenance duty rotation. The person on duty is called "the bucket person," as back in the days, a bucket was used to carry tools and spare parts around the museum.

[4]`https://tinyurl.com/`

[5]`https://bitly.com/`

then cite the link to that file on GitHub.[6] Markdown format is easy to learn, and it looks nice when viewed on GitHub. Alternatively, use HTML. To view HTML files on GitHub in the browser, add `https://htmlpreview.github.io/?` before their URL. In the example in Listing 8-5, I have used TinyURL to create short links for HTML playbook entries examples in the book's GitHub repository.[7]

SMS Alerts
Online SMS Services

There are services that specialize in SMS messages and phone calls, such as Twilio, Plivo, Nexmo, and Sinch. The market for these services is usually companies that use automated text messaging and phone calls in large volumes, for example, ride sharing apps and food delivery apps. Using these services cost money, but for the uses and scale that are relevant to our discussion, the costs are really insignificant – usually less than a cent per text message.

These services often offer a variety of products and various types of dashboards for their clients to configure the service and tailor it to their needs. What we need, however, is to simply make an HTTP request that will send us a text message. When it comes down to that, most services operate in a similar way: once you sign up, you get an ID and a token. These are used to verify your identity, so that nobody else will be able to send text messages on your behalf and on your dime. Then you will need to provide the number from which messages will be sent. The services will often either offer you to purchase a number from them or recommend another provider. Finally, you will need to install a helper library that

---

[6]See example here in the book's code repository: ch08/playbook/playbook0.md
[7]This is the full link: `https://htmlpreview.github.io/?https://github.com/apress/project-reliability-engineering/blob/master/ch08/playbook/playbook3.html`

simplifies the way in which your code talks to the service's API. Listing 8-11 demonstrates what that might look like with Plivo.[8]

Listing 8-11. Sending text messages with Plivo

```
import plivo

# Replace with your ID
AUTH_ID = 'XXXXXXXXXXXXXXXXXXXX'
# Replace with your token
AUTH_TOKEN ='XXXXXXXXXXXXXXXXXXXXXXXXXXXXXXXXXXXXXXXXX'
# Phone number you bought goes here.
# For the North America, don't forget
# the '1' at the beginning!
PROJECT_NUMBER = '15550000000'
# Your phone number goes here
ALERT_NUMBER = '15551111111'

client = plivo.RestClient(
  auth_id=AUTH_ID, auth_token=AUTH_TOKEN)
response = client.messages.create(
  src=PROJECT_NUMBER,
  dst=ALERT_NUMBER,
  text='Your project needs you!')
```

Services often recommend that the ID and token are not included in the code, but rather set as system variables. This is for security reasons, for instance, to prevent you from committing your credentials to GitHub. If you follow that recommendation, then instantiating the client simply looks like this:

```
client = plivo.RestClient()
```

---

[8]The library, along with its documentation, is here: https://github.com/plivo/plivo-python

You will need to consult with the specific service's API to figure out what those variables should be named. For Plivo, they are called PLIVO_AUTH_ID and PLIVO_AUTH_TOKEN. Remember that if the program is started on boot by the operating system, for example, with crontab, the environment variables are different than they are on a terminal session. In that case, the environment variables should be set at the top of the crontab file, like so:

```
PLIVO_AUTH_ID='XXXXXXXXXXXXXXXXXXXX'
PLIVO_AUTH_TOKEN='XXXXXXXXXXXXXXXXXXXXXXXXXXXXXXXXXX'
```

Getting started with one of these services can be a little frustrating. It's important to remember that makers are not the primary audience for them, so finding your way in their web sites and their documentation can feel a little alienating. However, the cost is really insignificant, and in return you not only get reliable alerts from your project, but you also open up a whole new channel for communicating with your project – text messages and voice calls.

SMS Alerts with Hardware

For an engineer being on an on-call duty for big tech service, getting an alert over a text message is usually just another route to ensure that the alert gets received: perhaps the engineer is in an area with no Wi-Fi and the cellular reception is limited to calls and SMS. For many maker projects, on the other hand, the challenge can be to get the alert sent in the first place. Projects are not always installed in the range of a Wi-Fi network. For projects that do rely on Wi-Fi, a stable network may the cause for issue in the first place. For that reason, sending alerts as text messages directly to the cellular network is a useful technique.

Many SBC projects incorporate an Arduino, or a similar microcontroller board, to handle more time-sensitive tasks, like interfacing with an ultrasonic range sensor or driving a motor. In this case, it may make sense to get a board that supports cellular communications and use it to also send the alerts. At the time of writing this book, the Arduino MKR GSM 1400[9] and Adafruit Feather 32u4 FONA[10] stand out as good overall solutions. They are also designed to be powered by a LiPo battery, which brings to mind another scenario where using them can be beneficial: to send an alert during a power outage, or when the main computer shuts down completely.

The code in Listing 8-12 shows how to configure the Arduino and send a text message.

Listing 8-12. Arduino code for sending SMS alerts

```
#include <MKRGSM.h>

const char PINNUMBER[] = "0000"; // Your SIM PIN
const char MYNUMBER[] = "15550000000"; // No. to text

GSM gsmAccess(true);
GSM_SMS sms;

void setup() {
  bool connected = false;
  while (!connected) {
    if (gsmAccess.begin(PINNUMBER) == GSM_READY) {
      // Connected
      connected = true;
    } else {
      // Not connected yet. Try again
      delay(1000);
    }
  }
}
```

---

[9]www.arduino.cc/en/Guide/MKRGSM1400
[10]www.adafruit.com/product/3027

```
void sendAlert() {
  sms.beginSMS(MYNUMBER);
  sms.print("Alert!\n");
  sms.print("Your project needs your attention\n");
  sms.endSMS();
}
```

The mechanism that triggers the alert, however, is not implemented in this example. This can be done in several ways based on the application. Here are a few options to consider.

An output GPIO pin on the SBC could be connected to an input GPIO pin on the Arduino (Figure 8-1). The SBC can set a GPIO pin high to let the Arduino know it should send an alert. The Arduino can test the pin either by polling or by setting up an interrupt. This method can be used to send an alert when the Wi-Fi is down.

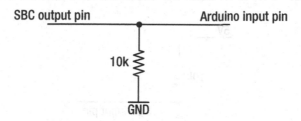

Figure 8-1. *Connecting an SBC to an Arduino for sending text alerts. Notice the pull-down resistor that is used to make sure the input voltage is always defined. This resistor can be omitted if the Arduino's internal pull-down resistor is used.*

If the project is not connected to the Wi-Fi in the first place, then all alerts would need to be sent by the Arduino. Therefore, we'd need a way to send a variety of messages. To accomplish that, it may be better to connect the Arduino to the SBC with a USB cable and transfer messages over serial communication. This way, we can send a more detailed message to the Arduino. It can be the actual text we want to send, or just an error code, and then the Arduino would hold the various texts and a mapping to their error codes.

To detect a power outage, the Arduino can be normally powered through its USB port, but also connected to a battery – in fact, it's recommended to have the Arduino connected to a battery when using the GSM module in order to handle the large current consumption. Instead of sensing a GPIO on the SBC, the Arduino can sense either its own 5V pin or one of the SBC's power pins. When the voltage on that pin drops, it means that a power outage has happened, and the Arduino should send out an alert.

Note   Both the Arduino MKR GSM 1400 and Adafruit Feather 32u4 FONA use 3.3V logic, so when sensing a 5V pin, some level shifting must be used, such as the voltage divider depicted in Figure 8-2.

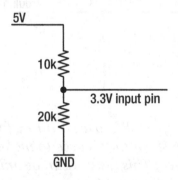

Figure 8-2. *Level shifter for sensing a 5V supply with a 3.3V input pin*

Last, the SBC can send out a heartbeat signal in the form of a level shift in an output GPIO pin or a signal over the serial connection. Then, the Arduino can be programmed to send the alert if the heartbeat signal has not been received. The amount of time that passes that should trigger the alert should be larger than the heartbeat interval: this is to avoid alerts being sent due to a small accidental delay in the heartbeat signal.

It's a good idea to just tell the Arduino to wait double the interval of the heartbeat signal, so if the heartbeat interval is 1 second, the Arduino can send an alert if 2 seconds have passed without a heartbeat signal being received. This technique is good for power outages as well as the situations where the SBC freezes or dies: for a Raspberry Pi, for instance, freezing due to a corrupted SD card is not unheard of.

IFTTT

Paging apps for mobile devices are a primary channel for alerting on-call engineers in tech companies. We will not cover these in this book for several reasons: to use these techniques, one must either use a third-party service, which cost a significant amount of money and are designed for a much bigger scale, or one can program their own app. This book is broad enough without getting into mobile app development, so we'll just skip this method. Moreover, for our purposes, the techniques we've covered in this chapter should be sufficient already.

However, this is an alternative. *IFTTT*[11] (If This Then That) is an extremely powerful service. It knows how to connect and talk to a large number of services, from Twitter, through Amazon Alexa, to online weather services like Weather Underground. With IFTTT, one can create applets that trigger an action in one service based on an event that happened in another service. One of the examples that is given in the IFTTT web site is sending an email if according to Weather Underground it's supposed to rain the next day.

Two features of IFTTT can be combined to create something that looks fairly close to a paging app. The first one is called *Webhooks*. It's an API maintained by IFTTT that can send and respond to GET and POST requests. The second one is the IFTTT mobile app that can display

---

[11]https://ifttt.com/

notifications triggered by push notifications. With these two services, we can set up an applet that sends a notification that is then displayed on our mobile device in response to an HTTP request coming from the project's program.

Note   This section is a little bit tutorial-like, something I am generally trying to avoid in this book. However, I found that setting up an IFTTT applet with Webhooks can be somewhat confusing. Let me save you some time by walking you through it.

To set this up, we need to start a new applet. For the "this" part, which is the event that triggers the applet, we choose "Webhooks." The API needs a name for the event. This, as we will see later, is expressed in the endpoint to which the request is sent. We will name our event "alert" (Figure 8-3).

For the "that" part, which is the action performed in response to the trigger, we choose "Notifications". We can choose either a simple notification, which is just plain text, or a rich notification, which can include a link. When the notification is received, clicking it opens a browser pointing to that link. For our use case, it makes perfect sense to make that link the relevant playbook entry. Therefore, a rich notification seems like a better choice.

In Figure 8-3, you can see that for the message itself, we chose some pretty generic text, but we also pressed the "Add ingredient" button to add the field "Value1". We did the same for the "Link URL" box and added the field "Value2". The value of the fields, as we will soon see, can be set by the HTTP request – we will make Value1 a free-form text that describes the issue and Value2 will be the link to the playbook entry.

Complete trigger fields
Step 2 of 6

Receive a web request

This trigger fires every time the Maker service receives a web request to notify it of an event. For information on triggering events, go to your Maker service settings and then the listed URL (web) or tap your username (mobile)

Event Name

```
page
```

The name of the event, like "button_pressed" or "front_door_opened"

Create trigger

Complete action fields
Step 5 of 6

Send a rich notification from the IFTTT app

This action will send a rich notification to your devices from the IFTTT app. Rich notifications may include a title, image, and link that opens in a browser or installed app.

Title

```
Alert!
```

Optional, bold text above the message   **Add ingredient**

Message

```
Your project triggered the following alert:
Value1
```

Add ingredient

Link URL

```
Value2
```

Optional, link may open in a browser or installed app   **Add ingredient**

Image URL

```

```

Optional   **Add ingredient**

Create action

Figure 8-3. *Screenshots for setting up the IFTTT alerting applet. On the left is step 2, in which the trigger, an http request, is configured. On the right is step 5, in which the action, a rich notification, is configured.*

Once we have finished creating the applet, we will need to retrieve our key. This can be found by going to the Webhooks page (https://ifttt.com/maker_webhooks) and clicking the "Documentation" button. This takes us to a page that displays our key, shows the API's endpoint and examples of how to use it, and lets us test the triggers directly from

245

that page. Now that we have an endpoint to work with, we can write code in our program that triggers the alert. Let's use Python for this example (Listing 8-13).

Listing 8-13. Python code that triggers an IFTTT applet using Webhooks

```
import urllib.request
import urllib.parse

MY_KEY = 'xxxxxx' # your key here
ALERT_EVENT = 'page'
ERROR_TEXT = 'project lost power'
PLAYBOOK_URL = 'https://tinyurl.com/pre-playbook01'

params = urllib.parse.urlencode({
   'value1': ERROR_TEXT,
   'value2': PLAYBOOK_URL
   })
data = params.encode('ascii')
url ='https://maker.ifttt.com/trigger/{}/with/key/{}'
url = url.format(ALERT_EVENT, MY_KEY)
with urllib.request.urlopen(url, data) as f:
   print(f.read().decode('utf-8'))
```

To make sure this example is consistent with the ones in the Webhooks documentation page, we set both the key and the event name as variables. Then we move on to encoding the parameters. A Webhooks request can include three parameters: value1, value2, and value3. These need to be in the request's body, which imply that requests with parameters need to be POST requests, while requests without parameters can be either GET or POST requests.[12] As we mentioned, we're going to set value1 to a text describing the reason for the alert.

The parameters go into a dictionary. This dictionary needs to be URL-encoded, since some characters, like white spaces, are not allowed in a URL or in a request's body. URL encoding replaces these characters usually by a sequence of three characters: '%' and two more characters representing the replaced character's ASCII value in Hex. This string is then encoded in ASCII, as expected by the HTTP protocol. This will be the request's body.

Next, we set up the URL by plugging our event's name and our key into the Webhooks URL template and make the request using urlopen(). Notice that the arguments are the URL and the body that contains the alert's text. Having the body as an argument tells urlopen() that this is a POST rather than a GET request. The request returns a text that says "Congratulations! You've fired the alert event". This text doesn't necessarily mean that the action was performed. It just means that the request came through.

IFTTT can be used to deliver alerts in other ways as well, and the options seem endless. It can use third-party services to send you a text message or call your phone. It can notify you through social media. It can even notify you by changing the temperature of your smart water heater, if you own one. Having said that, I would stick to the more conventional communication channels.

---

[12]That's actually not accurate – GET requests *can* have a body, but it's generally considered bad practice. As a rule of thumb, GET requests' parameters appear in the URL of the request, while the parameters of a POST request appear in the request's body.

Summary

In these last two chapters, we really treated our project the way Site Reliability Engineers in dot-com companies treat their systems. We covered three key aspects of the SRE discipline: logging, keeping records of the program's operation; monitoring, reviewing the machine and the programs' operation over time; and alerting, reaching the right person when intervention is needed. However, making sure that these processes are in place and running correctly is somebody's or, more often than not, multiple people's job. We simplified and scaled down these systems to work with a maker project, but for many maker projects and for some makers themselves, these techniques may still be over the top. I do encourage you to think about the scale of your project and what the needs are in terms of reliability, then consider the techniques we have discussed in this chapter, and scale them up or down to fit the needs of the project.

This concludes our journey in examining how the principles of SRE can be translated to the SBC maker project world. In the next chapter, we will look at some best practices for bringing our new tools together, reliability issues that apply specifically to the maker project world and are not derived from SRE, and some other useful tips.

CHAPTER 9

Best Practices

This last chapter is a collection of techniques and practices that I found useful in my work. These are various methods for making robust projects, and they are applicable at different stages of the project's life cycle, whether it's the project's design, development, debugging, or deployment. Almost each of the topics discussed here could probably fill its own book; however, this book would not be complete if we had not at least touched upon them.

Fake Classes

In Chapter 1, we discussed the advantages of using object-oriented programming. We showed how objects that belong to different classes but implement the same interface (duck typing) or derive from the same superclass (inheritance) can be treated by the program as if they were of the same class. This allows us, for example, to put objects of different types in an array and perform the same operations on all the objects or to readily swap one object for another.

This allows us to create a great tool for debugging: *fake objects*. A fake class has the same interface as the class that is supposed to be present in the fully functional project, but operates internally in the simplest way possible, producing either a pre-defined or a configurable output. This is useful for testing, debugging, or when the real object simply cannot operate.

© Eyal Shahar 2019
E. Shahar, *Project Reliability Engineering*, https://doi.org/10.1007/978-1-4842-5019-8_9

> **Note** In software engineering jargon, the terms "fake" (or "faux"), "stub," and "mock" have similar, yet slightly different meanings. What we refer here is closest in meaning to fake objects, so we'll stick to that term, disregarding any subtleties.

As an example, let's go back to our weather station. As you recall, we turned on a fan whenever the temperature was above a certain threshold. How can we test this logic without coming up with a way to actually change the temperature around the sensor? This is where a fake object can be useful. We can create a fake temperature sensor class that doesn't get its reading from a physical temperature, but rather gives a known value as its output. This output can be either a constant, a value that changes over time, or a value that can be changed using a dashboard. You will notice how techniques from almost every chapter in this book come into play as using the JavaScript implementation of the weather station project to demonstrate this. We'll start with the implementation of the fake sensor class itself (Listing 9-1).

Listing 9-1. Implementation of the fake temperature sensor class

```
class FakeTemp extends Sensor {
  constructor(cfg) {
    super(cfg);
    this.isFake = true;
    this.setTemp(cfg.temp);
  }

  measure() {
  }
```

```
setTemp(t) {
    this.lastRead = t;
    this.time = new Date();
  }
}
```

In the constructor, we add a data member to this subclass, isFake. It will help us down the road to identify which objects are real and which are fake. We also assume that the input configuration object contains a temp field that we use to set the sensor to the desired test temperature. Then we implement a measure() method that doesn't do anything: recall that in our measuring loop (last visited in Listing 3-20), every subclass of the Sensor superclass is expected to have a measure() method, so for the code to not fail, FakeTemp must implement this method as well. Last, we implement a setTemp() method that the constructor uses to set the temperature value and, later on, will allow us to control this fake class during runtime. Now, we need to revisit our dynamic instantiation code (Listing 5-12) and add the FakeTemp class (Listing 9-2).

Listing 9-2. Adding FakeTemp to the dynamic instantiation code

```
// ...
var sensorList = [];
for (let sensorCfg of config.sensors) {
  switch (sensorCfg.type) {
    // ...
    case 'FakeTemp':
      sensorList.push(new FakeTemp(sensorCfg));
      break;
  }
}
```

And now, if we actually want to use a FakeTemp class, all we need to do is swap the type of sensor in our configuration YAML file and include the desired temperature (Listing 9-3).

Listing 9-3. Changing the project's configuration file to include a fake sensor object

```
# Sensors configuration

sensors:
- name: temperature_east
  type: FakeTemp
  units: "deg C"
  temp: 25
# ...
```

This is already enough: we can set different temperatures in the configuration file, run the project, and see if the result matches our expectations. However, we will take this a little bit further and add real-time control over the fake class from the dashboard. To our Pug template (Listing 4-2), we will add another section dedicated to fake sensors (Listing 9-4).

Listing 9-4. Adding a fake objects section to the dashboard's Pug template

```
// ...
    div(id="sensors")
     // ...
    div(id="fans")
     // ...
    div(id="fakes")
      h2 fake
      each sensor in sensors
        if sensor.isFake
```

```
label(for=sensor.name)= sensor.name
input(
  type="range"
  name=sensor.name
  min="0"
  max="50"
  oninput="setFakeTemp(this)"
)
```

For every sensor that has the isFake field (and the isFake field is not false, by weird chance), an input of type range is added, better known as a slider. input elements have a name attribute, on which we will piggyback to map the element to the sensor. Any change to the slider will trigger a setFakeTemp(this) command to execute, with this being the slider element itself. The next step is to implement this setFakeTemp() function in the dashboard's JavaScript's file (Listing 9-5).

Listing 9-5. Implementing JavaScript code in the dashboard to send fake data to the server

```
function setFakeTemp(element) {
  ws.send(JSON.stringify({
    fake: {
      sensor: element.name,
      value: parseInt(element.value)
    }
  }));
}
```

Using WebSockets, we will send the server an object containing the name of the sensor, which we extract from the name attribute, and the desired value. We wrap this object in a dictionary under a key we named fake to help the server understand what we're trying to do. All that remains is to update the server code that handles incoming WebSockets

messages from the dashboard (recall Listing 3-20) and add the capability
to handle messages that set fake values (see Listing 9-6).

Listing 9-6. Server-side code that handles WebSockets messages to
set fake values

```
wsServer.on('connection', function connection(ws) {
  wsServer.broadcast(JSON.stringify({sensors: sensorList}));
  ws.on('message', function incoming(data) {
    msg = JSON.parse(data);
    if ('fake' in msg) {
      console.log(msg);
      for (sensor of sensorList) {
        console.log(msg.fake.sensor, sensor)
        if (msg.fake.sensor == sensor.name) {
          sensor.setTemp(msg.fake.value);
        }
      }
    }
    // ...
  });
});
```

And voila! We have a fake sensor that we can control in real time
and see if the rest of the project is doing what it's supposed to do. Fake
objects can be used during development, for example, when hardware
components are still not in the developer's possession, but I find that using
them is an extremely powerful technique during the debugging stage,
especially for projects that involve hardware.

By the way, if, while reading this book, you were asking yourself what
reliability engineering has to do with inheritance (Chapter 1), dashboards
and WebSockets (Chapters 2 to 4), and configuration files (Chapter 5), now
you know.

Exceptions and Errors
The Basics

Different programming languages and different schools of thought assign different meanings to the terms "exception" and "error," and this book is no exception.[1] An *error*, in my book,[2] is the thing that went wrong. It's a missing file, a failed HTTP request, an array that is invoked with an out-of-range index, or division by zero. An *exception* is the mechanism that allows errors to be intercepted, handled, and recovered from.

This mechanism operates in a similar manner in many languages – the try-catch-finally block. In this mechanism, code that has potential to fail is wrapped in a try clause. If it does fail, an exception is *thrown* (or *raised*, in Python). A catch clause (or except, in Python) is executed if an exception is thrown. This is the program's chance to handle the error and find a way to recover from it. It can also *rethrow* the exception to whatever code called the current function. A finally clause executes regardless of whether the try clause passed with or without exceptions. Even if an exception is raised and rethrown or a return is encountered, the finally clause is still guaranteed to execute.

While this may make the use of try-catch-finally blocks sound compelling, they should not be used liberally for three reasons: first, they are actually pretty computationally heavy; second, overuse of try-catch blocks tends to make the code less readable and more confusing ("why would this fail?"); and third, some exceptions, as explained in the next section, are better not caught.

---

[1] Pun totally intended.
[2] Yes, one more pun.

Operational vs. Programmer Error

When it comes to errors, we need to distinguish between programmer errors and operational errors. *Programmer errors* are simply bugs. Perhaps you misspelled a variable's name or messed up the indentation in your Python code. Those are errors you could, in theory, catch and recover from. Consider the JavaScript code in Listing 9-7.

Listing 9-7. Recovering from a JavaScript programmer error

```
b = {};
try {
  b.do(); // b doesn't have a method do()
} catch (err) {
  console.log('Error:', err)
  // Recovered. Program keeps running
}
```

But do you want to recover from this error? These errors are, in fact, problems with the program, and the first step to fixing those is to recognize their existence, whereas recovering from them will only achieve the opposite. Consider a more complicated case: using a dictionary as input to a function. We used this technique in Chapter 5 when we initialized objects with a configuration object as the constructor's input. Suppose that the configuration had a misspelled or a missing key, what would we want to happen? We could check that the input of a function is exactly as the function expects it, but what does an ill-formatted input argument actually means? It means that there's a mistake in the code that calls that function. Therefore, that piece of code should be fixed instead of adding more mechanisms to recover from such an error that would only hide the actual problem. If stderr is redirected to a log file and the program is configured to restart as we have discussed in Chapter 6, it's a good idea to let the program just crash and restart, and the log file would capture the information that will help you fix the error.

Note   In strongly typed languages, such as Java and C++, the programmer would need to work extra hard to call a function with an object of the wrong class as input. For this reason, testing for other potential errors, for example, a function's input argument being null, is more common and actually considered good practice. In loosely typed languages, like JavaScript and Python, it's possible – but much harder – to make sure that every input argument is of the right type.

Operational errors, on the other hand, should be considered as a normal part of the program's operation. Perhaps the program is trying to open a file that is missing or access an online service that is down. A classic example is right here in our weather station: if a temperature sensor gets disconnected or breaks and its wrapper object is unable to communicate with it, that is an operational error. Operational errors should be handled and recovered from, and the way to do that depends on the way the error presents itself, and these are, of course, different in Python and in JavaScript.

Python

All Python exceptions, from division by zero to a failed HTTP request, inherit from the Exception object. A Python try-except block can be as general as catching all exceptions of the Exception superclass, or specific, where various subclasses of the Exception class are indicated, and different recovery code is applied to each of them. The code in Listing 9-8 demonstrates how to catch different kinds of exceptions in Python.

Listing 9-8. Catching and handling different types of exceptions in Python

```python
import json
import urllib.request
import urllib.error
URL = 'some.url'

try:
    # May throw urllib.error.URLError
    response = urllib.request.urlopen(URL)
    # May throw json.decoder.JSONDecodeError
    data = json.loads(response.read().decode("utf-8"))
    # May throw KeyError
    table = data['table']
    # May throw IndexError
    a = table[50]
except urllib.error.URLError as e:
    print(('GET request error. Reason: {}')
        .format(e.reason))
except (KeyError, IndexError):
    print('JSON structure is not as expected.')
except Exception as e:
    print('Exception of type {} has occurred.'
        .format(type(e)))
```

Notice that some potential exceptions are not caught specifically, namely, json.decoder.JSONDecodeError, but they will be caught at the last except clause that catches all previously unspecified exceptions. Remember that this clause must be last. Otherwise, some exceptions will be caught and handled by this clause and not by a clause that appears later but handles those specific exceptions.

It's not always easy to figure out just by reading the documentation what type of exception a certain function can throw. Note how the type of the exception is extracted in the last except clause. Instead of guessing, you can force the program to fail during development and use this mechanism to identify the exception type and refine the program accordingly.

JavaScript

You can get away with quite a lot without getting an error in JavaScript. For instance, you can access a list with an index that is out of range:

```
a = [];
console.log(a[1]); // -> undefined
a[3] = 3.14;        // Out of range? not a problem
console.log(a);     // -> [ <3 empty items>, 3.14 ]
```

You can even divide by zero – that's not an error either:

```
b = 5 / 0;
console.log(b);     // -> Infinity
```

This puts extra responsibility on the programmer to make sure that this kind of code doesn't produce unwanted results.

However, when errors do occur, intercepting them is a little more involved in JavaScript than it is in Python. There are several different ways JavaScript functions express an operational error that we will discuss in the next sections. To make sure that the error doesn't crash your program, it's important to familiarize yourself with the command that poses the potential risk and identify the error reporting mechanism it uses.

Thrown Exceptions

Often, synchronous functions simply throw an exception when they fail, for instance, `fs.readFileSync()`, which we used in our weather station to read configuration data (recall Listing 5-12). The way to recover from this type of failure is using a `try-catch` block, as shown in Listing 9-9.

Listing 9-9. Recovering from a thrown exception

```
const fileName = path.join(__dirname, 'config.yaml');
var fileContent;
try {
  fileContent = fs.readFileSync(fileName, 'utf8');
} catch (err) {
  console.error(err);
  // recovery code goes here
}
```

If the exception happens within a function but we would prefer handling the error in the code that called it, we could rethrow the exception using `throw err`, with `err` being the error object. Then the caller would also call the function within a `try-catch` block (see Listing 9-10).

Listing 9-10. Rethrowing an exception in JavaScript

```
function callee() {
  try {
    fileContent = fs.readFileSync('test', 'utf8');
  } catch (err) {
    console.log('Let caller handle it. Rethrowing.');
    throw err;
  }
}
```

```
function caller() {
  try {
    callee();
  } catch(err) {
    console.log('Handling exception.');
  }
}
caller();
```

error Events

Some libraries are event-based, for instance, ws, which we used for real-time updates from the project to the web dashboard (recall Listing 3-6). In this paradigm, objects register to an error event with an event handler function, and when the event is triggered, the event handler is called. We can demonstrate this by modifying the code in Listing 3-6 and adding an error event handler (Listing 9-11).

Listing 9-11. Adding an error event handler to a WebSockets object

```
wsServer.on('connection', function (socket) {
  //...
  socket.on('error', function (err) {
    console.error(err);
    // handle error here
  });
});
```

Adding an error event handler is something that is easy to forget to do, but it's extremely important. Without it, the program would crash if there's an error.

Callback with an Error Argument

In this paradigm, an asynchronous function takes a callback function as an argument that is called once the execution is complete. Usually, the callback function is called with an argument that represents the error, if one occurred. We've seen an example of this in our weather station, when a sensor class was attempting to read from (i2cRead()) or write data to (writeByte()) the physical sensor over the I2C bus (recall Listing 1-15). Here's the relevant excerpt from that example (Listing 9-12).

Listing 9-12. Error handling while reading sensor data

```
class Si7021Temp extends Sensor {
  measure() {
    this.i2cBus.writeByte(0x40, 0xF3, 0, (err) => {
      if(err) {
        console.error(err);
        this.lastRead = -999;
        return;
      }
      setTimeout(() => {
        this.i2cBus.i2cRead(0x40, 3, new Buffer(3),
          (err, bytesRead, data) => {
          if(err) {
            this.lastRead = -999;
            return;
          }
```

Unlike functions that register to an error event, failing to provide a callback to a function or to check the error argument does not automatically mean that the program will crash if there's an error. However, if an error did happen and the error argument was not checked, normal execution is very likely to face some difficulties, since the failure is bound to have some implications, like the data argument might be empty, causing the program to crash down the road.

Promise Rejection

Some APIs focus on promises. When a promise is rejected, its callback function, specified by the catch() method, is called. Fetch() is a good example for an API that uses promises. Examine Listing 9-13.

Listing 9-13. Handling promise rejection

```
fetch(url)
  .then(function(response) {
    return response.json();
  }).then(function(data) {
    // process data here
  }).catch(function(err) {
    console.error(err);
    // recover from rejection here
  });
```

At the time of writing this book, rejected promises that are not handled simply cause an error message to be displayed. However, this is being deprecated, and in the future, an unhandled promise rejection will cause the program to terminate. This means that just as with error event handling, handling promise rejection is critical.

Software Recovery

Now that the exception is caught, what do you do? We vaguely said that the project should run some sort of "recovery code" without explaining what that means. In practice, it really depends on the project and what would be a sufficient solution. Here are some common recovery methods:

- When the machine cannot communicate with a sensor, a fake class can be instantiated and used instead.

- If the project relies on data from an online service and the request fails, the program can retry making the request at some later time.

- The program can also get the data from a backup source, such as an alternative online service, or local "canned" data stored in a file.

- If a configuration file is used, it is a good idea to also have an untouched default configuration file, in case an error is introduced to the configuration file while editing it.

- Some projects can disguise their intended functionality and upon failure do something completely different. Screen-based projects, for example, can switch to canned video, and art projects with interactive LEDs can switch to pre-programmed lighting patterns.

- Sometimes it just doesn't make sense to run the project at all. If a robot can't communicate with its motors, not much can be done. These are the cases where some physical error indicator, a blinking LED, for instance, is essential.

Version Control and Rolling Back

When on-call engineers get paged, it means there's a problem with their service that needs to be resolved as quickly as possible. Usually, these are no times for major code changes. Most often, they have three options: introduce minor code changes, edit configuration files, or *roll back*.

Rolling back means going back in time, undoing a specific change that was done in the code. This is possible through *version control* – systems that store the codebase and track the changes in it through time. In such systems, the code is stored in a *remote repository*. Developers work on local copies of the repository, *pushing* their code changes back to the remote repository, and *pulling* changes that their peers made to the code into their own local copy.

These days, the prevailing version control system is Git.[3] You are probably familiar with GitHub,[4] which is popular with the open source community. However, it's easy to forget that other platforms that use Git exist, both online and for local hosting.

Git shines when multiple programmers work on the same project. For example, a developer can create *branches* for new features of the program that they are working on and *merge* them into the *master* branch when they are ready. For the purposes of this discussion, however, we will deal with the most basic scenario: a sole programmer, using Git to keep a history and backup of their project. Figure 9-1 illustrates this workflow that we will describe in detail in the next few sections.

---

[3]https://git-scm.com/
[4]https://github.com/

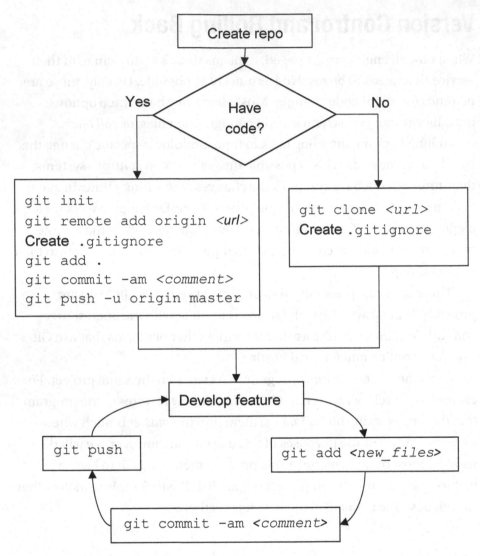

Figure 9-1. *The simplest Git workflow*

Getting Started

When we decide to use Git for a project, we first create a repository (or repo, for short) on the host – usually an online one like GitHub. Once we do that, we can get the repository's URL.

Starting with Existing Code

If code was already written, then the project's folder needs to be identified as a Git working copy with the terminal command

```
git init
```

Next, we point the working copy to the remote repository

```
git remote add origin <url>
```

origin refers to the original repository. When working on open source projects, it's common to work with multiple remotes, but that's rarely the case for maker projects.

We usually don't want all the files in the folder to be included in the repository. In Python code, we don't want *.pyc files, which are the files compiled by the Python interpreter. For Node.js projects, we don't want the folder node_modules where libraries are installed. The way to tell Git which files we don't want it to track is by listing them in a .gitignore file,[5] as shown in Listing 9-14.

---

[5]GitHub keeps a collection of useful .gitignore templates for many languages and frameworks: https://github.com/github/gitignore

Listing 9-14. An example of a .gitignore file

```
# .gitignore file. Comments are OK!

# If using a macOS computer for development:
.DS_Store
# For Python projects:
*.pyc
# For Node.js projects:
node_modules
```

Now we can add everything else to the repository

```
git add .
```

and *commit* the changes. When committing, all changes are saved in the working copy. An ID is given to the list of changes, so that the point in time when the commit happened can be later referred to.

```
git commit -am <comment>
```

The -a flag tells Git to automatically *stage*, which simply means save, all changes that happened since the last commit, including the deletion of any files. The -m flag denotes a comment, and every commit must have one. Committing a change only acts on the local working copy. To make the changes take place in the remote repository, we need to push them using the command

```
git push -u origin master
```

The first time we push to the remote repository, we need to specify which remote we'll be pushing to and to which branch using the -u (or --set-upstream) option. We've already established that we'll be working solely with origin as our remote. Using branches is outside the scope of this book. For this reason, when working on a personal maker project that makes basic usage of Git, the command git push -u origin master is usually what we would use.

Starting Fresh

If we decide to use Git before a single line of code was written, we can *clone* the empty repository we've created to the machine:

```
git clone <url>
```

This will create a folder on the machine. Had there been any code in the remote repository, that code would be copied to the local repository as well. Adding the remote and setting the upstream, as we did in the previous case, is done automatically with the clone command.

The Development Cycle

From this point a cycle starts where features are developed locally, and when the code is ready to be pushed to the remote repository, any new files are added with the command

```
git add <new_files>
```

The code changes are staged with the command

```
git commit -am <comment>
```

and finally pushed to the remote repository – it's not necessary to specify the remote and the branch again:

```
git push
```

Note   The workflow described here does not cover collaboration between multiple developers or even a development by a single developer on multiple machines – if these are things you care about, I recommend that you take the time to dive deeper into Git.[6]

Rolling Back

This brings us to a point where we can roll back – undo any changes that have caused our project to be unstable. We can undo all changes we made since the last commit with the commands

```
git reset HEAD --hard
git clean -fd
```

The reset command is used to point the local repository to a specific commit in the repository's history, and HEAD is shorthand for the very last commit. The --hard option tells Git to actually change the files in the local repository so that they match that commit.

We can also tell Git to try to undo a specific commit without touching changes that were done after it. This is done by first identifying the commit's ID. We can either find it in the commit history page on the host's web site or by typing

```
git log
```

This will print the commit history on the screen. If we were good about commenting coherently with every commit, we can identify the offensive commit by the comment we made and take note of its ID. Then, to undo that commit, we can use the command

```
git revert <commit_ID>
```

---

[6]Chacon, Scott, and Ben Straub. *Pro Git*. Berkeley, CA: Apress, 2014. Also available online at https://git-scm.com/book

If this is successful, the offensive code will be removed, and a new commit will be created. If not, either Git will protest, or we will have to get into the code and try to clean up the mess that happened during the failed attempt.

Git Best Practices

The best way to avoid having to roll back in the first place and to make sure rollbacks, when they are absolutely necessary, are done safely is to follow some of Git's best practices:

- Commit often.

- Preferably, commit stable code.

- Push stable code only.

- Comment clearly.

- Use comments to note stable code.

Hardware Reliability
Strain Relief

Cable connectors and the ports to which they connect create some of the most vulnerable areas in a system. When not treated correctly, they become physically strained from holding the hardware's own weight. Strain relief prevents any excessive forces from being applied to the connectors and instead absorbs these forces into the cable itself and the strain relief hardware. P-clamps and zip-ties (Figure 9-2) should be used liberally for this purpose. Zip-tie clamps are my personal favorites: they are screwed to the box or cabinetry that contains the hardware, and they secure the zip-tie to a fixed place. Good technique involves using strain relief hardware in a way that cables are prevented from forming a straight line between the connector and the potential source of strain, as shown in Figure 9-3.

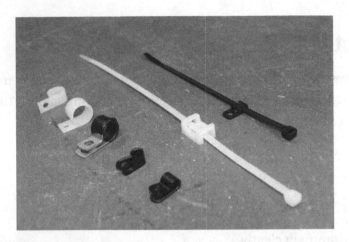

Figure 9-2. *Strain relief hardware: zip-ties with mounts and P-clamps*

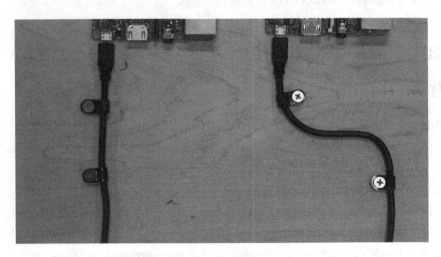

Figure 9-3. *Strain relief with P-clamps done wrong (left) and right (right). The cable on the left creates a straight line between the connector and the potential strain source. This is not as reliable as the cable on the right, where that line is broken.*

Remember that the electrical infrastructure should be decoupled from the structural infrastructure: never rely on electrical cables to keep parts of the system in their place.

Custom Shields

Projects often have components that must be separate from the computer. In such cases, it's usually best to avoid sticking jumper cables in the SBC's headers. Building a custom shield (or hat, or cape, or whatever it's called for your SBC of choice) is usually a more sustainable solution. A custom shield gives you an opportunity to

- Use terminal blocks for connecting wires from external components rather than soldering them to the board.

- Use headers to attach pre-assembled breakout boards.

- Use sockets for ICs.

- Add LEDs as status indicators.

- Add jumper headers and DIP switches for configuration.

Most of these features can be seen in Figure 9-4. It is a custom cape for the BeagleBone Black that I made for an Exploratorium exhibit called "Ship Chatter." This exhibit shows how the computers on ships' navigation systems communicate with each other.

Figure 9-4. *Custom BeagleBone Black cape, featuring (from right to left) terminal blocks for connecting two LCD screens, two LED indicators, a level-shifting breakout board mounted on headers, and an IC mounted on a socket.*

Real-Life Recovery Planning

Recovery also includes actions taken by you, or whoever maintains your project, in case of a hardware malfunction. Devote some time to think about spare parts: the number of units of each part you buy should be a function of its likelihood of breaking, a unit's cost, the budget allocated to the project's maintenance, and the hassle involved in ordering new units.

- Think about where the spare parts should be stored.

- Document which parts were used and where they can be purchased.

- Consider making a physical documentation sheet describing troubleshooting steps and how to replace parts and keep that sheet in the same place as the spare parts.

More Microservices

Microservices Revisited

We mentioned the concept of microservices in Chapter 8 when we built a logging microservice. We will not build more microservices in this section, since we covered the basics in Chapter 8, but I would like to discuss them a little further.

To recap, in a microservice architecture, different components of the project run as independent programs, potentially on different machines, and communicate with each other over the network. This can be useful in many situations, for example, when

- A centralized logging system is desired.

- Different parts of the project lend themselves better to different languages.

- The project has parts that are physically distributed and it's easier to control each of them with multiple machines.

- You want to separate the project's dashboard from the main program.

- Parts of the systems, like machines or users on their mobile devices, come in and out of the system.

A Case Study

The Exploratorium's Microscope Imaging Stations[7] (Figure 9-5) rely heavily on microservices. These are kiosks that let visitors control a scientific grade microscope while getting context-sensitive content that is driven by image processing algorithms. The kiosk application was developed with *Electron*,[8] a Node.js framework that allows developers to create desktop applications in JavaScript and program the user interface with HTML and CSS. Electron is a fantastic tool, especially in an environment where a prototype needs to roll out quickly and changes to the layout and content are done frequently.

Figure 9-5. *A microscope imaging station at the Exploratorium*

---

[7]Denise King, Joyce Ma, Angela Armendariz, and Kristina Yu, *Developing Interactive Exhibits with Scientists: Three Example Collaborations from the Life Sciences Collection at the Exploratorium*, Integrative and Comparative Biology, Volume 58, Issue 1, July 2018, Pages 94–102.

[8]https://electronjs.org/. Another similar tool is NW.js: https://nwjs.io/

The microscope itself, however, is behind a glass window, and the library that controls it is for Java programs. That meant that we had to bridge both the physical gap and the language gap between the microscope and the kiosk. To do that, we wrote a Java microservice that received messages over UDP from the kiosk and in turn sent commands to the microscope using the Java library.

Then we had to change the joystick that visitors use to control the microscope. The new joystick had to be connected to an Arduino that sent serial commands to the kiosk's computer. During development, running the serial JavaScript library in Electron on a Windows computer presented some challenges, which is a gentler way of saying that I couldn't get it to work. Writing the joystick adapter as a Python microservice not only saved me time but also opened more options: I created another microservice that also sent movement commands to the exhibit, but this one served a little web site, so I could now control the microscope with my phone. This did not interfere with the system as long as I didn't use my phone while a visitor was trying to use the joystick. I could also turn off my phone while the system was running without affecting it. I could even shut down or launch the phone-serving microservice while the exhibit was operating. The system did not care. This microservice is somewhat parallel to the fake objects we discussed earlier, but unlike those, the project's configuration files do not need to be changed, and the main program does not need to be restarted.

We also added image processing capabilities to the exhibit,[9] so that the machine could have an idea of what the visitor is looking at and provide relevant on-screen content. The algorithms were also written

---

[9]Joyce Ma, Eyal Shahar, Kevin Eliceiri, Guneet Mehta, and Kristina Yu, *Shedding Light: Integrating Bioimaging Technologies into the Design of an Interactive Museum Exhibit*, Proceedings of the 2019 Conference on Designing Interactive Systems (DIS '19). ACM, New York, NY, USA.

in Java using the *ImageJ*[10] and *OpenCV*[11] libraries, so they had to be incorporated into yet another microservice. That meant that the image processing microservice could run on a dedicated machine, improving the performance of the entire system.

Microservices Best Practices

There are some libraries out there, like gRPC,[12] that help standardize microservices and how RPCs (Remote Procedure Calls) are made, but I have never used them. I just push JSON objects around over UDP or HTTP requests, as we've done many times throughout this book.

If you decide to use microservices, I suggest that you

- Think carefully whether the communication should be over UDP or HTTP requests. UDP is fast, but packets may get lost, which makes it a better choice when the microservices run on the same machine. HTTP requests are slower, but more reliable. Also, HTTP requests are the way to go if the microservice serves a web dashboard.

- Be careful with Python. You'll have to use concurrency so that incoming communication doesn't block the rest of the program. Either threads and queues or `asyncio` are there to help you.

- Think carefully about the structuring of the JSON objects. Refer to Chapter 3 for inspiration.

---

[10]https://imagej.nih.gov/ij
[11]https://opencv.org/
[12]https://grpc.io/

- Use microservices conservatively and wisely. Turning every little component into a microservice will result in many programs and that can result in unnecessary confusion and overhead.

- If using version control, have all the code in one repository, with each microservice in its own folder. True, when working with multiple machines, that will result in unused code on some of them, but this is way more organized. You will need to `git pull` between committing and pushing to bring in changes you have done on other machines.

It's Best to Practice

Mechanisms for error logging and alerting and fault recovery only have value if they work, and the best way to verify that they actually do is by putting them to the test:

- Turn off your router to see if the project can deal with the network outage.

- Simulate a power outage by abruptly disconnecting the SBC from its power supply.

- Deliberately misspell URLs of online resources that the project uses to retrieve data to simulate an outage of external services.

- Disconnect both sensors and actuators while the project is running and on power up.

- If the project relies on external commands through the network or keyboard, try ill-formatted commands.

- Introduce errors to configuration files.

Did the project respond as you planned? Did your recovery mechanisms react as you intended?

And then there's always the scenario where human intervention is required. Practice these situations as well, and make sure there's a procedure that works. Make sure you have physical access to the project. Projects in public spaces often end up behind a lock: make sure you have the keys, or the contact information of the people who have them. Know where your spare parts are stored and ensure that you have access to them. Figure out where the power breakers and network equipment are.

If you can't attend to the project, can somebody else do that for you? Do they know what to do? For some projects, it can be crucial that you have someone you can trust to handle the situation when you're away, and these can be as high profile as an art project deployed in city hall or as personal as a cat feeder. In both examples, if you're travelling and the project fails, you really need somebody you trust to be there, have everything they need to access the project, and know how to respond. Practice various scenarios with them, even just to make sure they know how to manually feed your cats. Having said that, remember that many maker projects don't need this level of readiness, and in many cases, your project can just wait until you return from your travels.

Summary

This chapter brings our journey to a conclusion. We've covered some key concepts from the world of Site Reliability Engineering and explored ways to translate them into maker-scale projects, mostly on SBCs with focus on the Raspberry Pi.

Designing a project's software as an object-oriented architecture supports code readability, maintainability, and configurability by paralleling the software world and the hardware world. Since object-oriented programming can be more similar to the way humans think about the world, an object-oriented project lends itself more easily to be visualized on a dashboard for human use.

A web dashboard can provide insight into the machine's state in at any given moment. When something is wrong, viewing a dashboard is usually the very first step toward understanding what the source of the problem is, and a well-designed dashboard has the potential of pointing out the problem within the very first seconds of looking at it.

Configuring the project with a dedicated configuration file creates stronger code that does not require it to be changed if the hardware needs to be adjusted or replaced. It also facilitates easier debugging by enabling switching real element with fake ones. In conjunction to the program, a machine that is configured properly supports the project's software with a healthy environment for the project to run and providing mechanisms for recovering from power outages.

Logging, monitoring, and alerting can be tedious to set up, but they are crucial for notifying the developer that something is wrong with the project. They provide a timely connection between the project and those who care for it and also a way to travel back in time and identify problems and their sources.

No project is completely resilient to failure. Online services set a realistic goal for their service's availability that is usually expressed with "nines" – the number of nines that appear in the percentage of desired availability. For example, if a service is available 99.999% of the time, its availability is said to be "five nines." The company then uses the metrics it collects to see if the availability goal is met. If the availability goal is not met, improvements to the service need to be made, but if the availability is better than the goal, then no additional changes need to be done. This helps the company decide what reliability features are worthwhile working on. In our scope, developing and utilizing the features we discussed also take considerable amount of effort, but it's hard to find a way to quantify just how well the project is working and how well it should be working, so it's harder to determine whether investing time in developing reliability

281

features is worthwhile. It's up to you to find that balance, and that usually boils down to your intuition at the design stage, how you decide to overcome failures as you develop and test the project, and what you have learned from your experiences with previous projects.

Regardless of what you end up using for your projects, I hope you've learned some new things and changed the way you think about your work. If you are a professional maker, or an aspiring one, I believe that employing the techniques and thought processes that we have explored here will have a positive effect that will also propagate to other elements of your practice. You might even find that building reliability systems around your project can be interesting and fun just for the sake of it. This field is still young, and libraries and tools that address smaller-scale projects will probably develop in time, but making your own tools always has the extra value of learning while making, ending up with a product that is designed precisely for your own needs, and having the satisfaction of making the thing yourself – and isn't that what being a maker is all about?

Index

A

Abstract class, 11
Alerting, 201, 215, 217, 227, 245, 279
Application Program
        Interface (API), 41
Arduino, 144–153
    EEPROM, 144–152
    SD card, 152–153
Asynchronous code
        (*See* Synchronous *vs.*
        asynchronous code)
asyncio, 59–60

B

Bootstrap, 49
Broadcast (networking), 164
Broadcast (WebSockets), 57

C

Cascading Style Sheet (CSS), 90–98
    border-radius property, 105
    content property, 100
    data-driven, 98–100
    display property, 94, 95
    flexbox, 95–97
    position property, 97–98

selectors, 28–30
tables, 90–91
Text
    capitalization, 91–92
    fonts, 93
catch() method (*See* Exceptions)
Color gradients, 106–109
Command line arguments, 136,
      144, 209–210
    default help message, 142–144
    options, 136
    parsing, 138–142
    terminology, 136
    verbose mode, 137
Command substitution, 174, 181
Comma-Separated Values (CSV)
    file, 12, 213
Conditional operator, 88, 89
console
    cosnole.log(), 183
    Object, 201–202
Constructor argument, 133–134
Coroutines, 59–61, 63
Crash recovery
    forever.js, 176
    pm2, 176–177
    Python, 175
cron, 170–171, 173–175, 179

© Eyal Shahar 2019
E. Shahar, *Project Reliability Engineering*, https://doi.org/10.1007/978-1-4842-5019-8

crontab, 171, 172, 179, 231

Custom shield, 273–274

D

D3.js, 109

Dashboard (*See* Web dashboard)

DatagramHandler, 225

Data serialization, 129

Data visualization, 81, 106, 108, 213

datefmt argument, 196

    directives, 197

Decorators, 34

Default gateway, 162

Dictionary, 31, 69, 71, 78, 115, 127, 253, 256

DIP switches, 157–158, 273

DNS servers, 165

Document Object Model (DOM), 28

    elements, 89

Document Type Definition (DTD), 28

Domain name, 169, 170

Domain Name System (DNS), 165

    DDNS, 169–170

    resource records, 169

    servers, 165

Duck typing, 5–9

Dynamic Host Configuration Protocol (DHCP), 162, 163

Dynamic instantiation, 134–135, 251

E

Electrically Erasable Programmable Read-Only Memory (EEPROM), 144–145

    JSON, 145–150

    object serialization, 150–152

    put() method, 150

Endpoint, 39–41, 43, 47, 49, 52, 116, 244–246

Environment variables, 172, 173, 239

Errors

    callback with an error argument, 262–263

    error events, 261

    operational *vs.* programmer, 256–257

    promise rejection, 263

Exceptions

    catch clause, 255

    thrown exceptions, 260–261

    try-catch-finally block, JavaScript, 255

    try-except block, Python, 257

Express.js, 45–47

Extensible Markup Language (XML), 125–127

F

Fake classes, 249–254

Fetch(), 45, 112, 263

File descriptors, 184, 207

Flapping, 218, 227
Flask, 31–38, 83
    for-loops/conditionals, 36
    Jinja, 45
    template rendering, 34, 35
    web server, 37–38

G

Gauges, 112–116
Git (*See* Version control)
Google Charts, 109–116
    API, 110
    dataset property, 114
    DataTable object, 112
    draw() function, 113
    gauges, 112–116
    library loader, 111
    line graphs, 110–112
GPIO pin, 82, 126, 133, 141, 241
Graphical User
    Interfaces (GUI), 22
Graphic indicators, 104
    color gradients, 106–109
    gauges, 112
    LEDs, 104–105
    meters, 105–106
grep (command), 213

H

Hardware reliability
    custom shields, 273–274
    strain relief, 271–273

Hypertext Markup Language (HTML)
    classes, 54–55
    DOM (*See* Document Object
        Model)
    DTD (*See* Document Type
        Definition)
    tags, 27
Hypertext Transfer Protocol
    (HTTP), 22–24
    GET request, 23, 39
    POST request, 23
    requests, 22–24, 51–53
    response status codes, 24, 25

I

I2C, 2, 3, 65, 71
    openSync(), 15
    writeByte(), 16, 17
If This Then That (IFTTT), 243
    alerting applet, setup, 245
    GET/POST request, 247
    HTTP protocol, 247
    Python code, 246
    Webhooks, 243
Inheritance
    abstract class, 11
    subclasses, 9
    superclass, 9
    superclass's data member, 11–12
Interfaces, 7
Internet speed monitor, 120–121
IP address, 36–37, 163–164
    static, 167–168

J

Jade (*See* Pug)
JavaScript
    asynchronous code, 16
    console object, 201–202
    constructor function, 13–15
    ES6, 17–19
    Logging
        console object, 201–202
        Winston library, 202–204
    Object.assign(), 134
    Object.create(), 15
    properties, 14
    prototypes, 13
    setTimeout(), 17
    toFixed() function, 93
    toJSON() method, 72, 73
JavaScript Object Notation (JSON)
    communication
        design, 69–71
    configuration, 128
    object, 69–71
    entities, 127
    message parsing, 76–77
    pseudo-properties, 128–129
Jinja, 45
join() function, 12
JSONEncoder, 74–75
    default() function, 75
JSON.stringify()
        function, 71, 72
jQuery, 47–48
Jumpers, 155–157

K

Key-value pair, 69

L

Level shifter, 242
Light Emitting Diodes (LEDs), 104
Line graphs, 110–112
List comprehension, 12, 13, 63, 142
Literal, 127
Logger objects, 198–199
Logging
    callback, error arguments, 211
    configuration, 208–210
    data, 213
    email alerts, 219–222
    exceptions, 210–211
    initialization sequence, 212
    microservice (*See*
        Microservices)
    parameters, 213
    stdout/stderr, 184–186
Log handlers, email alerts
    credentials, 221
    SMTP handler, 220–221
Log levels, 188–189
    critical messages, 190–191
    debug and info messages,
        189, 190
    error messages, 190
    Python's logging module, 189
    severity, 188
    warning messages, 189, 190

Log rotation, 204
    configuration block, 205–206
    `RotatingFileHandler`/
        `TimedRotatingFile`
        `Handler`'s initialization,
        207–208
    stages, 205
    `WatchedFileHandler`, 207

M

Magic numbers, 123–124
Media queries, 100–102
Microframework, 31
Microscope imaging station, 276
Microservices, 222
    best practices, 278–279
    case study, 276–278
    logging client library, 225–226
    logging service, 222–223
    UDP (*See* User Datagram
        Protocol)
Monitoring, 226
    alerts throttling, 231–232
    simple monitoring system,
        227–230
    system metrics, 232–235
    `logrotate`, 233
Mustache, 31

N

Name servers (*See* DNS servers)
Network-Attached Storage (NAS), 120

Network configuration, 162–170
    accessing remotely, 167–170
Node.js, 45–47

O

Object-Oriented
        Programming (OOP)
    class, 1
    data members, 1
    inheritance, 9–13
    interface, 7
    instantiation, 3
    JavaScript, 13–17
    JavaScript ES6, 17–19
    member functions, 2
    methods, 2
    polymorphism, 5
On-call, 219, 239
Operational errors, 256, 257, 259

P

Playbook, 219, 235–237
    content, 235–236
    hosting, 236–237
Port forwarding, 168
Positional arguments, 136, 138
Programmer errors, 256–257
Project configuration
    Arduino (*See* Arduino)
    command line arguments (*See*
        Command line arguments)
    DIP switches, 157–158

Project configuration (*cont.*)
    file formats, 125–132
    handling errors, 154–155
    jumpers, 156–157
    magic numbers, 123–124
Promises, 42, 45, 263
    rejection, 263
Pull-down resistor, 156, 241
Pug, 31, 45–47, 113–114, 252–253
Pure abstract class, 11
Python
    asyncio, 59–60
    coroutines, 59
    event loop, 61
    exceptions, 257–259
    threads, 64
    websockets library, 61–65
Python modules
    argparse module
        add_argument() function, 139
        ArgumentParser object, 138
    logging module
        basicConfig() method,
            193–196
        date/time directive, 196
        formatting style, 193–194
        handlers, 199–201
        log message attributes,
            193–194
        Logger objects, 198–199
        msecs attribute, 197
        timestamp, 197
    sys module, 137

Q
querySelector(), 44, 48, 89
querySelectorAll(), 44

R
Random-Access
        Memory (RAM), 145
Raspbian, 159, 166, 167
Read-Only Memory (ROM), 145
Real-life recovery planning, 274
Remote access, 167–170
Remote Procedure Calls (RPCs), 222
Remote repository, 265, 268, 269
Resource record, 169, 170
Responsive design, 100, 103
    device orientation, 103–104
    media queries, 100–102
    sizing elements, 103
Rolling back (*See* Version
        control)
run_until_complete() function, 60

S
Scalability, 9, 218, 230
Secure Sockets Layer (SSL), 220
self method, 4
Server, 21–22
Setup documentation, 180–182
Shebang, 174, 182
Ship Chatter, 273–274
Signature, 133

Simple Mail Transfer Protocol
(SMTP), 219
Single Board Computer (SBC),
xxviii, 1, 6, 122, 144, 155,
156, 159, 164, 219, 241, 273
Singleton design pattern, 198
SMS alerts, 237
online SMS services, 237–239
SocketIO, 67–68
Software recovery, 264
Startup
command substitution, 174
__dirname constant, 173
environment variables, 172, 173
__file__ constant, 173
parameter expansion, 174
PATH variable, 172
shell script, 174
cron job, 171
Static files, 43, 83–84
Strain relief, 271–273
Subnet mask, 164, 167
Synchronous vs. asynchronous
code, 31
systemd, 178
target unit groups, 179
unit files, 178
System service, 177–180
boot sequence, 180
ExecStart, 179
ExecStopPost, 178
RestartSec, 179

T

Template rendering, 30–31, 44, 51,
55, 71, 77, 82, 113
Thrown exception, 260–261
Tidal Memory, 117–118
Tornado, 38
Transport Layer Security (TLS), 220
try-catch-finally blocks, 255

U

Uniform Resource
Identifier (URI), 23
Uniform Resource
Locator (URL), 23
Unit configuration file, 178
urlopen(), 247
useradd command, 161
User Datagram
Protocol (UDP), 223
User setup
pi, 160
root user, 159, 160
sudo, 160

V

Version control
clone command, 269
development cycle, 269
.gitignore file, 268
Git workflow, 266

W, X

Web dashboard, 21
   graphic indicators, 104
   Internet speed monitor, 120–121
   structure, 81, 82
Web framework, 22
Web Server Gateway Interface
   (WSGI), 37
WebSockets, 56
   browser, 65–66
   Node.js, 56–58

Python, 61–65
   socketIO, 67–68
Winston, 202–204, 219
Wired Pier, 119–120
Wrapper class, 8

Y, Z

Yet Another Markup Language
   (YAML), 125, 129–130, 134,
   227–228, 233

Printed in the United States
By Bookmasters

Printed in the United States
By Bookmasters